CISTERCIAN STUDIES SERIES: NUMBER EIGHTEEN

MERTON'S
THEOLOGY OF PRAYER

CISTERCIAN STUDIES SERIES

Board of Editors

CISTERCIAN STUDIES SERIES: NUMBER EIGHTEEN

MERTON'S
THEOLOGY OF PRAYER

John J. Higgins SJ

CISTERCIAN PUBLICATIONS

Spencer, Massachusetts

1971

Cistercian Studies Series   ISBN 0-87907-800-6
This volume, cloth   ISBN 0-87907-818-9
paper   ISBN 0-87907-918-5

Library of Congress Catalog Card Number: 70-175091

Ecclesiastical permission to publish this book was received from Bernard J. Flanagan, Bishop of Worcester, July 30, 1971, and James L. Connor sj, Provincial, Province of Maryland.

Printed in the Republic of Ireland by
Cahill & Co. Limited, Parkgate Printing Works, Dublin

To my Mother and Father

"Whatever I may have written, I think it all can be reduced in the end to this one root truth: that God calls human persons to union with himself and with one another in Christ. . . ."—Thomas Merton

CONTENTS

FOREWORD

EVELYN WAUGH ONCE SPOKE of an ascetic tradition that is deep within the American heart and that has taken at times rather unusual and unlovable forms. An indication of this might well be the current interest in Thomas Merton's inward-looking type of spirituality and especially in the new expression he gives to contemplative prayer which he describes as an awareness or an awakening of man to the presence of God within him.

It is somewhat surprising that to date no comprehensive or systematic treatment of Merton's spiritual writings have been published. The present work is an attempt to deal with this, specifically by offering a synthesis of Merton's understanding of prayer, which was undoubtedly the central and unifying theme throughout his writing. It is hoped that in this way researchers who are presently examining Merton will have a systematic basis for their studies.

This is an analytical study of Thomas Merton's theology of contemplative prayer, showing its centrality in man's spiritual life. Such a life, according to Merton, is essentially man's real life in that it consists of a continuous search for communion with God as well as a search for ways to manifest Him to one's fellow man.

It opens with a discussion of two basic concepts involved in Merton's spirituality, namely, "union with God" and "transformation of consciousness." For Merton, prayer has but one function and that is to bring man to a personal awareness of his union with God in Christ. However, man will achieve this awareness only if he discovers his true self since it is there that he becomes conscious of the God-man Who is present in the ground of his own being. As is evident from the third chapter, which describes contemplative prayer, this awakening to the presence of God within man, is really the result of man's total surrender of his being to God by means of the two-fold movement that is characteristic of Merton's contemplative prayer: man entering into the deepest center of himself and then passing through that center to his true self where he discovers the freedom that is his as a son of God. Here, man is no longer conscious of self, but having transformed his consciousness, now recognizes himself as a "self in God." To achieve this transcendent self, there is need for renunciation and sacrifice in man's life of prayer. For, it is these that give man the detachment necessary to recognize his own freedom as a son of God as well as the freedom of all those who share that Divine Sonship.

Merton's thought on contemplative prayer is critically evaluated in light of its originality and its contemporaneity as well as its value in providing a resolution to some of the real problems confronting modern man. Although such a theology of prayer tends to be theoretical rather than practical, its pragmatic value is noted in that it addresses itself to many of the contemporary issues in today's world and opens the way for increased dialogue with proponents of other religions. In light of these, Merton's contemplative prayer should have a relevant place in the life of today's Christians. For, at a time when there is a marked questioning and in many instances a noticeable de-emphasis on the value of personal prayer, contemplative prayer as propounded by Thomas Merton can offer a creative challenge to the man of today and make him more aware than ever before of the significance and the value of prayer in his life.

The primary thesis proposed in the introduction and demonstrated throughout the book is that contrary to the opinion of many today there is no radical change nor noticeable tension, nor open contradiction in Merton's thinking or writing. Rather, there is a gradual unfolding and a more explicit awareness in the full understanding of the central message of his spirituality, namely, man's life is a continuous seeking of God and finding Him by love and sharing that love with other men. Such a unified message is especially evident in his theology of contemplative prayer. To seek and find God by love and to share that love with other men through a concern for the paramount issues of humanity were the life-long preoccupations of Thomas Merton's life of prayer. Such a life should be analyzed and studied and acted upon by the Christian of today; for, every Christian is bound in some sense to be a man of prayer.

INTRODUCTION

ALTHOUGH AMERICANS are generally characterized by their pragmatism, Jacques Maritain is alleged to have remarked that beneath the intensely active life that characterizes these people there is a deep drive toward spiritual living as well as toward contemplation.[1] However surprising one may find such a remark, it cannot be denied that one of the most significant and relevant spiritual writers in contemporary America has been a man whose influence has been felt from within the physical isolation of a Cistercian monastery. With the death of Thomas Merton on December 10, 1968, America lost one of her most revolutionary thinkers and perceptive spiritual writers. The scope of his interests during the past twenty-five years covered a wide range and the writings that Thomas Merton left for society are prolific. His entire life was lived with a deep concern for the real and tragic issues of the present time. He was a man who was passionately aware both of the inward and outward crises confronting humanity; yet, he repeatedly addressed himself to such issues by pointing out the need and the importance of the contemplative dimension of man's life. As a monk, he was as physically remote as man can be from his fellow man; yet, it was such a separation that constituted the basis for his profound and creative dialogue with the world of

---

1. This sentiment was expressed by J. Maritain at one of the conferences of *La Semaine des Intellectuels Catholiques* held in Paris in May, 1950. Cf. Sister T. Lentfoehr, Introductory Comment to "Thomas Merton on Renunciation," *Catholic World*, CLXXI (1950), 420.

today. Even in his more recent years as a hermit, he was more in touch with today's troubled society and more truly present to the world and to his time by his love, by his compassion, and by his understanding, than many of his contemporaries. Indeed, this involvement with the real situation of people in the world and with their critical problems has been keenly felt in a very enduring sense, perhaps nowhere more noticeably and more forcibly than in the area of his spirituality. As one author recently noted: "No spiritual writer in modern times has had an impact upon the contemporary Catholic like Thomas Merton."[2]

Shortly before his death Merton remarked that man's life "is totally irrelevant, in order to find relevance in Him. And this relevance in Him is not something we can grasp or possess. It is something that can only be received as a gift."[3] For this reason, "the deepest level of communication is not communication, but communion."[4] Most simply, for Merton, life was a continuous search for communion with God as well as a search to manifest Him to his fellow man. His own life was a fulfillment of this in that he "sought solitude with God. He searched for that interior peace every man should have in order to be a functioning, integrated, normal individual."[5] And it was this total view that he tried to put forth in all his writings as he himself said:

> Whatever I may have written, I think it all can be reduced in the end to this one root truth: that God calls human persons to union with Himself and with one another in Christ, in the Church which is His Mystical Body.
>
> . . . But if I have written about interracial justice, or thermonuclear weapons, it is because these issues are terribly relevant to

2. Clifford Stevens, "Thomas Merton 1968: A Profile in Memoriam," *American Benedictine Review*, XX (1969), 7.

3. These words are from an extemporaneous talk Merton gave at the "Spiritual Summit Conference" held in Calcutta in October, 1968. Cf. *Washington Post* (January 18, 1969), C. 9.

4. *Ibid.*

5. Ed Rice, "Thomas Merton," *Sign*, XLVIII (1969), 36.

one great truth: that man is called to live as a son of God. Man must respond to this call to live in peace with all his brothers in the One Christ.[6]

In an age which places much value both on material prosperity and the need for instant communication, such a life and such a message might well have been considered a manifest contradiction. However, the sincerity of his conviction ultimately gave that life and that message a force that was quite persuasive.

While many persons have acknowledged such an influence, especially as evidenced in the number of tributes accorded him at the time of his death, the message, as indeed the man himself, has been misunderstood by not a few who feel that Merton himself experienced a tension between his commitment to the monastic life and his commitment to the real and impoverished world of today.[7] For some, the tension appears as an open contradiction in the man.[8] Still others note the radical change from the other worldly

6. Thomas Merton, "Concerning the Collection in Bellarmine College Library," statement made on November 10, 1963, *The Thomas Merton Studies Center* (Santa Barbara: Unicorn Press, 1971), pp. 3-4.

7. Rice, "Thomas Merton." Cf. also Naomi Burton, "I Shall Miss Thomas Merton," *Cistercian Studies*, IV (1969), 221, who first speaks of a struggle in Merton but later in the article asserts that the difficulty was really within herself as she tried "to reconcile his real need for seclusion and his real need to give himself to people." John Eudes Bamberger, "The Cistercian," *Continuum*, VII (1969), 229, speaks of a need for solitude and a need for human society in Merton and concludes: "And I suppose that is why, in fact, a pitched battle never developed. The entrenched, semi-conscious conflict between these two needs remained, active and intense, till the end." Luke Flaherty in his Master's thesis entitled "Mystery and Unity as Analogical Vision in Thomas Merton's *Cables to the Ace:* A Critical Explication," p. 3, speaks of Merton's "personal resolution of the inward-outward conflict as he turned finally away from the mysticism of introspection and toward the mysticism of unifying and unitary vision." Finally, Charles Dumont, "A Contemplative at the Heart of the World—Thomas Merton," *Lumen Vitae*, XXIV (1969), 634, says in speaking of the paradox between Merton's striving for solitude and for ever greater involvement in the world: "This did not happen without difficulties and exterior clashes, without interior conflicts."

8. Matthew Kelty, "Letter from Gethsemani," *Monastic Exchange*, I (1969), 87; Sarah Lansdell, "In Search of Thomas Merton," *The Courier-Journal and Times Magazine* (December 7, 1969), p. 54. Both Kelty and Lansdell,

devotion of his earlier works to a direct, deeply engaged, often militant concern with the critical situation of man in the world which is evidenced in his later writings.[9] The earlier writings, mainly concerned with the theme of "union with God," have at times been criticized for presenting the impression that such union with God can only come to a man who lives and works in a monastic setting.[10] However, one must be mindful that during this period Merton himself was preoccupied with arriving at a deep and intimate union with God in his own life. Such a union demands a solitude, a silence, a certain estrangement from the world. However, once he realized his own personal sonship with a loving God (communion), he also came to the realization of his oneness with all the other sons of God in the mystical Christ. And it was this

---

who quotes John Howard Griffin, speak of a contradiction between Merton's love for the solitary life and his love for people. Since both Kelty and Griffin knew Merton well, one can only assume that they are using the term figuratively. This problem of contradiction, as far as his writings are concerned, has been well summed up by Tarcisius Conner in an article entitled "Merton, Monastic Exchange and Renewal," *Monastic Exchange*, I (1969), 2, who says: "It has been frequently pointed out that he was a man of apparent contradiction. He would make some point, only later to assert what appeared to be diametrically opposed. . . . And yet this does not mean that his thought has not been expressed in clear and concise terms. It merely indicates that this thought is always fragmentary and always 'historical,' in the sense that it was always centered upon that portion of reality which he was confronting even though it still retained, at least in his own mind, a definite relationship with what has gone before and what is yet to come. But because his own personality was so dynamic and so enthusiastic, he tended to give the impression that what he said in each case was an adequate expression of the matter at hand. In actual fact, when this was pointed out to him, he himself would be the first to say that there were many other elements which had to be considered besides what he had said in this particular context."

9. Various terms have been used to describe this radical change in Merton. Frank Dell'Isola, "A Journey to Gethsemani," *Cross and Crown*, VIII (1956), 397, speaks of a "great change," "a New Merton." James Baker, "The Social Catalyst," *Continuum*, VII (1969) 259–61, speaks of a "startling change in attitude," "a dramatic change from spiritual isolationism to social involvement in the affairs of contemporary man." Daniel Callahan, "Unworldly Wisdom," *Commentary*, XXXIX (1965), 92, talks of a "different, and perhaps new, Merton."

10. Frank Dell'Isola, "The Conversion and Growth of Thomas Merton," *Cross and Crown*, XIV (1962), 57.

realization that led to his more explicit concern for the larger issues of humanity—the searching for new ways to bind men together in unity, in love, and in peace—that was so much a part of his later writings.

After an extensive reading of Merton's works as well as several conversations with some of the monks who lived with Merton at the Abbey of Gethsemani, the present writer feels that there is really no noticeable tension, no contradiction, no radical change in Merton's thinking or writing. The concerns of his later writings were really life-long convictions and were in evidence long before he entered the Cistercians.[11] To imply that he abandoned such concerns upon entering religious life is somewhat superficial. Indeed, in him there is a basic point of view that transcends all change, and even his most recent interests are prompted by this view. To say this, however, is not to deny that there is a process of growth or evolution in his writings both in the realization and the presentation of the central message of his spirituality, namely, that man's life is a continuous seeking of God and finding Him by love and sharing that love with other men.[12] To this extent his later

11. There is much talk among authors today about this cyclic development in Merton. Cf. Naomi Burton, who, in her Foreward to *My Argument with the Gestapo: a macaronic journal,* by T. Merton (New York: Doubleday, 1969), p. 8, says: "More and more it seems to me, the concerns of the last years of his life were the same concerns that occupied him in 1940. . . ." Likewise, Alice Mayhew, in "Merton Against Himself," *Commonweal,* XCI (1969–70), 71, says of Merton's interests: "In a number of ways he seems to come full circle, and in others one can see a straightforward and exciting line." Merton himself recognized this cyclic development. Cf. Thomas McDonnell, ed., *A Thomas Merton Reader* (New York: Harcourt, Brace and World, 1962), p. vii, where Merton says in his Introduction: "Much that is spelled out in later books and articles is already implied in THE SEVEN STOREY MOUNTAIN. But it cannot really be seen until it is found in more articulate statements—or perhaps more cryptic ones, . . ."

12. Many authors discuss or comment upon this development in the man or his writings. Cf. A. M. Allchin, "A Liberator, a Reconciler," *Continuum,* VII (1969), 364; Carr Worland, "Death of a Peacemaker," *Catholic Library World,* XL (1969), 423. Again, Merton also recognized this growth or evolution in himself and in his works. Cf. Thomas McDonnell, "An Interview with Thomas Merton," *U. S. Catholic,* XXXIII (1968), 32–33; Thomas Merton, *Raids on the Unspeakable* (New York: New Directions, 1966), p. 172.

B

writing is a logical outgrowth of his earlier writing. However, in all his works, "The point at issue is that all Christians, lay people, religious and priests, must play a constructive and positive part in the world of our time."[13] Yet, "We cannot live for others until we have entered this solitude. If we try to live for them without first living entirely for God, we risk plunging with them all into the abyss."[14]

And so, it seems that although he lived "in a society which for all its unquestionable advantages and all its fantastic ingenuity just does not seem to be able to provide people with lives that are fully human and fully real," Merton, nonetheless, felt no tension nor experienced any contradiction between his commitment to the monastic life and his commitment to the contemporary world.[15] Indeed, most paradoxically, his years as a hermit were also the years of his deepening concern for the world; likewise, the more involved he became with his fellow man, the more necessary was solitude for him. Somehow he recognized that the intense solitude of the contemplative life to which he was called gave him a unique perspective from which he could understand the world's anguish and share in its communion. He noted this not long before his death:

> . . . there is the nature of my own vocation to the monastic, solitary, contemplative life! Of course this monastic life does not necessarily imply a total refusal to have anything to do with the world. Such a refusal, would, in any case, be illusory. It would deceive no one but the monk himself. . . . But the monastic and contemplative life does certainly imply a very special perspective, a viewpoint which others do not share, the viewpoint of one who is not directly engaged in the struggles and controversies of the world. Now it seems to me that if a monk is permitted to be detached from these struggles over particular interests, it is only in

13. Thomas Merton, *Life and Holiness* (New York: Image Books, 1964), p. 107.

14. Thomas Merton, *No Man Is an Island* (New York: Image Books, 1967), p. 171.

15. Thomas Merton, *Faith and Violence: Christian Teaching and Christian Practice* (Notre Dame, Indiana: University of Notre Dame Press, 1968), p. 174.

order that he may give more thought to the interests of all, to the whole question of the reconciliation of all men with one another in Christ. . . .

A contemplative will, then, concern himself with the same problems as other people, but he will try to get to the spiritual and metaphysical roots of these problems—not by analysis but by simplicity.[16]

The present work is concerned with "The Theology of Prayer in the Spirituality of Thomas Merton." Its primary objective is to offer a synthesis of Merton's understanding of prayer, showing its centrality within the thought of his spirituality. While the originality of such a work lies in its being the first attempt at a synthesis of a contemporary theology of prayer drawn from the writings of the author, its significance is manifold.[17] First, it shows that contrary to the opinion of many today, as cited above, there is no real tension or radical change in the development of Merton's spirituality; rather, there is a gradual unfolding, a more explicit awareness in the full understanding of his central message, namely, man's life is a continuous seeking of God and finding Him by love, and sharing that love with other men. Such a unified message is evident, especially in his understanding of prayer, undoubtedly the central preoccupation in his own life as in his writings. Despite Merton's fame and influence, such a topic has not yet been treated in any comprehensive or systematic way. For the present, it is sufficient to describe prayer in Merton's view as "*a consciousness of one's union with God*" or "*an awareness of one's inner self.*"[18]

16. *Ibid.*, pp. 146–47.

17. Merton's recent book, *The Climate of Monastic Prayer*, Cistercian Studies Series, no. 1 (Spencer, Mass.: Cistercian Publications, 1969), is really not a systematic exposition or synthesis of the subject matter of prayer; rather, it is simply the fruit of his own years of study and experience in prayer.

18. The first description is found in Merton's book entitled *Spiritual Direction and Meditation* (Collegeville: Liturgical Press, 1960), p. 67. The second description is from a "Conference on Prayer" delivered to a group of Sisters. This writer listened to the taped recording of the conference while he was at Gethsemani. As shall be shown later the two descriptions are really synonymous.

Second, at a time when there is a marked questioning and de-emphasizing of the nature and value of prayer in contemporary society, there is a need and a desirability of presenting a theology of prayer that is both challenging and creative, yet also realistic. Merton's theology of prayer is such, in that he addresses himself specifically to the real spiritual problem confronting us today, the problem of alienation. It is this estrangement from himself, from society and from God, that has resulted in modern man's apparent incapacity for any kind of genuine spiritual experience.[19] While many writers either ignore the spiritual dimension of such a problem or find themselves incapable of apprehending and thus addressing themselves to the core of the problem, Merton boldly emphasizes that men cannot live together if they do not love one another, and they cannot love one another as brothers if they do not love God, their Common Father. Thus, man's love for his fellow man must come from his communion with God in prayer. For, in prayer man becomes aware of his inner or real self, and, in so doing, realizes that he cannot live merely for himself but must live for others; above all, he must live for God—in Him and with Him. Hence, it is only through a consciousness of his life of union with God in prayer that man can satisfy his desire for perfect freedom as a son of God and his desire for unity, peace, and love with the other sons of God. This is why, says Merton: "It is becoming increasingly evident that the only men in the world who are really happy are the ones who know how to pray."[20]

19. In an article entitled "Christian Action in World Crisis," *Blackfriars,* XLIII (1962), 259, Merton describes the moral evil in the world as due to man's alienation from God. In light of this he says, "The present world crisis is not merely a political and economic conflict. . . . It is a crisis of man's spirit." He then concludes, "The real problem of our time is basically spiritual." The same is also found in his article, "Christian Morality and Nuclear War," *Way,* XIX (1963), 15. In a recent article, "This Is God's Work," *Sisters Today,* XLII (1970), 3, Merton defines alienation as follows: "Alienation is the psychological condition of somebody who is never allowed to be fully himself. . . . There is no real personal meaning to his life, because everything he does belongs to somebody else."

20. Thomas Merton, "The Contemplative Life: Its Meaning and Necessity," *Dublin Review,* CCXXIII (1949), 32.

Third, closely allied to the problem of alienation is man's search for identity. In America today there is a serious and extended identity crisis. Man finds himself bewildered and disoriented. He is not himself; rather, he has lost himself in the illusions of mass society. He is depersonalized and incapable of authenticity. This Merton feels is due in large measure to the prevailing myth that technology is capable of solving all men's problems: "We find ourselves living in a society of men who have discovered their own nonentity where they least expected to—in the midst of power and technological achievement."[21] Because of this, man today has a desperate need for spiritual depth and authenticity in his life, as evidenced in the popularity of psychedelic drugs which attempt to satisfy man's appetite for inner integration and unity. Merton takes explicit cognizance of this search for identity when he stresses that, rather than force and human strategy, prayer and contemplation are the truest ways to the recovery of what is authentically one's own. For it is in prayer that man will find his real self, and in finding this true self, he will find God, the origin and goal of his being. Man, then, must discover his identity in prayer if he is to know himself and give himself fully and maturely to God, and thus keep the way open for present-day technological man to recover the integrity of his own inner being. It is for this reason that Merton asserts that "every Christian is bound to be in some sense a man of prayer."[22]

Fourth, for many of today's Christians, there appears to be an almost exclusive preoccupation regarding their relationship with other men. Undoubtedly, for some, there is a degree of contact with God in such relationships, especially in man's desire for social justice, for equality, and for peace. However, for Merton this is neither the only way nor the most basic way for man to approach

21. Thomas Merton, *The Living Bread* (New York: Farrar, Straus and Cudahy, 1956), p. xiv; a similar view is expressed in his book, *Conjectures of a Guilty Bystander* (Garden City: Doubleday, 1966), p. 253. Cf. also, Thomas Merton, *Mystics and Zen Masters* (New York: Farrar, Straus and Giroux, 1967), pp. 263–64.

22. Merton, *The Climate of Monastic Prayer*, pp. 29–30.

God. While one's neighbor is indeed an indication of the presence of God, so is one's self. Yet, the danger today is that men will see their holiness in activity to the neglect of prayer. Merton warns man against this frequently in his writings: "But just as in the past there has been a one-sided emphasis on the eschatological, so today we tend to see only the incarnational side and to forget the necessary dialectic between eschatology and incarnation."[23] Hence, at a time when the temptation to be satisfied with an almost exclusively horizontal dimension might compound man's troubles, Merton in his theology of prayer reiterates the transcendental element—the need for a direct experience of God. For this reason, especially, his contemplative prayer has a relevant place in the life of the contemporary Christian; indeed, without this direct and immediate relationship with God, man cannot exist fully.[24]

Finally, Merton's theology of prayer is a challenging response to an age that he sees as one of tremendous crisis as well as of tremendous hope. In analyzing modern man's restlessness and disillusionment, Merton recognizes the confusion, the unrest, and the struggle

---

23. Thomas Merton, "Ecumenism and Monastic Renewal," *Journal of Ecumenical Studies,* V (1968), 275. On his last trip, in his *Conference on Prayer* delivered at the Conference of Religious of India in Calcutta on October 27, 1968, Merton strongly emphasized this point: "You will not believe me when I tell you some of the things that are being said, of people going to a priest in confession, complaining of their inability to pray. The priest says, 'Why pray? I don't pray. Why should you? Prayer is irrelevant. Prayer is medieval. It is immaturity. . . .' 'Your action is your prayer and if your action is twenty-four hours a day, your prayer is twenty-four hours a day. . . .' This is the life of prayer which is relevant to the world. It is exceedingly dangerous. In America even some Catholic theologians have elected to go along with the popular theology: God is dead. The keynote is 'horizontal.' God is no longer transcendental. He is nowhere else but purely and simply in my neighbor." The conference was recently published under the title, "A Conference on Prayer," in *Sisters Today,* XLI (1970), 449–56, esp. 450.

24. Such emphasis on the contemporaneity of contemplative prayer is Merton's unique contribution to a theology of prayer. For the present, it suffices to recall the description of such prayer given above in footnote 17. In addition one might note the description given by Merton in an article entitled "Contemplation in a World of Action," written for *Bloominewman* (Newsletter of Newman Club of University of Louisville) on April 2, 1968— prayer is an "inner awareness of God's direct presence."

that surrounds man. There is cruelty, violence, and degradation confronting the man of today and Merton is quick to underscore this. Indeed, there is no more evident proof that man needs a life of prayer than this present condition of chaos. For the Christian immersed in such a society, there will be the added difficulty of finding himself in what Merton describes as the "Diaspora situation." More and more his faith will be menaced; he will become insecure—a marginal person existing in a secular and nonbelieving society.[25] And yet, despite such apparent pessimism in his outlook, there is no reason for Merton to despair of man or of human society. In fact, his ultimate answer to the most desperate situation of man is one of human and Christian hope. For, his task as a spiritual teacher is to try to educate man to a knowledge of that for which he was uniquely created, namely, prayer and contemplation, since it is through them that man becomes a sign of hope for the most authentic values to which his time aspires. It is for this reason, as well as for the other reasons mentioned above, that the present writer feels that Thomas Merton will achieve the distinction of making the contemporary world more aware than ever before of the significance and value of prayer in man's life.

In general, this will be an analytical study of Merton's theology of prayer. Although it will focus principally on the value and meaning of prayer in Merton's spirituality, in order that one better grasp the significance and centrality of his teaching on prayer, certain other essential and interrelated areas of concern in his spirituality will have to be considered. First, it will be necessary to

25. Merton, *Faith and Violence*, p. 209; also found in "How It Is—Apologies to an Unbeliever," *Harper's Magazine,* CCXXXIII (1966), 38. In his book *Seeds of Destruction* (New York: Farrar, Straus and Giroux, 1964), p. 322, Merton describes this "Diaspora" situation as follows: "Consequently it seems, to me that the meaning of the diaspora situation consists in recognizing this fact and in realizing how true it is that the Christian and the monk are actually in a position of working out their own salvation and that of the world together with the non-Christian and the non-monk, so that we actually have much to learn from them, and must be open to them, since it is always possible that life-giving grace may come to us through our encounter with them. This is what I mean by the Christian in the diaspora."

study Merton's concept of the spiritual life, which he considers "the life of man's real self."[26] Such will involve a discussion of two basic concepts involved in the foundational structure of his spirituality: "union with God" and "transformation of consciousness." After these foundational statements have been studied, there will follow a synthesis of Merton's understanding of "personal prayer" in which the meaning, the nature, and the significance of prayer in his spirituality will be analyzed in light of his central message, namely, man's life is a continuous seeking of God and finding Him by love, and sharing that love with others. In addition, the apostolic leanings of all prayer as evidenced in his concern for others will be investigated, as well as the relationship of personal prayer to liturgical prayer. It will be necessary to examine briefly certain fundamental ascetical themes in his spirituality, such as sacrifice and renunciation. Merton feels these are required, not merely as background for understanding his teaching on prayer, but also as essential elements in one's prayer life in that they support prayer. This will involve a study of Merton's attitude toward the world as well as a study of his own life of solitude and communion. Finally, Merton's ideas on contemplative prayer will be critically evaluated in light of their originality and contemporaneity for today's Christians as well as their value for providing a coherent and productive solution to some of the problems facing contemporary man. Here, as well as in the discussion of all his themes, Merton points out that, while the vocation of all Christians consists in a daily existential response to God's word, "It is for each one to find out for himself the kind of work and environment in which he can best lead a spiritual life."[27]

26. Merton, *No Man Is an Island*, p. 7.
27. *Ibid.*, p. 91.

CHAPTER I

UNION WITH GOD

THE FOUNDATIONAL STRUCTURE OF MERTON'S SPIRITUALITY
I: THE MYSTERY OF GOD

ONE OF THE TRUTHS emphasized by Merton in his writings is that "man has a fundamental duty to orientate his entire being and his life to God."[1] One wonders how many Christians today realize the depth of such a statement. For, in a sense, there is a tendency to orient one's being and life, not to God, but to one's fellow man—the result being that one's spiritual life is equated with some form of moral or ethical behavior. For Merton, however, the spiritual life of man was not primarily the work of man; rather, it was the work of God in man. And hence, one's moral and ethical life must lead to something beyond itself. It must lead "to the experience of union with God, and to our transformation in Him."[2]

THE MEANING AND GOAL OF SPIRITUALITY

In his book, *Life and Holiness*, Merton notes that sanctity, which can best be described as the ultimate perfection of the spiritual life, is constituted "first of all by ontological union with God in Christ."[3]

1. Thomas Merton, *A Balanced Life of Prayer* (Trappist, Kentucky: Gethsemani Abbey, 1951), p. 11.

2. Thomas Merton, *The Ascent to Truth* (New York: Harcourt, Brace, 1951), p. 8.

3. Merton, *Life and Holiness*, p. 57. Cf. also Thomas Merton, "Christ the Way," *Sponsa Regis*, XXXIII (1962), 146. In *No Man Is an Island*, p. 56, Merton simply says: "Sanctity does not consist merely in *doing* the will of

Such a description is especially noteworthy in that it contains within itself the essence of Merton's spirituality, namely, every Christian is called in some way or other to an intimate and perfect union with God in Christ. In addition, in describing sanctity in this way, it is evident that for Merton Christian holiness cannot be reduced merely to ethical behavior nor to some kind of moral conduct. Although there cannot be any genuine holiness without these dimensions, man must be careful to distinguish between the pseudo-spirituality of activism and the true spirituality of Christian action that is guided by the Spirit. Men today must realize that their call to holiness is primarily a call to share in the transcendence of God: "Hence we must first be transformed interiorly into new men, and then act according to the Spirit given us by God, the Spirit of our new life, the Spirit of Christ."[4] Holiness, therefore, is not so much a question of *doing*, but of *being*. Just as a monk is important more for what he *is* than for what he *does*, so, too, for every Christian: " 'Being' always takes precedence over 'doing' and 'having.' We must first be sons of the heavenly Father."[5]

Because man is called to this union with God in the depths of his own being, he finds his true identity, his full reality, in God alone. Indeed, as Merton notes, man is not fully man until he is "one spirit" with God.[6] And so, he must devote himself wholeheartedly to God. He must "become conscious of the fact that the only way

---

God. It consists in willing the will of God. For sanctity is union with God. . . ." In *The Ascent of Truth,* p. 187, Merton asserts: "Sanctity consists in a perfect union of mind and will with God." In both these definitions the *ontological* basis of union is evident.

4. Merton, *Life and Holiness,* p. 57; Merton, "Christ the Way," p. 146. In *The Sign of Jonas* (New York: Image Books, 1956), p. 255, Merton claims: "All creatures are holy insofar as they share in His being, but men are called to be holy in a far superior way—by somehow sharing His transcendence and rising above the level of everything that is not God."

5. Thomas Merton, *Monastic Peace* (Trappist, Kentucky: Abbey of Gethsemani, 1958), p. 9.

6. Thomas Merton, *New Seeds of Contemplation* (New York: New Directions, 1961), p. 140. In this context Merton notes in *Monastic Peace,* pp. 23–24: "It should be quite clear that living for 'God alone' in this sense by no means excludes the love of other men."

to live *is* to live in a world that *is* charged with the presence and reality of God."[7] Merton himself came to this realization as regards his own life: "Ultimately the only way that I can be myself is to become identified with Him in Whom is hidden the reason and fulfillment of my existence."[8] For Merton, then, there can be no doubt that God Himself is the source of one's spiritual life: "We live as spiritual men when we live as men seeking God."[9] Thus one can conclude that, according to Merton, holiness or sanctity is achieved when one lives his life in its fullness in conscious union with the living God.[10]

Although Merton is offering to the man of today what one might call an inward-looking spirituality or a spirituality of "being," nonetheless, it is a spirituality that is intended to give meaning and direction, not only to man's understanding of God, of others, of himself, but also to his very life and to his work. Above all, it is a spirituality that underscores the intimate *relationship* that should exist between man and God. Because of this, one could say that the

7. Thomas Merton, *The Seven Storey Mountain* (New York: Signet Books, 1948), p. 188.

8. Merton, *New Seeds of Contemplation*, pp. 35-36.

9. Thomas Merton, *Thoughts in Solitude* (New York: Image Books, 1968), p. 146. In *No Man Is an Island*, p. 84, Merton acknowledges God as the source of life. In a later article entitled "The Spiritual Father in the Desert Tradition," *Monastic Studies*, V (1968), 89, Merton says: "The only source of the spiritual life is the Holy Spirit." There is no contradiction here since in the latter he is talking about the explicit and ordinary communication of God to man which always takes place in the Spirit. The latter article can also be found in *Cistercian Studies*, III (1968), 3-23.

10. Thomas Merton, *The Silent Life* (New York: Farrar, Straus and Cudahy, 1957), p. 168. Obviously, one is not referring exclusively to the spiritual dimension of man's life. As Merton points out in *Spiritual Direction and Meditation*, p. 6, "the spiritual life . . . is the life of the whole person." Cf. *New Seeds of Contemplation*, p. 140, where Merton writes: "The 'spiritual life' is then the perfectly balanced life in which the body with its passions and instincts, the mind with its reasoning and its obedience to principles and the spirit with its passive illumination by the Light and Love of God form one complete man who is in God and with God and from God and for God." In *Thoughts in Solitude*, p. 55, Merton asserts: "A life is either all spiritual or not spiritual at all." Finally, in *No Man Is an Island*, p. 85, he says: "To have a spiritual life is to have a life that is spiritual in all its wholeness. . . ."

focus of such spirituality consists in revealing to contemporary man the double experience that he himself continually must undergo in the spiritual life: the experience of himself and his own destitution, and the experience of God whose mercy gives him salvation in Christ. Merton writes in *Thoughts in Solitude*:

> Then we discover what the spiritual life really is. . . . It is the silence of our whole being in compunction and adoration before God, in the habitual realization that He is everything and we are nothing, that He is the Center to which all things tend, and to Whom all our actions must be directed. That our life and strength proceed from Him, that both in life and in death we depend entirely on Him. . . .[11]

For Merton, the spiritual life is always inclusive of this two-fold experience. First, man must become keenly aware of the presence and goodness of God in his life and must enter into an intimate relationship with Him since the fulfillment of his destiny can be found only in Him. This knowledge of God, this experience of God, is the one thing that makes the nothingness of man finally begin to be.[12] However, this knowledge of God presupposes a true knowledge of self. Hence, man must likewise recognize his own dignity as a redeemed son of God if he is to transcend himself and achieve an intimate relationship with God. This Merton underscores in *The Climate of Monastic Prayer* when he says: "Instead we know him in so far as we become aware of ourselves as known through and through by him."[13] In Merton's view, then, there is a

11. Merton, *Thoughts in Solitude*, p. 52.

12. More shall be said about this knowledge in the following chapter in the discussion on man's transformation of consciousness. For the present, it is sufficient to show that in his most recent book, *The Climate of Monastic Prayer*, pp. 113–114, Merton says: "Our knowledge of God is paradoxically a knowledge not of him as the object of our scrutiny, but of ourselves as utterly dependent on his saving and merciful knowledge of us."

13. *Ibid.*, p. 113. Merton throughout his writings refers to the importance of self-knowledge for the spiritual life. Cf. *The Ascent to Truth*, p. 177, "the first step to sanctity is self-knowledge." See also Thomas Merton, "Examination of Conscience and Conversatio Morum," *Collectanea Ordinis Cisterciensium Reformatorum*, XXV (1963), 359: "There is no question whatever that self-knowledge is fundamental to all spiritual life."

continuity between this self-knowledge and this awareness of God, and it is to this extent that the spiritual life is the life of man's real self.[14] Finally, it should be noted that this knowledge of God, which is based upon knowledge of one's true self, is a knowledge which is affective. Therefore, in Merton's spirituality, man is made essentially for a *loving knowledge of God:* "Spiritual life is not mental life. It is not thought alone. Nor is it, of course, a life of sensation, a life of feeling, . . . Nor does the spiritual life exclude thought and feeling. It needs both."[15] Only in this way can man bring his entire being into communication and ultimately into communion with God.[16]

In view of such teaching on sanctity and the spiritual life, it

14. This continuity is also brought out in *Monastic Peace,* p. 19, where Merton says: "Our first task then is to know ourselves, to know the good that is in us, to know God's love for us, . . ."

15. Merton, *Thoughts in Solitude,* p. 29.

16. It is important to note here the interrelationship in Merton's spirituality among such terms as union, communion, awareness, prayer, charity. According to Merton, man's spiritual life can best be described in terms of an experience of his *union* with God (or similarly, as shall be shown later, of the discovery of one's own inner self in the divine image). This experience is had, first of all, in *prayer,* which is basically an awareness of one's union with God. It is, however, more fully realized in contemplation, which Merton describes in his book, *Seasons of Celebration* (New York: Farrar, Straus and Giroux, 1965), p. 26, as "the intimate realization of one's perfect union with Christ 'in one Spirit.' " As shall become evident from the subsequent discussion in the present chapter, this perfect union is referred to by Merton as man's mystical or transforming union or man's *communion* with God. Such communion is essentially a union of perfect love or *charity* in that its realization or awareness consists primarily in loving God with a love that is disinterested and totally free. Hence, God, Who is really beyond all knowledge, is known in contemplation through love. Such a perfect identity of love between man and God in contemplation should also overflow in a love for all other men in Christ. This Merton notes in *New Seeds of Contemplation,* p. 65, when he states: "For contemplation is not ultimately perfect unless it is shared." Hence, one can say that, for Merton, man's ultimate goal in the spiritual life is the awareness or realization of his union with God in Christ by perfect charity. Such a statement in no way negates the fact that it is charity that constitutes the essence of Christian perfection. This latter point shall be treated in more detail in the third chapter. For the present, it is sufficient to remind the reader that this point should be kept in mind whenever the present writer speaks of man's "experience of his union with God" as the goal of the spiritual life.

follows that every Christian should have some experience of God as a living and personal reality in his life. In fact, if the man of today is to live a full and integrated Christian life, his contact with God must be such that he experiences a union with Him as well as a transformation of consciousness. Such are the two principles underlying Merton's spirituality. Obviously, the two principles are related closely and cannot be divided in reality without destroying man's spiritual life itself. However, for purpose of clarification, they shall be analyzed separately. The first principle, "union with God," will be studied in the remainder of the present chapter, while the second principle, "transformation of consciousness," will be examined in the following chapter. In this way the basic foundational statements of Merton's spirituality will be treated amply, and one will be able to understand better the centrality of prayer and the interrelation of prayer and asceticism, both of which will be discussed in the subsequent chapters.

The spiritual man, then, has but one goal in life, according to Merton, and that is to realize the end for which he was created, namely, personal and intimate union with God in Christ by love.[17] Continually throughout his writings Merton concerns himself with this deep search for union with God and with pointing out the relationship that must exist between man's love for God and his union with Him: "The more we love God, the more closely are we united to Him and the more perfect are our lives."[18] Since it is

17. Most recently, Thomas Merton, in *Zen and the Birds of Appetite* (New York: New Directions, 1968), pp. 131–32, asserts: "Paradise is not the final goal of the spiritual life . . . the ultimate end is the Kingdom of God." Later in the book, p. 132, he describes the Kingdom of God as the "work of the Mystical Christ, the New Adam, in whom all men as 'one Person' or one 'Son of God' will transfigure the cosmos and offer it resplendent to the Father." It is in view of this that this writer has described the ultimate goal of the spiritual life, not merely as an awareness of union with God, but an awareness of union with God in Christ by love.

18. Thomas Merton, "The Primacy of Contemplation," *Cross and Crown*, II (1950), 5. Cf. also, "Thomas Merton on Renunciation," *Catholic World*, CLXXI (1950), 426–27; Thomas Merton, *The New Man* (New York: Mentor-Omega Books, 1961), pp. 110–111. Furthermore, Merton emphasizes that if

basically an awareness of this union with God that man searches for in prayer, it is necessary to understand the full meaning of this concept in Merton's theology.[19]

In his book, *Conjectures of a Guilty Bystander*, Merton writes: "Man is the image of God, not His shadow."[20] Such a revelation constitutes in Merton's theology the basis for what one might call man's *natural union with God*. Following the Fathers of the Church as well as the traditions of Cistercian spirituality, Merton taught that man by his very essence has a natural capacity for divine union.[21] Inasmuch as he has been created in the image of God and created for pure love, man is destined by God for a perfect union of likeness with Him. Throughout his own life, Merton searched to discover precisely what this union meant and in many of his writings he expressed what it really meant to say that man was

man is to grow in love and union with God, then the love of one's fellow man is also necessary. Cf. Thomas Merton, "Christian Freedom and Monastic Formation," *American Benedictine Review*, XIII (1962), 309.

19. Merton, *Spiritual Direction and Meditation*, p. 67.

20. Merton, *Conjectures of a Guilty Bystander*, p. 149. For Merton this doctrine of the image of God is the only valid basis for an authentic Christian anthropology, a topic that will be discussed in the final chapter. For the present, it is important to note how Merton is influenced by the Fathers regarding this doctrine. While several of the Fathers stress this idea of the image of God in their teaching (i.e., Clement of Alexandria, *Stromata* 2:19–PG 8/1047; Origen, *Homilia in Leviticum* 4:3–PG 12/436), Merton is predominantly influenced by Augustine, who, in his *De Trinitate*, 14:8–PL 42,1044, regards man as the image of God by reason of his rational nature itself. Thus, Augustine, in *De Trinitate* 14:15–PL 42,1055, sees the divine image as orientating man's spirit toward contemplative union with God.

21. Regarding the Fathers, cf. the previous footnote. As regards the Cistercian tradition, Aelred of Rievaulx, who followed Augustine's teaching, exercised a great influence on Merton regarding this doctrine, especially insofar as he saw the image as a constitutive element of the soul's nature and hence unable to be destroyed (*Speculum Caritatis*, 1:4–PL 195/508). Likewise Aelred notes that insofar as the image is rooted in man's being, it gives him a capacity for God (*Speculum Caritatis*, 1:3–PL 195,507).

made in the image of God and thus made for perfect union with Him. Most succinctly, he describes this state of natural union with God as "an immediate existential union with Him residing in our soul as the source of our physical life."[22]

Among the elements constituting this natural unity of man in the Divine Image, Merton notes first of all that man has an obediential potency of being drawn to God in perfect identification. In addition, two further elements, rooted in man's nature, constitute him in God's image and make him capable of perfect union with God. These are his capacity for perfect freedom and for pure love—"for at the very core of our essence we are constituted in God's likeness by our freedom, and the exercise of that freedom is nothing else but the exercise of disinterested love—the love of God for His own sake, because He is God."[23] For Merton it is above all because of his freedom that man possesses this natural union with God; for, man is free only to the extent that he is like God, only in proportion as he shares in the freedom of God.[24] It is precisely this aspect of man's nature which renders him capable of loving God and thus fulfilling himself, as Merton describes:

> The freedom that is in our nature is our ability to love something, someone besides ourselves, and for the sake, not of ourselves, but of the one we love. There is in the human will an innate tendency, an inborn capacity for disinterested love. This power to love another for his own sake is one of the things that makes us like God, because this power is the one thing in us that is free from all determination. It is a power which transcends and escapes the inevitability of self-love.[25]

22. Merton, *The New Man*, p. 84. Here he also refers to this union as the "natural presence of the uncreated Image."

23. Merton, *The Seven Storey Mountain*, p. 365. Cf. also, *New Seeds of Contemplation*, p. 202.

24. Thomas Merton, *The Secular Journal of Thomas Merton* (New York: Dell Publishing Company, 1959), p. 171; Merton, *No Man Is an Island*, p. 35.

25. Unpublished material from the original manuscript of *The Seven Storey Mountain*. Cf. *A Thomas Merton Reader*, p. 341. For Merton, love is the fulfillment of man's freedom. Cf. Thomas Merton, "Is the 'Contemplative Life' Finished?" *Monastic Studies*, VII (1969), 12.

Man, then, according to Merton, has but one objective if he is to realize his union with God and that is to love God with a love that is pure and disinterested and free. It was for this that man came into the world and it is in this way that he must respond to the source of love, God Himself, Who is beyond and yet within him. This is the full implication in Merton's assertion: "To say that I am made in the image of God is to say that love is the reason for my existence, for God is love."[26]

Therefore, as regards this natural union of man with God, one might note, by way of conclusion, first of all, that: "One of the things rooted in our nature which constitutes us in God's image is out innate liberty."[27] second, because man is free, he is capable of rendering to God the highest degree of love possible, namely, loving Him for His own sake. It is in this way that man responds to the free love of God for him, and thus finds his own true dignity. Hence Merton writes: "Man's greatest dignity, his most essential and peculiar power, the most intimate secret of his humanity is his capacity to love. This power in the depths of man's soul stamps him in the image and likeness of God."[28] Finally, man's capacity to achieve this communion with God lies in his surrendering himself to God's love, in losing himself in God. It is all this that is implied in man's first union with God when Merton says: "For Him we are made."[29]

Although man is united to God by nature, for Merton, he has in a sense failed to realize this fundamental orientation towards God in that his human nature has been weakened by original sin. In fact, this natural union of man with the Divine Image is inaccessible; it cannot be actualized without grace insofar as original sin has covered over man's innate capacity for divine union.[30]

26. Merton, *New Seeds of Contemplation*, p. 60.

27. *A Thomas Merton Reader*, p. 341.

28. Thomas Merton, *Disputed Questions* (New York: Farrar, Straus and Cudahy, 1960), p. 98.

29. Merton, *The Ascent of Truth*, p. 53.

30. In *Zen and the Birds of Appetite*, p. 116, where Merton speaks of Paradise as "the state in which man was originally created to live on earth," he goes

Merton sees the sin of Adam as a failure to be true to his own nature causing the Divine Image in him to be disfigured and mutilated. "He lost," says Merton, "his *rectitude*, and from then on it became impossible for him without grace, to be true to himself, or true to the obediential potency for union with God . . ."[31] Because of this sin, fallen man, although still retaining the *image* of God, insofar as it is of the very essence of his being, has lost his likeness to God: "Fallen man, then, is one in whom the Divine Image, or free-will, has become a slave to itself by making itself its own idol. The image of God is distorted by "unlikeness."[32] In light of this, man has become deeply false to his inmost reality, to his true or inner self to the person he was meant to be—made in the image and likeness of God. This Merton points out in his Introduction to *The Monastic Theology of Aelred of Rievaulx:*

> The image of God in man—the openness to love, the capacity for total consent to God in Himself and in others—remains indestructible. But it can be buried and imprisoned under selfishness. The image of God in man is not destroyed by sin but utterly disfigured by it. To be exact, the image of God in man becomes self-contradictory when its openness closes in upon itself, when it ceases to be a capacity for love and becomes simply an appetite for domination or possession: when it ceases to give and seeks only to get. . . . In monastic terms: the inclination to love, which is at the core of man's very nature as a free being, is turned in on itself as its own object and ceases to be love.[33]

---

on to say, p. 137: "Paradise has been lost . . . Paradise cannot be opened to us except by a free gift of the divine mercy. Yet it is true to say that Paradise is always present within us, since God Himself is present, though perhaps inaccessible." In *The New Man*, p. 69, Merton notes that man still retains the *innate capacity* for divine union.

31. Thomas Merton, *The Spirit of Simplicity Characteristic of the Cistercian Order*. An Official report demanded and approved by the General Chapter together with Texts from St. Bernard of Clairvaux on Interior Simplicity. Trans. and commentary by a Cistercian Monk of Our Lady of Gethsemani (Thomas Merton) (Trappist, Kentucky: Abbey of Our Lady of Gethsemani, 1948), p. 78.

32. Merton, *The Silent Life*, p. 18.

33. Thomas Merton, Introduction to *The Monastic Theology of Aelred of Rievaulx*, by A. Hallier (Spencer, Mass.: Cistercian Publications, 1969) p. x.

In a real sense, then, man has, for Merton, "become alienated from his inner self which is the image of God."[34] For this reason, Merton sees all sin as a radical "refusal to be what we are, a rejection of our mysterious, contingent, spiritual reality hidden in the very mystery of God. Sin is our refusal to be what we were created to be—sons of God, images of God."[35]

However, this alienation from God, the result of Adam's Fall, has been rectified in the Incarnation of Christ, a mystery which holds pre-eminence in Merton's theology as he himself has stated:

> For although like all other mysteries it flows from the highest of all, the mystery of the Trinity, yet with regard to us the Incarnation is the most important of all because it is through Christ that we are incorporated into the life of the three Divine Persons and receive into our souls the Holy Spirit, the bond of perfection, Who unites us to God with the same Love which unites the Father and the Son.[36]

Essentially Merton sees this mystery as a *re-creation* or *restoration* of the divine likeness and freedom in man. Having lost his capacity for realizing his union with God to the extent that the divine image in him has been distorted, man now recovers the original perfection intended for human nature by God. Christ, Merton holds, has now "restored man to his original existential communion with God, the source of life."[37] Without in any way minimizing the demands of this mystery in one's life, namely, man's reverence for all creation and his respect for all men in whom he must see in mystery the presence of Christ, Merton attempts to show that the primary purpose of Christ becoming incarnate was to effect a new union between God and man.[38] Therefore one can conclude that what has

---

34. Merton, *New Seeds of Contemplation*, p. 280.

35. Merton, *Life and Holiness*, p. 12.

36. Merton, *The Ascent to Truth*, p. 313.

37. Merton, *The New Man*, p. 91.

38. Cf. Thomas Merton, "La formation monastique selon Adam de Perseigne," tr. by C. Dumont, *Collectanea Ordinis Cisterciensium Reformatorum*, XIX (1957), 16, where he says: "L'Incarnation, . . . est le climat d'amour divin, . . . cet amour dans lequel la force mysterieuse et infinie de l'Esprit-Saint travaille secrètement à donner naissance à de nouveaux Christ."

been said about man being created in the image and likeness of God and thus being destined for union with God is incomplete and somewhat meaningless for a Christian unless it is viewed in its proper relation to the Person of the Incarnate Word, Jesus Christ, Who came to form a new union between man and God.[39]

MAN'S SUPERNATURAL UNION IN CHRIST

Therefore, man is called to a higher and more intimate union with God in Christ. This new union Merton calls man's *supernatural union in Christ* or man's union with God by grace.[40] In *The New Man* he defines this union as "an immediate existential union with

39. Here it is important to note that Merton, (following the Fathers of the Church and Bernard) holds that creation itself is orientated to Christ, not only in the sense that He is its term and fulfillment but also in the sense that He is its source and beginning. Commenting on this, he says in *The New Man*, p. 81: "And we too, from the very moment we come into existence, are potential representations of Christ simply because we possess the human nature which was created in Him and was assumed by Him in the Incarnation, saved by Him on the Cross and glorified by Him in His Ascension." Again on p. 82, he writes: "The very fact that men were made in the image of God meant that they were already potentially united with the Word of God Who was to come and take human nature to Himself." This union Merton calls the "natural presence of the uncreated Image within us" (*The New Man*, p. 84). In one of his last conferences, "A Conference on Prayer," p. 452, Merton again referred to this presence of Christ: "Even before the Lord dwells in us by His Spirit there is a deeper presence which comes, in a certain sense, from the fact that we are created in Him, and . . . live in Him—our being is in Christ even ontologically. God wills us to come into being in Christ." One can conclude, then, that for Merton Christ is naturally present to man in his physical life and, as shall now be shown, spiritually present to man in his supernatural life. Hence, man's supernatural life is in no sense destructive of his natural life; rather, it perfects and fulfills it. It should be noted that both presences are actualized together, although they can be considered theoretically separate. Cf. *The New Man*, p. 103.

40. Merton identifies man's life of grace with his life in Christ in *Spiritual Direction and Meditation*, p. 66. In light of this, grace is simply "our divine sonship in Christ," as he notes in *Monastic Peace*, p. 25, or "God's own life, shared by us" as he points out in *The Seven Storey Mountain*, p. 167. A more existential definition of grace is found in *Life and Holiness*, p. 30: "For all practical purposes we might as well say that grace is the quality of our being that results from the sanctifying energy of God acting dynamically in our life."

the Triune God as the source of the grace and virtues in our spirit."[41]
As such, it implies, first of all, an actualization of the divine image
in man and of his basic orientation towards God. Moreover, in this
new re-creation there is a further revelation of God's love; for, His
love is now concretized in the love of Jesus Christ. It is through Him
that the divine image in man is restored to a likeness. And so man's
natural life is now elevated and fulfilled; he becomes a new creature,
a new man regenerated by the Holy Spirit in Christ. He now shares
God's supernatural life through his incorporation into Christ; his
"life is hidden with Christ in God."[42]

In describing this new union, Merton notes that it is not merely a
moral union in which man tries to imitate Christ's virtues or to
produce His dispositions, nor is it some kind of a psychological
identification in which man constantly is thinking of Christ and
trying to imagine what might have been Christ's sentiments.
Rather, it is a spiritual union in which "Christ mystically identifies
His members with Himself by giving them His Holy Spirit."[43] In
his book, *New Seeds of Contemplation*, Merton says of this union:

> A "new being" is brought into existence. I become a "new man"
> and this "new man," spiritually and mystically one identity, is at
> once Christ and myself. . . . This spiritual union of my being with
> Christ in one "new man" is the work of the Holy Spirit, the
> Spirit of Love, the Spirit of Christ.
>   . . . The union of my soul with God in Christ is not of this
> ontological or inseparable character. It is, on the contrary, an
> accidental union: yet it is more than just a moral union or an
> agreement of hearts. The union of the Christian with Christ . . . is
> a mystical union in which Christ Himself becomes the source and

41. Merton, *The New Man*, p. 85.

42. Merton, *Seasons of Celebration*, p. 67. Earlier in the book, pp. 48–49,
one notes the meaning of the redemption which Merton describes as follows:
"The redemption is Christ Himself . . . living and sharing His divine life with
His elect. To be redeemed . . . is also to live in Christ, to be born again of
water and the Holy Spirit, to be in Him a new creature, to live in the Spirit."
Cf. also Thomas Merton, "Time and the Liturgy," *Worship*, XXXI (1956),
2–3.

43. Merton, *The New Man*, p. 99.

principle of divine life in me. Christ Himself, . . . "breathes" in me divinely in giving me His Spirit.[44]

In referring to this union as spiritual, Merton is emphasizing that this union takes place in the order of grace; man becomes identified with Christ through the Spirit. Hence, man is said to be divinized in Christ insofar as Christ becomes the center and source of his being. Because Christ communicates His life to man, man receives His Spirit Who reveals to him the reality of Christ's presence and thus enables him to be united to God in his own person as a true son of God by adoption.

The new man, possessed by the Spirit of Christ, must try to penetrate the inner meaning of his life in Christ in order to see the full significance of its demands as Merton points out:

> The Holy Spirit . . . not only makes us understand something of God's love as it is manifested to us in Christ, but He also makes us live by that love and experience its action in our hearts. When we do so, the Spirit lets us know that this life and action are the life and action of Christ in us. And so the charity that is poured forth in our hearts by the Holy Spirit brings us into an intimate, experiential communion with Christ.[45]

As a son of God, he must realize what it means to possess once again the likeness of God within him; he must examine what it means to live by the Spirit in his life. In addition, he must come to the realization that this Spirit unites him not only to God as Father, but also to all other men, who share this Spirit, as brothers in the one

---

44. Merton, *New Seeds of Contemplation,* pp. 158–99. Two points should be noted. First, Merton here speaks of the union as being mystical. Obviously, he is using the term in a wide sense, since man's mystical union with God is the culmination or perfection of his spiritual union as will be shown below. Second, he here refers to this union as accidental only to differentiate it from the Hypostatic Union which he previously noted, p. 158, is ontologically perfect—"a union of essences in one subsisting Personal entity Who is the Eternal God." Elsewhere, Merton calls man's spiritual union an ontological union. Cf. *supra,* pp. 1–2, footnote 3.

45. Merton, *No Man Is an Island,* p. 137.

Christ.[46] Both these aspects are underscored in *Seasons of Celebration* when Merton says of the Spirit: "He makes Christ live in us when the love that comes to us from Christ becomes our love and remains in us while it also remains in Him. This same love, this same Spirit, unites us all to one another in Christ."[47]

The Spirit, however, does not accomplish His work in man if man remains completely passive and inert. If man is to enter fully into the mystery of his supernatural union in Christ, he must respond to God's gift of grace and consent to live as a son of God. Such consent must be elicited by man's own free will, as Merton implies, when he says: "If we would live like sons of God, we must reproduce in our own lives the life and the charity of His only begotten Son."[48] It is the exercise of this new freedom as a son of God that makes man capable of achieving his true likeness to God. And what is required of man to exercise this freedom in his life is an openness to the Spirit in *faith* and in *love*. Merton writes: "It is the easiest thing in the world to possess this life . . . ; all you have to do is believe and love.[49]

Man's supernatural union in Christ, then, must be constituted by faith and by love. "In a word," says Merton, "the whole Christian life consists in seeking the will of God by loving faith and carrying

46. In "Christian Freedom and Monastic Formation," p. 309, Merton points out the close relationship between this two-fold union: "and those are most closely united to their brothers who are at the same time most closely united to God." In addition, the importance of such a union with one's fellow man is also brought out in his book, *What Are These Wounds? The Life of a Cistercian Mystic, Saint Lutgarde of Aywières* (Milwaukee: Bruce, 1950), p. 140, where he asserts: "Fraternal union is given us as one of our principal means for arriving at mystical union with God."

47. Merton, *Seasons of Celebration*, p. 43; similarly found in Merton's article, "Church and Bishop," *Worship*, XXXVII (1963), 119. Such a description is really a description of one's Christian life as Merton shows in *The Living Bread*, p. 4: "The Christian life is nothing else but Christ living in us, by His Holy Spirit. It is Christ's love, sharing itself with us in charity. It is Christ in us, loving the Father, by His Spirit. It is Christ uniting us to our brothers by charity in the bond of this same Spirit."

48. Merton, *No Man Is an Island*, p. 57.

49. Merton, *New Seeds of Contemplation*, p. 160.

out that will by faithful love."[50] According to Merton, there is an especially intimate connection between the two. In view of this fact, faith cannot be looked upon merely as an assent of the mind to certain truths; rather, says Merton, "it is the gift of our whole being to *TRUTH itself*, to the Word of God."[51] Man essentially believes not because he wants to know, but because he wants to be— to be his true self, which can be found only in God.[52] Faith, then, in Merton's view, cannot be looked upon merely as the moment in one's spiritual life when man accepts God. It is man's whole life inasmuch as it brings him into vital contact with God and then preserves his union with God in Christ. Insofar as that union is with a God Who is Love, it follows that as man's faith becomes more intensive, it also becomes more deeply penetrated with love and more vitalized by charity.[53] For only a man of faith is sufficiently open to receive God's love.[54] In turn, the man who has received this love must reach out to everyone else who is imbued with this same Spirit of Christ. Merton notes: "Our faith is given us not to see

50. Merton, *Life and Holiness, p.* 36; similarly found in Thomas Merton, "The Testing of Ideals," *Sponsa Regis,* XXXIII (1961), 96.

51. *Ibid.,* p. 73. Also found in Thomas Merton, "The Life of Faith," *Sponsa Regis,* XXXIII (1961–62), 168.

52. The relationship between man's true self and his union with God will be the subject matter of the following chapter in which the problem of self-transformation will be discussed. Here it is sufficient to point out the relationship between *faith* and *existence* for Merton. In *Thoughts in Solitude,* p. 113, he writes: "By faith I find my own true being in God." Cf. also *Conjectures of a Guilty Bystander,* p. 19, and Thomas Merton, "The Night Spirit and the Dawn Air," *New Blackfriars,* XLVI (1965), 690.

53. Merton's view on faith as "communion with God" is well expressed in *New Seeds of Contemplation,* pp. 135–40.

54. Here one notes the intimate connection between faith and love in this union. Merton emphasizes this in several of his writings. Cf. *Disputed Questions,* p. 123: "The tremendous work of Christian love is also at every moment a work of faith." Thomas Merton, "Pâques; une Vie Nouvelle," *La Vie Spirituelle,* tr. by M. Toole, C (1959), 346: "Une foi vivante au Christ est inséparable de l'amour du Christ." In "The Psalms and Contemplation," *Orate Fratres,* XXIV (1950), 434, Merton says: "Faith is penetrated by love. It only establishes a living contact between the soul and God in so far as it is vitalized by charity." Cf. Thomas Merton, *Bread in the Wilderness* (New York: New Directions, 1953), 117–18.

whether or not our neighbor is Christ but to recognize Christ in him and to help our love make both him and ourselves more fully Christ."[55]

Therefore, the man who is receptive to God's love for him—who possesses this *loving faith*—must in turn live a life of *faithful love*. He must reveal the great mystery of God's love for him. This Merton recalled in one of his final conferences given in India when he said:

> This love is the very root of our being. Therefore what we are called to do is to live as habitually and constantly as possible with great simplicity on this level of love which proceeds from the depths of our own being where Christ reigns and loves. This is a dimension of life which no one can take away unless we close the door ourselves and no one can bring it in unless we open the door to Christ, opening our hearts to Christ and dwelling there.[56]

Man, therefore, as a son of God, who is created to love God, must live his entire life as a response of love. This he does fully when he not only accepts God's love in faith but also shares his faith in God through love. It is only in this context that love, which is meant to be communicated, can be understood as the key to the meaning of life and as the root of our being. For, it is through a love based on faith and a faith permeated with love that man comes into contact with his own deepest self and with the self of his fellow man in Christ.[57]

To realize his union with God in faith and love, therefore, must be the ultimate reason for the existence of each Christian and the end of all his actions. Because such union is mediated through Jesus Christ, man, then, must actively participate in the mystery of

55. Merton, *Disputed Questions*, p. 125.

56. Merton, "A Conference on Prayer," p. 452.

57. Merton brings this point out rather well in his book, *Disputed Questions*, p. 123: "As we grow in love and in unity with those who are loved by Christ (that is to say, all men), we become more and more capable of apprehending and obscurely grasping something of the tremendous reality of Christ in the world, Christ in ourselves, and Christ in our fellow man."

Christ; he must enter into it; he must make that mystery his own. For, it is only in Christ that he can receive the Spirit and thus be led back to the Father, Who is Love. In Merton's spirituality, therefore, Christ will hold central place for the man who is seeking union with God. For, it is Christ Who teaches man the way to love God by showing him how God has really loved him. Merton himself was intensely aware of this life in Christ in his own striving for union with God. Speaking of the monastic life, he said:

> The monk must always be conscious of the fact that, without Christ, there would be no salvation, no happiness, no joy, because man would be irrevocably cut off from God, the source of all life and joy. He must realize, above all, how utterly useless is human effort to please God, without Christ....
>
> Here then is our situation—without Christ we are entirely cut off from God, we have no access to Him.... With and in Christ all our lives are transformed and sanctified.[58]

MAN'S MYSTICAL UNION IN GOD

In view of this sharing in the mystery of Christ in all its dimensions, every Christian is capable of perfect assimilation to Christ in a union of loving faith. Every man, then, must become spiritually identified with Christ Who is the principle of his union with God. However, this very identification implies a responsibility to develop and to grow in one's new life. Hence, the union with God, which is at the basis of Merton's spirituality, is of necessity something dynamic. It implies growth and development in the individual Christian in that such a person must continuously learn to live more fully, more prefectly, and more completely in Christ in order that the Spirit of Christ might carry out in his life actions worthy of Christ. This, Merton notes in an article about his own conversion:

58. Thomas Merton, *Basic Principles of Monastic Spirituality* (Bardstown, Kentucky: Abbey of Gethsemani, 1957), pp. 13–14; Thomas Merton, "Seeking our Redeemer," *Sponsa Regis*, XXVIII (1956–57), 142–43.

If they [Christians living in the world] are to live as true members of Christ and radiate the divine influence among the men with whom they are in contact, they will be obliged to develop rich interior lives of union with God, and this union will have to be deep enough to weather the demands of hard work and constant contact with things that would defile a weaker spirit.[59]

In view of this, one can say that man's purpose in life is to grow continuously, through a participation in the life of the divine Spirit, in union with the risen Christ, toward the complete maturity and perfection that is the full manifestation of Christ in one's life, namely, Christ living in man and uniting men to one another in His own life and unity.[60]

It is in this way that man will dispose himself for the culmination of his supernatural union—his perfect possession of God through love of Christ. This is achieved in this life in what Merton calls man's mystical or transforming union with God, which he defines as "the perfect coalescence of the uncreated Image of God with our created image not only in a perfect identification of minds and wills in knowledge and love but also above all knowledge and all love in perfect communion."[61] In this perfect communion with God one notes that there is, first of all, a perfect possession of one's whole being by Christ. "In other words, He is substituting His life for our life, His thoughts for our thoughts, His will for our will."[62] Through such a process of transformation, man finds the real meaning of his life in Christ. For here he fully realizes his divine

59. Cf. Thomas Merton, "The White Pebble," *Sign*, XXIX (1950), 27.

60. Cf. Thomas Merton, "Growth in Christ," *Sponsa Regis*, XXXIII (1961–62), 197.

61. Merton, *The New Man*, p. 85. Earlier in the book p. 35, he shows that the perfection of man's divinization lies in his mystical identity with God. The terms, "transforming" and "mystical" are used synonymously to describe this perfection of man's union with God. Cf. *The Ascent to Truth*, p. 71, where he describes *mystical* union as "a union with God in perfect charity." Later in the same book, p. 260, he describes *transforming* union as a "perfect union of love with God, through Christ, in the Holy Spirit."

62. Merton, *Seasons of Celebration*, p. 134; similarly found in his article, "Self-Denial and the Christian," *Commonweal*, LI (1949–50), 651.

Sonship and thus becomes his true self, as Merton points out in *No Man is an Island* when he writes: "Each one of us becomes completely himself when, in the Spirit of God, he is transformed in Christ."[63] In this union, therefore, man truly achieves the end for which he was created; he is "perfectly conformed to the likeness of Christ."[64]

Secondly, this transformation involving man's total being, results, as Merton notes, essentially in a union of perfect love, and therefore it is a supreme manifestation of man's liberty: "Hence love alone makes the creature equal to its God, and therefore capable of perfect union with Him."[65] For Merton this transformation has already begun. He writes:

> The degree and intensity of our transformation depends precisely on our union with the Holy Spirit, on the purity of the image within us. This, in turn, is a matter of charity. We are transformed by love, and transformed in proportion to the purity of our love for God and for other men.[66]

Therefore, man's mystical or transforming union with God is not merely a union of wills, but rather what Merton calls a perfect communion or a oneness in charity which makes man "one spirit" with God with the result that man lives by God's life and loves with His love. The individual is now said to love God in God, to love Him for what He is in Himself. Most simply, he loves God for His own sake and not for the good that he gets from Him.[67]

63. Merton, *No Man Is an Island*, pp. 136–37.

64. Merton, *The New Man*, p. 94.

65. Thomas Merton, *The Last of the Fathers; Saint Bernard of Clairvaux and the Encyclical Letter, Doctor Mellifluus* (New York: Harcourt, Brace, 1954), p. 82. Cf. *supra*, p. 6 for clarification of the role of love in man's perfect union with God.

66. Merton, *The New Man*, p. 95. One should note that this necessity of love for one's fellow man is an important aspect of mystical union and is stressed throughout Merton's writings. Cf. *A Thomas Merton Reader*, p. 150: "The ascent of the individual soul to personal mystical union with God is made to depend, in our life, upon our ability to love one another."

67. Merton, *The Ascent to Truth*, pp. 260, 279–80. For Merton the likeness of God in man is fully restored when man's freedom is perfectly united with

Although there is a perfect identity of love between man and God in such mystical union, Merton is careful to note that man does not lose his own proper identity:

> Even when the soul is mystically united with God there remains, according to Christian theology, a distinction between the nature of the soul and the nature of God. This perfect unity is not then a fusion of natures, but a unity of love and of experience. The distinction between the soul and God is no longer experienced as a separation into subject and object when the soul is united to God.[68]

On the contrary, it is in this mystical union with God that man's human personality is brought to its highest perfection, to its most complete actualization and identity where all its deepest potentialities are fulfilled.

Finally, it is important to note that, according to Merton, the realization of this mystical or transforming union with God should be the desire of every Christian who is seeking to live a full and integrated life in Christ. Because such union is the fulfillment of man's spiritual union in Christ, it logically follows that its realization too, must be a part of the goal to which man must tend as a Christian created in the image of God.[69] Indeed, for Merton: "To

---

the divine freedom. This man achieves when he acts with a pure and disinterested love. This point is emphasized by Merton in "The Catholic and Creativity: Theology of Creativity," *American Benedictine Review*, XI (1960), 197–213.

68. *A Thomas Merton Reader*, p. 515. In his book, *What Are These Wounds?*, p. 14, Merton comments on this union as follows: "However, the union between the soul and God in love is so close and so complete that the only remaining distinction between them is the fundamental distinction between two separate substances. Otherwise, they are identical: that is to say, the soul has 'become God,' and God has 'become the soul,' and the only trace of distinction that remains between them is the fact that what is God's by nature is the soul's by participation and by God's free gift, that is by love. God *is* love. The soul *has* love. But once the soul reaches transforming union its acts are not only Godlike, but they become *God's own acts*."

69. Thomas Merton, "The Transforming Union in St Bernard and St John of the Cross," *Collectanea Ordinis Cisterciensium Reformatorum*, X (1948), 109.

be a Christian, then, is to be committed to a deeply mystical life."[70]
Hence, in Merton's theology, this highest form of union with God
to which man can attain on earth, namely, the love of God for His
own sake, does not belong to an elite group but is the prerogative
of all men baptized in Christ, as he himself has emphasized:

> The mystical life is essentially the normal way of Christian per-
> fection. . . . The mystical life is one to which all Christians, in
> general, receive a remote call. On the other hand, manifest
> mystical prayer, infused contemplation in the strict sense of the
> word, may perhaps be listed, though normal, as a *special* vocation.
> It is not for all in the same sense as the mystical life is for all.
> However, the mystical life, by its very nature, includes at least a
> latent element of infused prayer, and the call to the mystical life
> implies a call at least to masked contemplation (mystics who do
> not know it).[71]

This, then, is Merton's teaching on the first foundational principle,
man's union with God—involved in his spirituality. Man, in his
basic structure, has an existential capacity for God. He is created to

70. Merton, *Life and Holiness,* p. 58; Merton, "Christ the Way," p. 147.
Cf. also, Merton, *What Are These Wounds?,* p. 106.

71. Thomas Merton, "Is Mysticism Normal?" *Commonweal,* LI (1949–50)
98. Cf. Thomas Merton, *What Is Contemplation?* (London: Burns, Oates and
Washbourne, 1950), p. 6, where he says that everyone may desire the gift of
infused contemplation. It is important to understand these statements of
Merton, as much criticism has been brought against him as a propagandist of
mysticism for the masses. Cf. Aelred Graham, "Thomas Merton/A Modern
Man in Reverse," *Atlantic Monthly,* CXCI (1953), 72; also Virginia M.
Shaddy, "Thomas Merton and *No Man Is an Island,*" *Catholic World,*
CLXXXIV (1956), 54, who criticizes Merton for advocating mysticism as
the only way of Christian living. What Merton proposed was that all
Christians have a *remote call* to mystical union (the perfection of their supernatural union in Christ). Such a call includes some form of infused contemplation; at least, what Merton calls masked contemplation. Manifest mystical
prayer, however, is still a special vocation. Cf. *Life and Holiness,* pp. 58–59,
where Merton says: "To be a Christian then is to be committed to a deeply
mystical life. . . . This does not mean, of course, that every Christian is or
should be a 'mystic' in the technical modern sense of the word. But it does
mean that every Christian lives, or should live, within the dimensions of a
completely mystical revelation and communication of the divine being."

love God; for, at the very core of his being is a freedom that Merton calls the image of God within him. This image of God constitutes man's *natural union with God*. However, in order that this image in man might attain a perfect likeness to God in love, God has given to man His own Son, enabling man to share the freedom of the sons of God. This coming of the Word, whereby man is given a share in the divine life by the action of the Spirit, constitutes the basis for man's *supernatural union in Christ* or his *union with God by grace*. Finally, when the Word loves the Father in us, then man's freedom is transfigured in and by His Spirit, and his love becomes identical with God's love. Such love of God for His own sake constitutes the final perfection of man's supernatural union, namely, his *mystical or transforming* union with God. Merton sums it up most succinctly in *The New Man:*

> If we are only truly real "in Him" it is because He shares His reality with us and makes it our own. The reality which brings us into such intimate dependence on Him by nature is elevated by grace to a "unity of spirit," which, when it is fully perfected, amounts to a mystical identity.[72]

Such is the reason why Merton could say: "Whatever I may have written, I think it can all be reduced in the end to this one root truth: that God calls human persons to union with Himself and with one another in Christ. . . ."[73] The realization, therefore, of his *union with God* is the one truth that must underlie a Christian's entire life if that life is to be a return to the Father, Who is the source of his existence, through the Son, Who is the Perfect Image of the Father, in the Holy Spirit, Who is the Love of the Father and the Son. In Merton's spirituality, therefore, the most important and the most enduring work of a Christian must be accomplished in the depths of his own soul. For, it is there that ultimately man is interiorly transformed and achieves his perfect union with God.

72. Merton, *The New Man*, pp. 97–98.
73. Thomas Merton, "Concerning the Collection in Bellarmine College Library," p. 3.

Once he is drawn to such union with God in Christ by the Holy Spirit, he can then express fully his love and his new being to others. And this Merton would hold is the summit of one's spiritual life: "Hence I want to say that the highest form of life is this 'spiritual life' in which the infinitely 'fontal' (source-like) creativity of our being in Being is somehow attained, and becomes in its turn a source of action and creativity in the world around us."[74]

The Christian, then, has but one function in life and that is to be his real self, a son of God created in the image and likeness of God. To achieve this, he must search for the God Who is the source of his spiritual life. He shall find Him, as shall be shown in the following chapter, when he finds his own true self; for "He is nearer to us than we are to ourselves."[75]

74. Merton, *Faith and Violence,* p. 115; Thomas Merton, Comments in *War Within Man,* ed. by E. Fromm (Philadelphia: Peace Literature Service of American Friends Service Committee, 1963), p. 47.

75. Merton, *The New Man,* p. 16.

CHAPTER II

TRANSFORMATION OF CONSCIOUSNESS

"THE SINCERITY OF ALL PRAYER whether liturgical or private," says Thomas Merton, "depends on the fundamental acknowledgment of our actual spiritual state."[1] Man must have, therefore, some realization of who he is. In the preceding chapter, it was shown that each man is called in some way or other to an intimate union with God in Christ by charity. It is now necessary in this chapter to bring out the implications involved in such a union. If this union between man and God is to reach perfection in a mystical or transforming union, then man must somehow come to recognize both himself and God. For this reason, man's perfect communion with God demands an authentic and serious search for God, a continuous effort on the part of man to "realize" God and to discover the reality of the hidden presence of God in his life. This search each man must undertake for himself; for, paradoxically, he will discover that the God he is searching for is hidden within the depths of his own self, and hence, can only be found by man in so far as he finds Him in himself.[2] For, although He is an infinitely transcendent God, He is nonetheless immanently present to man; and although He is a God Who is beyond man, He is also a God Who is within the very ground of man's being. Therefore, in finding this God, man will also find himself.[3]

1. Merton, *The New Man*, p. 131.
2. Merton, *Thoughts in Solitude*, p. 112.
3. Merton, *Faith and Violence*, p. 64; Thomas Merton, Introduction to

D

MAN'S SEARCH FOR GOD

Man's search for the perfect possession of God in Christ is the secret of Merton's spirituality. In fact, as he once pointed out: "The whole work of man in this life is to find God."[4] For this reason, it is important that one understand the nature and reality of this search in Merton's theology.

Because God is present within the depths of man's being, in order to find God, man must find himself in the sense of becoming conscious of his true self.[5] Such a search, according to Merton, consists in a double movement: man's entering into the deepest center of himself, and then, after passing through that center, going out of himself to God:

> Unless we discover this deep self, which is hidden with Christ in God, we will never really know ourselves as persons. Nor will we know God. For it is by the door of this deep self that we enter into the spiritual knowledge of God. (And indeed, if we seek our true selves it is not in order to contemplate ourselves but to pass beyond ourselves and find Him.)[6]

The Prison Meditations of Father Alfred Delp, by A. Delp (New York: Herder and Herder, 1963), p. xxv. In *New Seeds of Contemplation,* p. 36, Merton also points this out: "If I find Him I will find myself." He immediately adds, however, "and if I find my true self I will find Him." This apparent paradox will become evident as the nature of man's search for God is discussed in the following pages.

4. Merton, *The Living Bread,* p. 97.

5. This is one of Merton's paradoxical statements. In *No Man Is an Island,* p. 13, he writes: "We cannot find ourselves within ourselves, but only in others." However, he then adds, "yet at the same time before we can go out to others we must first find ourselves." It is in this sense that man's search for God must begin with himself. This point was emphasized by Merton quite early in his writings. Cf. "The Contemplative Life: Its Meaning and Necessity," p. 28, where he says: "The fact is, however, that if you descend into the depths of your own spirit . . . and arrive somewhere near the center of what you *are,* you are confronted with the inescapable truth that, at the very roots of your existence, you are in constant and immediate and inescapable contact with the Infinite power of God."

6. Merton, *The New Man,* p. 32; also, pp. 70, 77. In *Mystics and Zen*

It is in light of this that Merton says that self-realization is "less an awareness of ourselves than an awareness of the God to whom we are drawn in the depths of our own being."[7]

Before examining in detail this double movement involved in man's search for God, it is important to note three characteristics of this search. First, according to Merton, even the beginning of such a search is essentially a gift from God. This he points out in *No Man Is an Island* when he says: "We cannot begin to seek Him without a special gift of His grace."[8] In referring to this discovery as a gift to man, Merton is trying to emphasize the fact that man does not seek God in the same way that he seeks an object or thing which can be seized and understood by his mind. Since God is present within man and offers Himself as a gift to him, man can only seek Him and become aware of Him by "listening," by becoming attentive to the fact that he is known and loved by God, by recalling that his very being is penetrated with God's knowledge and love for him. This Merton underscores in his last book, *The Climate of Monastic Prayer:*

> Our knowledge of God is paradoxically a knowledge not of him as the object of our scrutiny, but of ourselves as utterly dependent on his saving and merciful knowledge of us. It is in proportion as we are known to him that we find our real being and identity in Christ. We know him in and through ourselves in so far as his

Masters, p. 153, Merton refers to such a process as "introversion" and acknowledges its Augustinian influence. It is in light of this double movement that Merton can say in *Thoughts in Solitude,* p. 74: "But we do not find Him merely by finding our own being." Normally, man must enter the very center of his being and then pass beyond himself to God. As shall be shown in the following chapter, the recognition of this double movement can be accomplished in a single act when man becomes immediately aware of the divine image in the very center of his being. This, according to Merton, is *contemplation* as he notes in *The New Man,* p. 76.

7. Merton, *The New Man,* p. 75. Cf. also *New Seeds of Contemplation,* p. 47.

8. Merton, *No Man Is an Island,* p. 13. Likewise in *New Seeds of Contemplation,* p. 36, Merton says: "The only One Who can teach me to find God is God Himself Alone." Later in the same book, p. 39, he writes: "Our discovery of God is, in a way, God's discovery of us."

truth is the source of our being and his merciful love is the very heart of our life and existence.[9]

Hence, the first thing that man must remember in seeking God is that this search is not some sort of a Promethean exploit in which man is trying to find something outside of himself. On the contrary, it simply means that man must somehow realize that he himself is possessed by God in the inmost depths of his being. This is why Merton says: "In the end, no one can seek God unless he has already begun to find Him. No one can find God without having first been found by Him."[10]

Secondly, man will never reach the realization that he is possessed by God unless he first realizes his own nothingness and emptiness. This entails a surrendering of one's exterior self completely to God's love and a forgetting of oneself as an object of reflection to such an extent that man loses everything that is centered on his illusory and superficial self and thus gains the truer and deeper self that is the image of God within him.[11] It is in the resulting emptiness and nakedness of this inmost self that man will be filled with God's love and thus be perfectly one with him. To this extent there is a fullness in his nothingness as Merton points out in *Zen and the*

9. Merton, *The Climate of Monastic Prayer*, pp. 113–114. It is for this reason that Merton in his book, *Life and Holiness*, p. 29, stresses that "our seeking of God is not all a matter of our finding him by means of certain ascetic techniques. It is rather a quieting and ordering of our whole life by self-denial, prayer, and good works, so that God himself, who seeks us more than we seek him, can 'find us' and 'take possession of us.'" See also, Thomas Merton, "Called Out of Darkness," *Sponsa Regis*, XXXIII (1961), 69.

10. Merton, *The Silent Life*, p. vii.

11. In his diary, *The Sign of Jonas*, p. 143, Merton identifies this finding of himself in God with losing himself: "God has taught me to find myself more in Him or lose myself more: it comes to the same thing." In *Zen and the Birds of Appetite*, p. 76, he notes that all higher religions achieve this realization through self-emptying and not through self-attainment: "That is why it is felt necessary by these traditions to speak in strong negative terms about what happens to the ego–subject, which instead of being realized in its own limited self-hood is spoken of rather as simply vanishing out of the picture altogether. The reason for this is not that the person loses his metaphysical or even physical status, or regresses into non–entity, but rather that his *real* status is quite other than what appears empirically to us to be his status."

Birds of Appetite: "It is in so far as 'emptiness' and 'nakedness' are also pure gift that in Christian terms they equal fullness."[12] Thus, man's loss of self in order that there may be "no self" but that of God becomes in Merton's theology, not a self-alienation, but the highest and most perfect self-realization.[13]

Finally, Merton notes "*that a man cannot enter into the deepest center of himself and pass through that center into God, unless he is able to pass entirely out of himself and empty himself and give himself to other people, in the purity of a selfless love.*"[14] Man's search for God, therefore, also involves an opening of oneself to others not only in the sense that it must lead toward a deeper and full integration of charity to them and toward a communication to them in and through the Holy Spirit, but also in the sense that the perfect realization of one's true self as a person who has been sought and found by God's love, cannot be discovered alone but must include others.[15] The reason for this is that the man who is known and loved by God finds himself one with Christ. Merton writes: "The discovery of ourselves in God, and of God in ourselves, by a charity that also finds all other men in God with ourselves is, therefore, not the discovery of ourselves but of Christ."[16]

12. Merton, *Zen and the Birds of Appetite*, p. 137. Both here and in *The Climate of Monastic Prayer*, p. 127, Merton underscores the idea of emptiness as gift. In the latter book, he says: "We cannot argue that 'emptiness' equals 'the presence of God' and then sit down to acquire the presence of God by emptying our souls of every image. It is not a matter of logic or of cause and effect. It is not a matter of desire, of planned enterprise, or of our own spiritual technique." This idea is also found in *New Seeds of Contemplation*, p. 39. The characteristic of gift must always be evident in God's presence in man.

13. Thomas Merton, "Monastic Vocation and Modern Thought," *Monastic Studies*, IV (1966), 29–30.

14. Merton, *New Seeds of Contemplation*, p. 64.

15. Merton, *Seasons of Celebration*, pp. 223–24 Here, Merton writes: "But we do not seek Him the way we seek a lost object, a 'thing.' He is present to us in our heart, our personal subjectivity, and to seek Him is to recognize this fact. Yet we cannot be aware of it as a reality unless he reveals His presence to us. He does not reveal Himself simply in our own heart. He reveals Himself to us through one another." Cf. also Thomas Merton, "Seeking God," *Sponsa Regis*, XXVIII (1956–57), 118.

16. Merton, *No Man Is an Island*, p. 12.

A Christian, then, in Merton's view, is searching for God only when he is aware both of God and of others in God in his life and only when he realizes through love that he has been transformed in Christ by God. The problem today, Merton believes, is that many Christians fail to realize this truth. They "too often fail to realize that the infinite God is dwelling within them, so that He is in them and they are in Him. They remain unaware of the presence of the infinite source of being right in the midst of the world and of men."[17] He then goes on to say: "What is required of Christians is that they develop a completely modern and contemporary *consciousness* in which their experience as men of our century is integrated with their experience as children of God redeemed by Christ."[18]

MEANING OF CONSCIOUSNESS

In Merton's spirituality it is this idea of consciousness that provides the solution to man's search for union with God.[19] By means of it, man is enabled to undertake the double movement that is involved in his discovery of God, namely, his entering into himself and his transcending himself. For Merton, such consciousness can be described basically as a self-awareness. However, it is

17. Merton, *Faith and Violence*, p. 222.

18. *Ibid.*, p. 279.

19. The term is first used by Merton in his book, *No Man Is an Island*, p. 38, when he distinguishes man's psychological conscience, which he calls "consciousness," from man's moral conscience. He then goes on to show, p. 39: "The psychological conscience has its place in our prayer, but prayer is not the place for its proper development." However, the importance of consciousness in prayer is later asserted in *Spiritual Direction and Meditation*, p. 67, when he points out that if prayer does not awaken in man a consciousness of his union with God, then it has not achieved the full effect for which it is intended. The apparent contradiction is resolved when one examines Merton's final use of the term in *Seasons of Celebration*, p. 70, where he implies that consciousness is not introspection but compunction or a liberation of ourselves which "takes place in the depths of our being, and lets us out of ourselves from the inside. This liberation from concentration on ourself is the beginning of a conversion, a *metanoia*, a real inner transformation."

important to note the unique and distinctive meaning that he attaches to this self-awareness. For him it is not to be equated with some kind of reflexive awareness in which man becomes so preoccupied with his own self as subject that awareness of self becomes all important. This type of Cartesian self-awareness is, according to Merton, too solipsistic, as he notes in *Zen and the Birds of Appetite:* "Modern consciousness then tends to create this solipsistic bubble of awareness—an ego-self imprisoned in its own consciousness, isolated and out of touch with other such selves in so far as they are all 'things' rather than persons."[20] When man regards himself as such a purely isolated subject surrounded by objects, it is inevitable that sooner or later he will regard his own being as a quasi-object.[21]

Over against this type of Cartesian self-awareness, Merton

20. Merton, *Zen and the Birds of Appetite,* p. 22. Merton goes on to show in the same book two dangers resulting from an emphasis on this type of consciousness. First, there is the inevitability of the "death of God theology" which asserts that all experience of the reality of God and of His relevancy for man today is illusory. In fact, man has no need of God, and so long as he imagines that he needs Him, he is alienated from the reality of his own world. For Merton, God as such an object of thought is unthinkable. Hence, as long as man tries to reach God as an object by starting from the thinking self, God will surely die. He says, p. 23: "God as object is not only a mere abstract concept, but one which contains so many internal contradictions that it becomes entirely non-negotiable except when it is hardened into an idol that is maintained in existence by a sheer act of will." This point is likewise emphasized in *Faith and Violence,* p. 253. Cf. also Thomas Merton, "The Death of God, I: The Death of God and the End of History," *Theoria to Theory,* II (1967), 3–16. Second, in Merton's estimation, so long as man remains a Cartesian thinking-self, it is impossible for him to really enter into the ground of his being and to transcend himself (the double movement involved in his search for God). Interestingly enough, Merton shows, p. 28, that the present wide-spread use of drugs as sort of an escape or short-cut to inner transformation is really "a *deus ex machina* to enable the self-aware Cartesian consciousness to extend its awareness of itself while seemingly getting out of itself. In other words, drugs have provided the self-conscious self with a substitute for metaphysical and mystical self-transcendence."

21. One notices here the root of Merton's interest in Eastern Mysticism, especially in Zen Buddhism. He himself acknowledges that this interest is due partly to a reaction to Cartesianism. Cf. *Conjectures of a Guilty Bystander,* p. 285.

proposes a type of consciousness which really underlies this subjective experience in that it is an immediate experience of being in which the subject as such disappears; and yet, at the same time, this consciousness goes beyond all reflexive awareness of one's egoself since man becomes preoccupied with a pursuit for his transcendent self.[22] Since God is present to man in the very act of his being, each Christian must recognize his act of being as a direct participation in the Being of God. He must cease to assert himself as the center of consciousness and discover God as the deepest center of consciousness within him.[23] In contrasting this consciousness with the previous Cartesian consciousness, Merton says:

> It starts not from the thinking and self-aware subject but from Being ontologically seen to be beyond, and prior to the subject-object division. Underlying the subjective experience of the individual self there is an immediate experience of Being. This is totally different from an experience of self-consciousness. It is completely non-objective. It has in it none of the split and alienation that occurs when the subject becomes aware of itself as a quasi-object. The consciousness of Being . . . is an immediate experience that goes beyond reflexive awareness. It is not "consciousness of" but pure consciousness, in which the subject as such disappears.[24]

In this form of consciousness the individual can be said to be aware of himself only to the extent that he sees himself as a self that must be dissolved and lost in God. Merton calls the resulting experience

22. Merton, *Mystics and Zen Masters*, p. 268. In *Conjectures of a Guilty Bystander*, p. 221, Merton writes: "One who has experienced . . . what it means to *be* has in that very act experienced something of the presence of God. For God is present to me in the act of my own being, an act which proceeds directly from His will and is His gift. My act of being is a direct participation in the Being of God.

23. Merton, *Zen and the Birds of Appetite*, p. 69. Earlier in the same book, p. 26, Merton describes this new consciousness in these words: "the empirical self is seen by comparison to be 'nothing,' that is to say contingent, evanescent, relatively unreal, real only in relation to its source and end in God, considered not as object but as free ontological source of one's own existence and subjectivity. . . . Being is not an abstract objective idea but a fundamental concrete intuition directly apprehended in a personal experience that is incontrovertible and inexpressible."

24. *Ibid.*, pp. 23–24.

of such consciousness a *transcendent experience* in that the self is no longer conscious of itself as a subject but rather experiences itself as a "no-self" or really a transcendent self which "is metaphysically distinct from the Self of God and yet perfectly identified with that Self by love and freedom, so that there appears to be but one self."[25]

Once the self has achieved this dissolution or loss, it has entered into the very center or ground of its being where it is totally empty, and it is there that it is capable of going beyond itself by becoming filled with the presence of God. In this transcendent experience it becomes evident that the individual subject really undergoes a radical change, an inner transformation, or what Merton refers to as a "transformation of consciousness" from an awareness of his empirical self (also called man's false self or ego-self) to an awareness of his transcendent self (also referred to as man's true self or his person).[26] The individual is no longer conscious of himself as an

25. *Ibid.*, pp. 71–72. Previously in the same paragraph, he describes such a transcendent experience as "an experience of metaphysical or mystical self-transcending and also at the same time an experience of the 'Transcendent' or the 'Absolute' or 'God' not so much as object but Subject. The Absolute Ground of Being . . . is realized so to speak 'from within'—realized from within 'Himself' and from within 'myself,' though 'myself' is now lost and 'found' 'in Him.'"

26. It is this transformation of consciousness or inner transformation that Merton sees as the essential witness value of contemplatives in today's world. More shall be said about this in the fourth chapter. For the present, it is sufficient to note that for Merton the monk is a person who is continually in search of God and who endeavors through an inner transformation to attain to a deepening of the consciousness of his true self in the presence of God. In recent years, Merton has written widely on this topic. Cf. Thomas Merton, "Marxist Theory and Monastic Theoria," unpublished conference delivered at Bangkok on December 10, 1968, where he says: "The essential of the monastic life . . . is something deeper than a role. It is somewhere concerned with this business of total inner transformation." Thomas Merton, "Monastic Experience and East-West Dialogue," notes from an unpublished paper delivered at Calcutta in October, 1968; Thomas Merton, "Renewal and Discipline in the Monastic Life," unpublished article written in February, 1968; Thomas Merton, "Letter to Friends—June 23, 1968," which was later published under the title, "On the Future of Monasticism," *L'Osservatore Romano*, IV (January 23, 1969), 5. Such a concept appears closely similar to what the earlier monastic fathers implied in their concept, "purity of heart," or man's total surrender to God by a renunciation of all false self images.

isolated ego but sees himself in his inmost ground of being as dependent on Another or as being formed through relationships, particularly his relationship with God. By forgetting himself both as subject and as an object of reflection, man finds his real self hidden with Christ in God. And so, as his self-consciousness changes, the individual is transformed; his self is no longer its own center; it is now centered on God.[27] There is death of the self-centered and self-sufficient ego and in its place there appears a new and liberated self who loves and acts in the Spirit. Man is now empty of all ego-consciousness; he is a Transcendent Self—a person who has gone beyond his individual self and has found his true self in the presence of God. Hence, it is through this dynamic process of inner transformation or transformation of consciousness that man empties himself and transcends himself, and thus ultimately becomes his true self in Christ. This Merton notes in *Zen and the Birds of Appetite:*

> This dynamic of emptying and of transcendence accurately defines the transformation of the Christian consciousness in Christ. It is a kenotic transformation, an emptying of all the contents of the ego-consciousness to become a void in which the light of God or the glory of God, the full radiation of the infinite reality of His Being and Love are manifested.[28]

One can affirm, then, that for Merton the problem of man's searching for his union with God is basically a problem of man's finding his true identity. For Merton describes identity as that which "you really are, your real self."[29] In actual fact, the man who is seeking union with God is seeking to recover possession of his deepest self—the self that is discovered after all other partial and exterior selves have been discarded as masks. Most simply, he is seeking to discover who he is in relation to God. And, when such

27. For Merton, the tragedy today is that man's consciousness is alienated from this center due to original sin. This is why man must undergo a transformation of consciousness. Cf. Merton, *Zen and the Birds of Appetite*, pp. 12, 31.

28. *Ibid.*, p. 75.

29. Thomas Merton, *The Waters of Siloe* (New York: Image Books, 1962), p. 366.

a man draws near to God, he does not lose his identity; he becomes, rather, his real self or his true self. However, if this transformation, which is ultimately accomplished by God's merciful love in man, is to be realized by man, then he must work together with God in creating his new identity in the sense that he must desire it and work to find it with God and in God.[30]

TRUE-FALSE SELF

The first step of this transformation, then, is for man to begin with what he actually is and to recognize his present alienated condition as a man who is far from God. "Before we can realize who we really are, we must become conscious of the fact that the person we think we are, here and now, is at best an imposter and a stranger."[31] This external or superficial self, which Merton calls man's empirical or egotistical self, is false and illusory, since it is, to a great extent, a mask and a fabrication for man's true identity which is hidden in the love and mercy of God. In speaking of this false self, Merton says:

> Everyone of us is shadowed by a false self. This is the man I want myself to be but who cannot exist, because God does not know anything about him. And to be unknown to God is altogether too much privacy.
> My false and private self is the one who wants to exist outside the reach of God's will and God's love—outside of reality and outside of life. And such a self cannot help but be an illusion.[32]

The danger today, as Merton sees it, is that man will settle to live by such an illusory self, and hence, yield to a superficial personalism which identifies the "person" with this external or empirical self

30. Merton, *New Seeds of Contemplation*, p. 33.

31. Merton, *The New Man*, p. 73. Cf. Merton, *New Seeds of Contemplation*, pp. 280–81, where Merton asserts: "We have to start from our alienated condition. . . . But at the same time we must remember that we are *not* entirely what we seem to be, and that what appears to be our 'self' is soon going to disappear into nothingness."

32. Merton, *New Seeds of Contemplation*, p. 34.

and devotes itself to the cultivation of such a false self. For Merton, this is a great mistake. For, when this happens, man reaches the most tragic of frustrations and errors—he becomes alienated from his inner self which is the image of God.[33] The result is the rugged individualism prevalent in today's world where man's ego has become the center of all his strivings for selfish gain and for satisfaction. Man today is so self-centered that he is, according to Merton, "an isolated human unit functioning and acting for himself and by himself."[34] Commenting on this danger, Merton says in his book, *Disputed Questions:*

> Individualism is nothing but the social atomism that has led to our present inertia, passivism and spiritual decay. Yet it is individualism which has really been the apparent ideal of our western society for the past two or three hundred years. This individualism, primarily an economic concept with a pseudospiritual and moral facade, is in fact mere irresponsibility. It is, and has always been, not an affirmation of genuine human values but a flight from the obligations from which these values are inseparable. And first of all a flight from the obligation to *love*. . . . The individual, in fact, is nothing but a negation: he is "not someone else."[35]

Hence, for Merton, such a superficial external self cannot be man's real self in that it estranges man from God and alienates him from that which is most real and most authentic in his own being. "There is," says Merton, "no real love of life unless it is oriented to the discovery of one's true, spiritual self, beyond and above the level of mere empirical individuality with its superficial enjoyments and fears."[36] Therefore, man cannot remain content to seek a self-

---

33. Merton, *Faith and Violence*, p. 113; see also his Comments in *War Within Man*, by E. Fromm, p. 46.

34. Merton, *Seeds of Destruction*, p. 163; cf. Thomas Merton, *Redeeming the Time* (London: Burns and Oates, 1966), p. 172.

35. Merton, *Disputed Questions*, p. x. In a most recent article by Thomas Merton, "Prayer, Personalism, and the Spirit," *Sisters Today*, XLII (1970), 129–36, he further notes the difference between individuality and personality in terms of the exclusivity of the individual.

36. Merton, *Faith and Violence*, p. 112; similarly found in his Comments in *War Within Man*, p. 45.

fulfillment that fulfills nothing but this illusory self. Because man is made in the image and likeness of God; he is a spiritual or self-transcending being, and so, there is only one way for him to find out who he really is and that is by transcending his empirical self and finding within himself the true "I," the inner self, who is united to God in Christ.[37]

Man, therefore, must reject this external and false self; he must become detached from all the illusions that he has fabricated about this selfish and limited self, if he is to reach an awareness of this inner self as well as of God. Such renunciation of everything that is centered on this empirical self underscores the necessity of self-emptying in his life, as Merton explains in *Zen and the Birds of Appetite*:

> The path to transcendent realization is a path of ascetic self-emptying and "self-naughting" and not at all a path of self-affirmation, of self-fulfillment, or of "perfect attainment. . . ." Hence it becomes overwhelmingly important for us *to become detached from our everyday conception of ourselves as potential subjects for special and unique experiences, or as candidates for realization, attainment and fulfillment.*[38]

In Merton's view, therefore, the ego-subject, instead of being realized in its own limited self, must simply vanish. With its disappearance, however, man does not regress into non-entity. Rather, this loss of self enables him, paradoxically, to find himself. For, in renouncing his false self, man enters more deeply into the center of himself and in his emptiness and nakedness he finds his "true self." In actual fact, he has transcended his empirical self and recovered a self that is "beyond self." He is no longer aware of himself as a subject of inordinate needs which he seeks to satisfy; rather, having liberated himself from such attachments, he is now capable of surrendering himself to God and of opening himself to God's love and mercy.

37. Merton, *New Seeds of Contemplation*, p. 7; similarly expressed in his article "Notes on Contemplation," *Spiritual Life*, VII (1961), 200.

38. Merton, *Zen and the Birds of Appetite*, pp. 76–77.

Once man experiences the awakening of this real inner self, which is the perfect image of God stamped with the likeness of Christ within him, it is then possible for him to realize his true identity in Christ. Hence, for Merton, it is the discovery and the acceptance of this "empty" self that leads to a discovery of one's true self—the self that is necessary if man is to draw near to God Himself. It is this self Merton speaks about when he writes: "In order to find God, Whom we can only find in and through the depths of our own soul, we must first find ourselves."[39] In Merton's view, then, this true self, the self as we exist in the eyes of God, becomes in turn the stepping stone to man's awareness of God: "The recognition of our true self, in the divine image, is then a recognition of the fact that we are known and loved by God."[40] For, once man has experienced his own inmost being, he is disposed for the supernatural gift of God's love which makes him capable of experiencing God as present within himself. This Merton emphasizes in his *New Seeds of Contemplation:*

> But although God is present in all things by His knowledge and His love and His power and His care of them, He is not necessarily realized and known by them. He is only known and loved by those to whom He has freely given a share in His own knowledge and love of Himself.[41]

It is in light of this that Merton sees man's inner self as a kind of mirror in which God reveals Himself and in which His image is reflected. This is why, in his opinion, man must enter into himself, find his true self, and then pass "beyond" this inner self to God. This he asserts in *The New Man:* "It is more 'natural' for us to be 'out of ourselves' and carried freely and entirely towards the

---

39. Merton, *The New Man*, p. 44.

40. *Ibid.*, p. 76. Here a clarification is undoubtedly necessary. For Merton the true self is the self that is created in the image and likeness of God. Normally, man first becomes aware of this inner self and then in a subsequent act of knowledge recognizes himself as a person known and loved by God. However, all this is accomplished in a single act in the gift of contemplation.

41. Merton, *New Seeds of Contemplation.* p. 40.

'Other'—towards God in Himself or in other men—than it is for us to be centered and enclosed in ourselves."[42] In this way, man's nothingness becomes a fullness. Totally empty of self, he is now one in being with God in Christ. It is this Merton writes about in his Preface to the Japanese edition of *The Seven Storey Mountain* when he says:

> The ALL is nothing, for if it were to be a single thing separated from all other things, it would not be ALL. This precisely is the liberty I have always sought: the freedom of being subject to nothing and therefore to live in ALL, through ALL, for ALL, by Him who is ALL. In Christian terms, this is to live "in Christ" and by the "Spirit of Christ," for the Spirit is like the wind, blowing where He pleases, and He is the Spirit of Truth. The "Truth shall make you free."
> But if the Truth is to make me free, I must also let go my hold upon myself, and not retain the semblance of a self which is an object of a "thing." I, too, must be no-thing, And when I am no-thing I am in the ALL, and Christ lives in me.[43]

The man, then, who has realized his inner self in the perfect image of God, has, in fact, been transformed into God. His deepest potentialities have been fulfilled. He has become his real self in union with God. Such a man has been brought fully in the mystery of Christ by the Holy Spirit. He is alive to the presence of Christ within him. And, for Merton, it is this man who has achieved his true identity as he recently noted in his *Conference on Prayer:* "Who am I? My deepest realization of who I am is—I am one loved by Christ. . . . The depths of my identity is in the center of my being where I am known by God."[44] It is in such an existential encounter with God in Christ that man recovers his deepest and most authentic freedom—the freedom that belongs to him as a

---

42. Merton, *The New Man*, p. 77.

43. Thomas Merton, "Introducing a Book," *Queen's Work*, LVI (1964), 10.

44. Merton, "Conference on Prayer," p. 452. Previously, in *The Living Bread*, p. 68, Merton acknowledged that "Christ is our own deepest and most intimate 'self,' our higher self, our new self as sons of God."

son of God, the freedom that enables him to be open to Christ and follow His Spirit, and thus love God without limit. He no longer finds it necessary to seek his own self-fulfillment; rather, he is content simply to be and to find his fulfillment in his being which is rooted in Christ. "We are fulfilled," says Merton, "by an Identity that does not annihilate our own, which is ours, and yet is 'received.' It is a Person eternally other than ourselves who identifies Himself perfectly with ourselves. This Identity is Christ, God."[45] It is the man who possesses such freedom, who, in Merton's view, is the authentic Christian person in the full sense of the word. He has been found and actualized in union with Christ.[46] Indeed, unless man recognizes that the Christian sense of the person is ultimately found in the recovery of man's likeness to God, in Christ, by the Spirit, he does not fully realize what it means to be a person in the deepest sense of the word and he fails to reach a true self-realization in his life.[47] Without such self-realization, he remains alienated from himself, from others, and from God; and hence, he is incapable of achieving a perfect union with God.

45. Merton, *Bread in the Wilderness*, p. 76. This idea of man finding his fulfillment in Christ is also found in the story of his own conversion. Cf. Thomas Merton, "The White Pebble," in *Where I Found Christ: The Intimate Personal Stories of Fourteen Converts to the Catholic Faith*, ed. by J. A. O'Brien (New York: Doubleday and Co., 1950), p. 250: "But it is only in Christ, in the whole Christ, that each individual personality can be completely perfected and fulfilled. For Christ is our life, and until we live perfectly in Him, and He in us, we still fall short of the man we were intended to be, because something of our life is still lacking to us."

46. Merton, *Zen and the Birds of Appetite*, p. 75; also p. 128, where he describes the person as "the image of God stamped with the likeness of Christ." Cf. Thomas Merton, *Silence in Heaven: A Book of the Monastic Life* (New York: Studio Publications in association with Thomas Y. Crowell, 1956), p. 23, where he describes the human person as "a free being with capacities that can only be fulfilled by the vision of an unknown God." In *Redeeming the Time*, p. 59, Merton writes: "The person is the individual not only as member of the species but as 'image of God,' that is to say as the *free and creative source of a gift of love and meaning* which, if it is not made and given, is irreplaceable and cannot be given by another."

47. Thomas Merton, "The Good News of the Nativity: A Monastic Reading of the Christmas Gospels," *Bible Today*, XXI (1965–66), 1371.

PROBLEM OF ALIENATION

It is in view of this that Merton, especially in his more recent writings, focusses his attention upon the problem of man's alienation from his true self.[48] In his estimation, there are countless Christians, today, who are created in the image of God, and yet know nothing of Him. They possess an Infinite God within them and yet are so preoccupied with self in the worst sense that they are not aware of their real identity in Christ. Although they are called to the true freedom of the sons of God, they have lost sight of the God Who has called them. They are, says Merton, "men who are so alienated from themselves and from God that they are no longer capable of genuine spiritual experience."[49] Because of a false emphasis in our culture on fulfilling one's narcissistic self, these men have become depersonalized and incapable of authenticity; and hence incapable of any full and personal self-realization. They are completely estranged and divided against what is most real and authentic in themselves; with the result that they have not discovered their point of contact with God.[50] In addition, because

48. Cf. Merton, "Marxist Theory and Monastic Theoria," where Merton describes alienation as follows: "The idea of alienation is basically Marxist, and what it means is that man living under certain conditions is no longer in possession of the fruits of his life. His life is not his. His life is lived according to conditions determined by someone else." This idea of being subject to someone else is also brought out in another article by Merton entitled, "Identity Crisis and Monastic Vocation," written in October, 1964: "The term alienation is used of a human being who is systematically kept, or who allows himself to be kept, in a social situation in which *he exists purely and simply for someone else.*" Finally, in his article, "Is the 'Contemplative Life' Finished?" Merton says: "To be alienated is to be a prisoner in something of which you cannot possibly take an active personal part." *Contemplation in a World of Action,* p. 350.

49. Merton, *New Seeds of Contemplation,* pp. 11–12; similarly found in his article "Notes on Contemplation," p. 203.

50. The idea of alienation being closely allied to an emphasis on one's false self is brought out by Merton in his *New Seeds of Contemplation,* p. 21, as well as in an article entitled, "Rain and the Rhinocerous," *Holiday,* XXXVII (1965), 12. In *Opening the Bible,* written during Advent, 1967, Merton again points out the relationship between the false self and alienation, p. 41, when he asserts:

E

everything in modern life is calculated to keeping man from really entering into himself and transcending himself, men today are incapable of a true openness with one another that would express itself in a genuine communion. Rather, they have substituted or adopted unauthentic and illusory relationships in place of such communion. They play what Merton calls the pantomime of "collective togetherness, in which all possibility of authentic personal existence is surrendered and one remains content with one's neutral quasi-objectified presence in the public mass."[51]

Indeed, so deep is this alienation and so devastating its effects, not only is contemporary man estranged from his true self, he is also enslaved by the delusions of human society all about him. In the highly developed structure of technology in which he lives, man feels no need for the presence of God to fulfill his person and being. Instead, he becomes an atomized individual in a general mass—"the mass man"—one who is totally lacking in responsibility and who cannot think for himself because he has lost himself to the empty routine and alienating pressures of commercialism and technology. For Merton, such a man:

> . . . lives not only below the level of grace, but below the level of nature—below his own humanity. No longer in contact with the created world or with himself, out of touch with reality of nature, he lives in the world of collective obsessions, the world of systems and fictions with which modern man has surrounded himself. In such a world, man's life is no longer even a seasonal cycle. It's a linear flight into nothingness, a flight from reality and from God, without purpose and without objective, except to keep moving, to keep from having to face reality.[52]

"In other words, we affirm our unity on a shallow and provisional level by shutting out other persons and by closing off the deepest area of inner freedom where the ego is no longer in full conscious control. . . . Thus, cut off from our true inner selves, we remain alienated beings, semifictitious masks."

51. Merton, *Mystics and Zen Masters*, p. 267.

52. Merton, *Seasons of Celebration*, p. 51; also found in his article, "Time and the Liturgy," p. 4. In his book, *Conjectures of a Guilty Bystander*, Merton attributes the alienation among men, p. 60, "to technology and to the moral collapse of a materialist world." This in no way denies what has already been

While Merton would readily admit that there is nothing wrong with technology in itself, he also feels that it is a myth to think that technology, by itself, can solve men's problems. "Technology," he asserts, "was made for man and not man for technology."[53] In his view: "The ultimate end of all techniques, when they are used in the Christian context, is charity and union with God." [54] However, such an objective is scarcely achievable today in that technology has become "nothing more than an expensive and complicated way of cultural disintegration."[55] It has failed to deepen and perfect the true quality of man's existence—his being. This, Merton says it can do only on one condition: "that it remains subservient to his *real* interests; that it respects his true being; that it remembers that the origin and goal of all being is in God."[56]

It is over against this exaggerated emphasis on technology in man's culture with its obsession on *doing* (activity), that Merton proposes his spirituality of being. For, as he notes in *Conjectures of a Guilty Bystander:* "Without a sense of *being* and a respect for being, there can be no real appreciation of the person."[57] As was indicated above, it is the man, who recognizes the full Christian sense of the

---

stated, namely, that alienation is also due to an over-emphasis on one's false self. As noted above, alienation is caused both by estrangement and enslavement.

53. Merton, *Conjectures of a Guilty Bystander,* p. 222; cf. also his article, "Can We Survive Nihilism?" *The Saturday Review of Literature,* L (1967), 19. In the former citation Merton refers to the illusion prevalent in modern society of equating mechanical progress with human improvement. This has resulted in society's over-emphasis on *doing* as opposed to *being;* hence, the reverse interest on *being* in Merton's spirituality (cf. Chapter I). It is here in his concern with authentic personal identity and the problem of alienation that one notices the influence of Existentialism in Merton's spirituality, especially the Existentialism of Kierkegaard; cf. Merton, *Mystics and Zen Masters,* pp. 255–80; also found under the title, "The Other Side of Despair: Notes on Christian Existentialism," *Critic,* XXIV (1965–66), 12–23.

54. Merton, *No Man Is an Island,* p. 93.

55. Merton, *Conjectures of a Guilty Bystander,* p. 73. Cf. also Thomas McDonnell, "An Interview with Thomas Merton," *Motive,* XXVII (1967), 41, in which Merton says: 'It is our technology, for example, that threatens us with dinosaurism and self-destruction."

56. Merton, *Conjectures of a Guilty Bystander,* p. 253.

57. *Ibid.,* p. 308.

person, that finds his true-self—the "I," who "is Christ Himself, living in us: and we, in Him, living in the Father."[58] Because this inner self of man is inseparable from Christ in a mysterious and unique way, man is also inseparable from all other persons who live in Christ. There now remains to point out how, according to Merton: "The discovery of this 'true self' is also a discovery of one's responsibility to other such selves, one's brothers in Christ, one's fellow men."[59]

UNION WITH OTHER MEN

In Merton's view, the force that holds together man's union with God and with his fellow man is charity. This he writes in *The New Man:* "And the charity of Christ, which springs from the Father as from its hidden and infinite source, goes out through us to those who have not yet known Him, and unites them ,through Christ in us, to the Father."[60] For Merton, because charity is synonymous with Christ's life in man, the person who lives perfectly in Him must also be able to reach out to others in a relationship of true, genuine love. This means that man must somehow enter deeply into the mystery of God's love for his fellow man. He must try to identify spiritually and interiorly with other men to the extent that he no longer regards them as "objects" on which he expresses his sentiment or bestows favors. Instead, he tries to become the person he loves; he tries to see that person as another self, as one who is also loved by Christ.[61] It is in this way that man really loves others in and for God.[62]

58. Merton, *Disputed Questions,* p. 207.

59. Merton, "Monastic Vocation and Modern Thought," p. 29.

60. Merton, *The New Man,* p. 111. Cf. also *No Man Is an Island,* p. 134, where Merton asserts: "All charity comes to a focus in Christ, because charity is His life in us. He draws us to Himself, unites us to one another in His Holy Spirit, and raises us up with Himself to union with the Father."

61. Cf. *The Wisdom of the Desert: Sayings from the Desert Fathers of the Fourth Century,* trans. by Thomas Merton (New York: New Directions, 1960), pp. 17–18.

62. For Merton this is the climax of love. As he notes in *Conjectures of a*

In Merton's view, to love others with such perfect charity is not an easy task. It involves a kind of death of one's own being, a sacrifice of one's self. Yet, Merton emphasizes that this is part of the emptiness that is entailed in man's search for union with God: "*a man cannot enter into the deepest center of himself and pass through that center into God, unless he is able to pass entirely out of himself and empty himself and give himself to other people in the purity of a selfless love.*"[63] It is in light of this that Merton can conclude: "Love alone gives us the true dimensions of our own reality."[64] For, man is created in the image and likeness of God, Who is Love, and hence, the union with God that he is searching for must ultimately be a question of love. And the love of other men is important if man is to transcend himself and grow without illusions in this authentic love of God: "It is by loving Him . . . that we grow in our capacity to love others."[65]

In conclusion, then, it can be stated that it is the duty of each Christian to strive for an awareness of his union with God in Christ. In order to achieve this, man's life must be a continuous search for

---

Guilty Bystander, p. 121: "The demands of the Law of Love are progressive. We begin by loving life itself, by loving survival at any price. Hence, we must first of all love ourselves. But as we grow we must love others. We must love them as our own fulfillment. Then we must come to love them in order to fulfill them, to develop their capacity to love, and finally we must love others and ourselves in and for God." Here one notices the similarity to the four stages of growth in love expressed by Bernard of Clairvaux in his *De Diligendo Deo,* 15, 39 (PL 182/998,) tr. R. Walton, *The Works of Bernard of Clairvaux,* vol. 5: *Treaties II,* Cistercian Fathers Series, no. 13, (Spencer, Mass., Cistercian Publications, 1972).

63. Merton, *New Seeds of Contemplation,* p. 64.

64. Thomas Merton, "Notes on Love," *Frontier,* X (1967–68), 214.

65. Merton, *The Living Bread,* p. 147. Cf. also *Bread in the Wilderness,* p. 92, where he says: "The more we are united to Him in love the more we are united to one another, because there is only one charity embracing both God and our brother." In his article, "Christian Freedom and Monastic Formation," p. 309, Merton cites this relationship between man's love for God and his love for his brothers as one of the basic principles of Cistercian mysticism. As he notes in "The Monk Today," "The two loves are in fact one, and they are in no sense obstacles to each other."

God in the sense that he comes to the realization that he is a person who is possessed and loved by God, a person who has been created in the image and likeness of God. And this God, Who is *within* him, is Christ. Hence, for Merton, God will be discovered only in so far as man can find Him within himself. Such a discovery involves a double movement: man entering into the deepest center of himself and then, after passing through that center, going out of himself to God.

Man must go beyond focusing upon his false or empirical self and discover his real identity in the true or transcendent self; for it is in this real inner self that man becomes one with God in Christ. Merton writes: "It is this inner self that is taken up into the mystery of Christ, by His love, by the Holy Spirit, so that in secret we live in Christ."[66] The man who has discovered this true self is no longer a victim of the alienation in contemporary society. He has transcended the rugged individual or the mass-man in today's world. He has become a "person"—one who has discovered that the essential mystery of his vocation is to be a son of God. "Whoever we are, whatever may be our state of life," says Merton, "we are called to the glory and freedom of the sons of God. Our vocation is union with Christ. We are co-heirs with Him of His own divine glory. We share His divine Sonship."[67] Alive to the Christ-life in him, he is a free man, completely open to God and to his fellow man. He is one with Him and with them in a union of love that is real, a love that is the gift of his inmost self to the other in that it is a gift of the Christ in him. This Merton emphasizes in *New Seeds of Contemplation* when he says: "Therefore when you and I become what we are really meant to be, we will discover not only that we love one another perfectly but that we are both living in Christ and Christ in us, and we are all One Christ. We will see that it is He Who loves in us."[68] For Merton, therefore, the Christian who has found his true self is the man who has become intensely

66. Merton, *New Seeds of Contemplation*, p. 295; see also, Thomas Merton, "The General Dance," *Jubilee*, IX (1961), 10.

67. Merton, *What Are These Wounds?*, p. 190.

68. Merton, *New Seeds of Contemplation*, p. 65.

aware of his life in Christ as well as of the necessity for love in his life. He sees his life as one of both self-transcendence and of communion. He realizes, as Merton notes, that: "It is not a matter of *either* God *or* man, but of finding God by loving man and discovering the true meaning of man in our love for God. Neither is possible without the other."[69] This point Merton brought out most poignantly and most forcibly in a letter written the year before his death and published posthumously. He said:

> But indeed we exist solely for this, to be the place He has chosen for His presence, His manifestation in the world, His epiphany . . . if we once began to recognize, humbly but truly, the real value of our own self, we would see that this value was the sign of God in our being, the signature of God upon our being. Fortunately, the love of our fellow man is given us as the way of realizing this. . . . It is the love of my lover, my brother or my child that sees God in me, makes God credible to myself in me. And it is my love for my lover, my child, my brother, that enables me to show God to him or her in himself or herself. Love is the epiphany of God in our poverty.[70]

It is important to note that for Merton man will never be capable of such a communion of love with his fellow man on this deepest level until the inner self in him has been sufficiently awakened to confront the inner self of the other person.[71] It is this *awakening of his inner self* that man searches for in his life of prayer, as shall be shown in the following chapter in which the meaning and significance of prayer in Merton's spirituality will be discussed in light of his central message, namely, man's life is a continuous seeking of God and finding Him by love, and sharing that love with others.

69. Merton, *Faith and Violence*, p. 262.

70. Thomas Merton, "As Man to Man," *Cistercian Studies*, IV (1969), 93–94; similarly found as "Dieu n'est pas un problème," *Collectanea Cisterciensia*, XXXI (1969), 22–23. Both articles are publications of a letter written August 21, 1967.

71. Cf. *Mystics and Zen Masters*, p. 276, where Merton says: "Man cannot be genuinely open to others unless he first admits his capacity to hear and obey the Word of God." Also found in his article, "The Other Side of Despair: Notes on Christian Existentialism," p. 22.

CHAPTER III

CONTEMPLATIVE PRAYER

ITS MEANING, NATURE, AND SIGNIFICANCE IN MERTON'S SPIRITUALITY

IN HIS ARTICLE entitled "Contemplation in a World of Action," written in March, 1968, Thomas Merton notes that man's love for his fellow man tends to be superficial and deceptive unless man explores the inner ground of his own human existence. He then goes on to note that traditionally it has been the idea of personal prayer that has been associated with this deepening of one's personal being and with man's capacity to understand and to serve others.[1] There is little doubt as far as Merton is concerned that prayer and contemplation are the most valid ways to the recovery of what is authentically man's own.[2] For it is in them that man seeks to deepen the clarity and the truth of his own inner awareness. In view of this, it is the purpose of the present chapter to examine the meaning, the nature, and the significance of Merton's concept of *contemplative prayer* and thus show its centrality in his spirituality. For it cannot be denied that Merton, both as a person and as a writer, saw very clearly the place for and the use of prayer in the spiritual life insofar as he recognized that it was in prayer that man becomes aware of his union with God in Christ. Further-

1. Thomas Merton, "Contemplation in a World of Action," article written in March, 1968, in *Contemplation in a World of Action* (Garden City, N.Y.: Doubleday, 1971), pp. 157–65.
2. Cf. Thomas Merton, "Community, Politics, and Contemplation," ed. by Naomi Burton Stone, *Sisters Today*, XLII (1971), 245, where he notes: "It is in prayer that we are truly and fully ourselves."

more, he also realized that it was in prayer that man would be led to the fullness of charity in his life.[3]

The preceding chapters considered the two fundamental themes in the spirituality of Thomas Merton, namely, the mystery of God and the mystery of man. An understanding of both are essential for approaching Merton's teaching on prayer in that prayer is a spiritual activity which brings God and man into communion with one another. In discussing these principles, it was noted that man's spiritual life consists primarily in an experience of his union with God in Christ. Such experience involves man in a continuous search for God in the sense that he must enter into the deepest center of himself, and then, after passing through that center, must surrender himself to God. Once man has realized this fully, then he recognizes his true self in the divine image. He is aware of himself as a person who is known and loved by God. Such a realization, however, can only be achieved, as Merton notes, when there is a full awakening of man's inner self to God.[4] Hence, man's search for God lies essentially in his becoming aware of himself as a person possessed by God. And so, he must learn to rest in God, to listen in silence to the God Who has already found him. It is this that points out both the significance and the necessity of contemplative prayer in man's life, the function of which is to bring man into a conscious communion with God in Christ.[5]

3. Cf. *supra*, p. 5, footnote 16.

4. As was noted in the previous chapter, this inner self is the perfect image of God. Hence, when this self or real "I" awakens, man finds within himself the Presence of God Whose image he is. Here one sees implicitly the need for prayer in Merton's spirituality. Such an idea is brought out more explicitly in *The New Man*, p. 34, where Merton says: "but the Spirit of God Himself dwells in us as the Gift of God, and He is there to be known and loved. He even desires His presence to be recognized in contemplative prayer."

5. Merton, *No Man Is an Island*, p. 45, where he asserts: "The whole function of the life of prayer is, then, to enlighten and strengthen our conscience so that it not only knows and perceives the outward written precepts of the moral and divine laws, but above all lives God's law in concrete reality by perfect and continual union with His will."

THE MEANING OF CONTEMPLATIVE PRAYER

Before discussing the nature of contemplative prayer, it would be worthwhile to examine its meaning in Merton's spirituality.[6] For, in stressing the importance of this type of prayer for all Christians, Merton is not advocating that the contemplative life in a restricted sense is vitally necessary for all men, nor is he proposing that contemplative prayer, in the sense of infused contemplation or mystical prayer will be readily achieved by all men.[7] Rather, for Merton, the term, *contemplative*, when applied to prayer, refers more to the *orientation* that one's life of prayer must take.[8] Because all men have a need to listen to God in silence, man must develop

6. In *The Wisdom of the Desert: Sayings from the Desert Fathers of the Fourth Century*, p. 20, Merton notes: "What we could call today contemplative prayer is referred to as *quies* or 'rest' . . . [and] has persisted in Greek monastic tradition as *hesychia*, 'sweet repose.' " Hence, Merton's interest in hesychasm. Cf. Thomas Merton, "Hesychasm," *Diakonia*, II (1967), 380–85, in which he underscores both the dangers and the values of contemporary hesychasm.

7. In his Introduction to *A Thomas Merton Reader*, p. viii, Merton explicitly states that he does not hold such propositions. Later in the same book, p. 313, he writes: "In this world in which all good things are talked about and practically none of them are practiced, it would be unwise to make contemplative prayer a matter for publicity, though perhaps no harm has been done, thus far, by making its name known. God Himself knows well enough how to make the thing known to those who need it, in His designs for them." For future clarification on this point, cf. *supra*, p. 22, footnote 71.

8. It should be noted, however, that the term, contemplative prayer, is sometimes equated with contemplation by Merton. Cf. Merton, *Spiritual Direction and Meditation*, pp. 44, 83. Nonetheless, more often it is used to refer to the orientation man's prayer must take, as for instance in the same book, p. 66, where meditation is considered a part of contemplative prayer. In this wider sense, the term is synonymous with monastic prayer, which Merton, in his book, *The Climate of Monastic Prayer*, p. 42, says "is not so much a way to find God, as a way of resting in him whom we have found. . . ." It is in light of this latter interpretation that Merton writes in *New Seeds of Contemplation*, p. 234, that "contemplative prayer is only truly what it is called when it becomes more or less habitual." It is in this wider sense of *orientation* that the term, contemplative prayer, is used in this chapter as well as throughout the book. When referring exclusively to infused contemplation or to mystical prayer later in the present chapter, the writer will use the term "contemplation."

a personal outlook or attitude of prayer and try to live consciously in an atmosphere of prayer. However, according to Merton, what matters in prayer is, not so much the witnessing for God, but the surrendering to God; for, the contemplative orientation lies essentially in emptiness. Man must descend into the depths of his own emptiness and await the word by which God will speak to him and create in him a new being—a being that is totally free insofar as it is like God. Merton hinted at this kind of orientation early in his writings, as for instance, when he wrote in *The Seven Storey Mountain*:

> And now I think for the first time in my whole life I really began to pray—praying not with my lips and with my intellect and my imagination, but praying out of the very roots of my life and of my being, and praying to the God I had never known, to reach down towards me out of His darkness and to help me to get free of the thousand terrible things that held my will in their slavery.[9]

In addition, it should be noted that it is in the context of this contemplative orientation to prayer that Merton finds the term, "mental prayer," although used by him in his earlier writings, somewhat misleading.[10] Since "contemplative prayer" includes man's whole being, it cannot be confined to man's mind, as he points out in *The Climate of Monastic Prayer*:

> We rarely pray with the "mind" alone. Monastic meditation, prayer, *oratio*, contemplation and reading involve the whole man, and proceed from the "center" of man's being, his "heart" renewed in the Holy Spirit, totally submissive to the grace of Christ. Monastic prayer begins not so much with "considerations" as with a "return to the heart," finding one's deepest center, awaken-

---

9. Merton, *The Seven Storey Mountain*, p. 114.

10. Thomas Merton, "What Is Meditation?" *Sponsa Regis*, XXXI (1960), 181, where he says: "Meditative thought is simply the beginning of a process which leads to interior prayer and is normally supposed to culminate in contemplation and in affective communion with God. We can call the whole process (in which meditation leads to contemplation) by the name mental prayer."

ing the profound depths of our being in the presence of God who is the source of our being and our life.[11]

Hence, one can say that, in Merton's view, prayer is some kind of "inner awareness of God's direct presence" or an "awakening of one's inner self."[12] Although such a view has been expressed in different terms at various times throughout Merton's writings, one always finds the fundamental note of *awareness of man's real condition* somehow expressed. For example, in *The Sign of Jonas* (1953), he speaks of contemplative prayer as "the recognition that we are the Sons of God." In his book, *Spiritual Direction and Meditation* (1960), prayer is described as "a consciousness of one's union with God." A year later in an unpublished manuscript entitled "Selections on Prayer," Merton speaking of prayer says: "The discovery of God within us leads ultimately to the discovery and fulfillment of our own true being in God." Again, in a taped "Conference to Sisters on Prayer," prayer is described most simply as "an interior opening of the inner self to recover the freedom of the sons of God." Finally, in his most recent book, *The Climate of Monastic Prayer* (1969), he asserts: "Prayer then means yearning for the simple presence of God, for a personal understanding of his word, for knowledge of his will and for a capacity to hear and obey him."[13] When one recalls from the preceding chapters that the discovery of one's inner self in the divine image is also the realization of man's union with God, one can readily see the similarity in all Merton's descriptions of prayer. In light of this, one can conclude by saying that "contemplative prayer," which for Merton is essentially a listening, is meant to open man's heart to God by enabling him to surrender his inmost depths to God's

11. Merton, *The Climate of Monastic Prayer*, p. 44.

12. The first description is from Merton's article, "Contemplation in a World of Action," *Contemplation in a World of Action*, p. 162; the second from a taped "Conference to Sisters on Prayer," which this writer heard during his stay at the Abbey of Gethsemani.

13. Merton, *The Sign of Jonas*, p. 284; *Spiritual Direction and Meditation*. p. 67; "Selections on Prayer," unpublished manuscript written during Lent, 1961; "Conference to Sisters on Prayer;" *The Climate of Monastic Prayer*, p. 92.

presence within him. For this reason, it involves both renunciation and self-transcendence, if it is to re-establish the proper conditions for the awakening of man's inner self, for his conscious union with God.[14]

While this awakening or awareness of man's conscious union with God is ultimately achieved in contemplation, according to Merton: "Every meditation, every act of mental prayer, even if it may have some immediate practical purpose, should also bring us into direct communion with God."[15] Hence, he speaks of prayer simply as those moments in which the individual becomes more conscious of God in his life.[16] In discussing the nature of "contemplative prayer" it is important to note the manner and the extent of this conscious awareness during the various phases of prayer as described by Merton.

THE NATURE OF CONTEMPLATIVE PRAYER

An experience of his union with God in Christ is the goal, then, to which man must orient his entire life, especially insofar as his

14. Since renunciation is an essential aspect of Merton's contemplative prayer, it shall be discussed at length in the following chapter. The remaining part of the present chapter will concern itself with the nature of contemplative prayer and its significance as seen in its relationship to the apostolate and to the liturgy.

15. Merton, *Spiritual Direction and Meditation*, p. 62; see also Thomas Merton, "Meditation—Action and Union," *Sponsa Regis*, XXXI (1960), 194–95. In the same article, p. 194, Merton asserts: "Meditation can therefore be considered in relation to two ends, one of which leads to the other. The immediate end of our mental prayer may be the understanding of some particular truth, the resolution to embrace a particular course of action, the solution of a spiritual problem, all of which prepare us for the reception of a very definite and particular grace necessary for the practical fulfillment of our daily duties. But the ultimate end of all mental prayer is communion with God." Cf. Merton, *Spiritual Direction and Meditation*, p. 61. That this awareness is ultimately achieved in contemplation is brought out by Merton in his article, "Notes on Contemplation," p. 198, when he says: "Contemplation is the awareness and realization, even in some sense *experience* of what each Christian obscurely believes: "It is now no longer I that live but Christ lives in me."

16. Merton, *The Seven Storey Mountain*, pp. 204–205.

spiritual activity is concerned. In view of this, there can be no uncertainty as to the ultimate end that man must seek in prayer, which is central to such spiritual activity, and that is union with God.[17] Therefore, man's whole life of prayer must consist in a dynamic and loving attention to the presence of God and an awareness of his own dependence upon Him. Man belongs to God and it is in prayer that he must come to realize that the depths of his own being and life are meaningful and real only to the extent that they are open to God. It is this that Merton emphasized in one of his earlier articles when he said: "Mental prayer need not make us *see* the God we seek, but it should always confirm us in our determination to seek Him and no other. . . . In this sense God and the way to God become more and more perfectly 'defined' as we advance in mental prayer."[18]

According to Merton, such unitive and loving knowledge of God begins in meditation. However, in Merton's contemplative prayer, this beginning is not merely a preparatory step leading ultimately to contemplation; rather, it is a very essential and integral part of a continuous whole. For it is right from the start of his life of prayer that man begins to penetrate the inmost ground of his being and to awaken to the discovery of his inmost self in God. This is why Merton, although admitting the importance of both the intellect and the will for achieving this loving spiritual contact with God in Christ, emphasizes that man must include his whole being in his meditation:

In meditative prayer, one thinks and speaks not only with his mind and lips, but in a certain sense with his whole being. Prayer

17. Such an objective has been described by Merton at various times in his writings. Cf. Merton, *A Balanced Life of Prayer*, p. 2: "The supreme object of prayer is the fulfillment of God's Will." Such is perfectly achieved when man reaches perfect union with God in Christ. Cf. Thomas Merton, "The Humanity of Christ in Monastic Prayer," *Monastic Studies*, II (1964), 3, where he says that "the object of all Christian prayer is union with the Father, through the Person of the Son, by the Holy Spirit."

18. Merton, *Spiritual Direction and Meditation*, p. 61; "Meditation—Action and Union," p. 194.

is then not just a formula of words, or a series of desires springing up in the heart—it is the orientation of our whole body, mind and spirit to God in silence, attention and adoration. All good meditative prayer is a *conversion of our entire self to God.*[19]

For Merton, then, meditation can never mean some sort of futile introspection or preoccupation with self-understanding.[20] Indeed, it is such reflexive thinking that Merton finds one of the greatest obstacles to prayer today. Nor, can man's meditation mean simply the effort to know God better intellectually: "The purpose of meditation is not merely to acquire or to deepen objective and speculative knowledge of God and of the truth revealed by him."[21] In meditation, there is only one way that man can come to know God and that is by realizing that his very being is penetrated with God's knowledge and love for him.

Meditation, therefore, is really the experiencing to a degree of Someone Whom we already possess. Such a realization is brought about, first of all, by man's experiencing his own nothingness and helplessness in the presence of God. By gradually descending into the center of his own wretchedness before God and coming face to

19. Merton, *Thoughts in Solitude*, p. 48. Cf. also *Spiritual Direction and Meditation*, p. 43, where Merton writes: "Reflection [which he identifies with meditation in the preceding paragraph] involves not only the mind but also the heart, and indeed our whole being." In fact, in another book, *Monastic Peace*, pp. 28–29, Merton goes on to show that it is because prayer embraces man's whole being that it is possible for man to live consciously in an *atmosphere* of prayer and thus pray constantly.

20. Cf. Thomas Merton, "The Life That Unifies," ed. by Naomi Burton Stone, *Sisters Today*, XLII (1970), 65, where he writes: "I want to make it quite clear that the whole essence of contemplative prayer is that the division between subject and object disappears. You do not look at God as an object and you don't look at yourself as an object. You don't stand back and look at yourself; you are just not interested in yourself."

21. Merton, *The Climate of Monastic Prayer*, p. 108. Cf. Merton, "Prayer, Personalism and the Spirit," p. 129, where he also notes this fact when he says: "And of course when I say 'meditation' I do not mean mental prayer. Mental prayer is only a phrase—you cannot pray with your mind. You pray with your heart or you pray with the depths of your being."

face with the existential reality of his own emptiness, man confronts the deepest reality of his relationship with God Who is present in his being. Thus, he abandons and surrenders himself to God. Such a kenotic type of openness to God came to be called by Merton in more recent years *"prayer of the heart"* in that it has its roots in the deepest ground of man's being.[22] What man must do in meditation, therefore, is to discover his heart, that is, he must awaken the profound depths of his being in the presence of God and become aware of the ground of his identity before God and in God. Most simply, man must seek God by becoming aware of himself as a person who is possessed by God in the inmost depths of his being. Therefore for Merton: " 'Meditation' or 'prayer of the heart' is the active effort we make to keep our hearts open so that we may be enlightened by him and filled with this realization of our true relation to him."[23]

Finding one's heart and recovering an awareness of one's inmost identity become, then, one and the same thing, and imply, as far as Merton is concerned, the recognition that man's external self is to a great extent illusory and false. However, since even this recognition is essentially a gift or grace from God, what man must do in meditation is simply to dispose himself to *receive* this grace whenever God wishes to grant it to him.[24] This he does by trying to deepen his consciousness of his basic relationship to God as a creature before his Creator and as a sinner before his Redeemer. By trying

22. In *The Climate of Monastic Prayer*, p. 48, Merton says that the concept of "the heart" "refers to the deepest psychological ground of one's personality, the inner sanctuary where self-awareness goes beyond analytical reflection and opens out into metaphysical and theological confrontation with the abyss of the unknown yet present." Again, in an article entitled "Renewal and Discipline in the Monastic Life," written in February, 1968, Merton says in speaking of prayer: "What has to be rediscovered is the inner discipline of 'the heart,' that is to say, of the 'whole man'—a discipline that reaches down into his inmost ground and opens out to the invisible, intangible, but nevertheless mysteriously sensible reality of God's presence, of His love, and of His activity in our hearts." *Contemplation in a World of Action*, p. 113.

23. Merton, *The Climate of Monastic Prayer*, p. 123.

24. *Ibid.*, p. 97.

to recognize his own indigence and spiritual poverty as well as his need for God, man can come to the realization that he has "no other reason for being, except to be loved by him as Creator and Redeemer, and to love him in return."[25] Because there can be no true knowledge of God that does not imply a deep grasp and acceptance of this two-fold relationship, man must bring to his meditation two fundamental attitudes—*compunction* and *dread*. Since the beginning of serious contemplative prayer brings man into the presence of God, man needs, first of all, an awareness of his own insufficiency and contingency as a creature who stands in need of a Creator. Such is the meaning of compunction according to Merton.[26] Its purpose is to *liberate* man from any false self-illusions and from concentration upon his exterior self, and turn him towards God. Merton describes this attitude as follows:

> The inward movement of compunction is not so much a matter of hiding ourselves, as a liberation of ourselves, which takes place in the depths of our being, and lets us out of ourselves from the inside. This liberation from concentration on ourself is the beginning of a conversion, a *metanoia*, a real inner transformation.[27]

Second, as a sinner who has repudiated his basic relationship with God and acted contrary to the truth of his real condition as a person made in the image and likeness of God, man must also come to prayer with an awareness of his own infidelity and falsity and with a certain amount of doubt and real guilt at his pretense and unauthenticity. This profound awareness on the part of man of his own failure before God is the meaning of dread in man's life, which Merton describes in much detail in *The Climate of Monastic Prayer*:

> The experience of "dread," "nothingness" and "night" in the heart of man is then the awareness of infidelity to the truth of our

25. *Ibid.*, p. 114.

26. Merton, *Spiritual Direction and Meditation*, p. 81.

27. Merton, *Seasons of Celebration*, p. 70.

F

life. More, it is an awareness of infidelity as unrepented and without grace as *unrepentable*. It is the deep, confused, metaphysical awareness of a *basic antagonism between the self and God* due to estrangement from him by perverse attachment to a "self" which is mysterious and illusory.[28]

It is only when one has descended through compunction and dread to the center of his own nothingness as a creature and as a sinner that he can be led by the Spirit to find God. For, it is in this complete emptiness that man is fully *liberated* in the sense that, not only does he experience the meaninglessness of his own existence, but also he gradually comes to the real meaning of his life as experienced in the fullness of God's love. Hence, one can conclude that for Merton man's prayer begins with the acknowledgment of his own nothingness and wretchedness; but, as shall be evident in the subsequent development of the present chapter, it is through this *emptiness* that man is called into intimate communion with God in the true and deepest freedom that is his as a son of God.[29]

In the beginning of "prayer of the heart" or meditation, there is little or no awareness of God in the sense of experiencing His presence. It is only after he enters into himself and empties himself through compunction and dread that man comes to "*a conscious realization of the union that is already truly effected between souls and God by grace.*"[30] And as he grows in this consciousness, he becomes more aware of the deepest root of his life of prayer, namely, the Christ-life within him.[31] He begins to consciously *identify* with the

28. Merton, *The Climate of Monastic Prayer*, p. 132. It is obvious that such dread is really a grace or gift from God that purifies man and thus enables him to encounter God.

29. It is important to note the prominence of freedom along with awareness in "prayer of the heart." Cf. Merton, "Is the 'Contemplative Life' Finished?", p. 13, where he points out that man's encounter with God in prayer is also the discovery of his deepest freedom as a son of God.

30. Merton, *Spiritual Direction and Meditation*, p. 67.

31. In his article, "The Humanity of Christ in Monastic Prayer." Merton emphasizes the Christocentrism of contemplative prayer. After pointing out that all Christian prayer is centered on the Person of Jesus Christ, Merton

person of Christ by experiencing as real factors in his own life of prayer the mysteries of Christ.[32] For this reason, Merton lays great stress on meditating or reflecting on the mysteries of Christ and especially on Christ's Passion as a means of growing in one's consciousness of the presence of God within him. By sharing Christ's vision of reality, by listening to His response to it, man is brought by the Spirit to a deeper identification with the Incarnate Word, and thus is led to a further knowledge of the living God and to a deeper experience of Who He really is.[33] Moreover, this consciousness or awakening of which Merton speaks is basically a *loving* knowledge for man cannot rest or listen to God unless, together with a deep faith in His presence, he also desires that presence.[34] It is this faith in and continued desire for the presence of God that constitutes the basic motivation underlying "contemplative prayer" in Merton's spirituality.[35]

---

raises the question as to whether contemplative prayer should be directed to Christ as God and not as man. He concludes that because all contemplative prayer is directed to the Father through the Person of Christ, the God-man, as He now is in the glory of the Father: "There is no question whatever of 'excluding' the humanity of Christ from contemplative prayer in order to contemplate His divinity! On the contrary, humanity and divinity are contemplated in inseparable unity in the Person of the glorified Son of God."—p. 10.

32. *Ibid.,* p. 7, where Merton points out that: "All Christian prayer develops and becomes perfect by penetrating deeply, in the Spirit, into the hidden Mystery of Christ." Later, in the same article, p. 14, he writes: "Meditation on the mysteries of the life and death of Christ is, then, to be seen as part of the *transitus* or *pascha* by which we 'pass over' to contemplation of the invisible light shed in our hearts, through the Holy Spirit, by Christ in glory."

33. Merton, *Spiritual Direction and Meditation,* p. 96; see also Thomas Merton, "The Subject of Meditation," *Sponsa Regis,* XXXI (1960), 270. One should note here the Christological and Trinitarian dimensions in "contemplative prayer."

34. Merton, *The Sign of Jonas,* p. 117; *New Seeds of Contemplation,* p. 43.

35. Interestingly enough in his book, *No Man Is an Island,* p. 48, after emphasizing the "gift" aspect of prayer, a gift, which, he notes, is not given to all men, Merton goes on to say: "Perhaps it is given to few because so few desire it."

Finally, it should be noted that the precise way in which each man reflects upon these mysteries in order to become more conscious of God's presence within his own being depends in large measure upon his temperament and his natural gifts. Yet, there is no doubt that in Merton's view a contemplative orientation to one's prayer life requires certain characteristics of all Christians who practice it. Among these, he would emphasize that such prayer must be sought in an atmosphere of tranquility and of solitude, not necessarily in the sense of physical isolation, but rather in the sense of interior withdrawal and recollection that brings with it a sense of love, of wonder, and of admiration.[36] It is in such an atmosphere that man can most easily desire God and attend to God's presence within him. Because of this need for withdrawal and recollection, Merton feels that meditation cannot be practiced without constant and strict discipline, especially in the beginning of one's prayer life. However, such discipline should never imply the obligation that all men must follow one identical rigid system of techniques.[37]

Likewise, if man is to identify with Christ in prayer, then he must approach his life of prayer with a sense of sincerity, in which having acknowledged the unauthenticity and falsity of his exterior self, he becomes capable of finding the authentic true self that is created to share the life of God in Christ. It is this sense of sincerity that Merton feels is the most important quality of true prayer.[38] Above all, the prayer of every Christian must abound in a sense of realism and practicality. Because meditation is a personal and intimate form of prayer, it should encompass all of the reality that confronts the individual—his life, his experiences, his duties, his difficulties: "The prayer of the heart must penetrate every aspect

36. For Merton recollection is not merely the absence of sensible objects; it also includes the idea of presence. In *No Man Is an Island*, p. 165, he says of recollection: "And it makes us present to God, present to ourselves in Him, present to everything else in Him. Above all, it brings His presence to us."

37. *Ibid.*, pp. 93–94. It is important to note here that, for Merton, one's outlook or attitude towards prayer is more important than any system or techniques of praying that man uses.

38. *Ibid.*, p. 156.

and every activity of the Christian's existence."[39] In fact, says Merton: "Meditation has no point and no reality unless it is firmly rooted in *life*."[40] Man's entire existence must enter into his life of prayer if his life is to be related to God.[41] For this reason, Merton throughout his writings urges the man of prayer to link up the truths and mysteries of Christ's life to his own present reality.[42] It is only through such characteristics that man will *awaken* his interior self and thus prepare himself for the deepening awareness of the presence of God that will ultimately lead to a constant loving attention and dependence on God, which is the ultimate end of Merton's contemplative prayer.[43]

As man progresses in his life of prayer, then, there is growth both in his awareness and in his receptivity of God. One dominant attraction begins to emerge in his life and that is the deep sense of his

---

39. Merton, *The Climate of Monastic Prayer*, p. 55.

40. *Ibid.*, pp. 136–37. Cf. Merton, *No Man Is an Island*, p. 48.

41. In *Spiritual Direction and Meditation*, p. 97, Merton says: "The peculiar value of mental prayer however is that it is completely personal and favors a spiritual development along lines dictated by our own particular needs." Here one sees the place for prayer of petition in the early stages of prayer. In *Thoughts in Solitude*, p. 100, Merton points out that "the life of prayer is founded on prayer of *petition* no matter what it may develop into later on." This asking and receiving is the most elementary and ordinary level of man's relationship with God. As man loses himself and becomes less aware of himself and more aware of the God within him, petitionary prayer, to a great extent, yields to other levels of prayer, such as thanksgiving and praise and adoration. In these latter types of prayer man is no longer concerned with himself but with God. In his article, "Contemplation in a World of Action," Merton speaks directly of prayer of petition and its function in contemplative prayer and notes that in contemplative prayer it is praise and thanksgiving that become more important than petition. The reason should be apparent. In contemplative prayer, man realizes that in God everything is really present to him; hence, by trusting in God to take care of his necessities, he can worry a great deal less about the details of his daily needs.

42. Merton, *Spiritual Direction and Meditation*, esp. Part II. Cf. also Merton, "The Humanity of Christ in Monastic Prayer."

43. Merton, *New Seeds of Contemplation*, p. 217. Cf. also *A Balanced Life of Prayer*, pp. 20–21, where Merton speaks of the proximate aim that man must strive for in prayer as "a vital and loving awareness of the presence of God."

own identity as a person who is open to God.[44] There is, says Merton, an awakening in us of "a consciousness of our union with God, of our complete dependence upon Him, for all our vital acts in the spiritual life, and of His constant loving presence in the depths of our souls."[45] Ultimately, the full realization of this is achieved in contemplation where man no longer is conscious of himself as an object of God's love but is conscious only of the God Who is present within his being. However, as Merton shows, the growth from this "prayer of the heart" to its fulfillment in mystical contemplation is a gradual movement through affective and even more obscure and more receptive forms of prayer. Although Merton does not discuss in any detail such intermediary stages in his recent book, *The Climate of Monastic Prayer*, he does underscore their importance in his earlier writings.[46] In *What Are These Wounds*, he speaks of the simplicity of affective prayer for those who have progressed in their life of prayer and says:

44. Cf. Thomas Merton's unpublished conference, "Prayer," given at Darjeeling in 1968. Here, growth in prayer is viewed in terms of man's openness to God.

45. Merton, *Spiritual Direction and Meditation*, p. 67.

46. In *The Climate of Monastic Prayer*, p. 64, Merton mentions such stages in passing when he says: "It is true that one may profit by learning such methods of meditation, but one must also know when to leave them and go beyond to a simpler, more primitive, more 'obscure' and more receptive form of prayer. If this 'obscure' prayer becomes painfully dry and fruitless, one will do better to seek help from psalmody or from a few simple words of the Scriptures, than by resorting to the conventional machinery of discursive 'mental prayer.'" One can only assume that the absence of any detailed treatment of such stages of prayer is due to the fact that Merton at the time of his death was really searching for a new synthesis of the nature of "contemplative prayer" in terms of his interest in Existentialism and Eastern Mysticism (i.e., in light of the double movement of entering into one's inmost center and transcending that center. The first step in the movement obviously includes "prayer of the heart" while the latter involves "mystical contemplation"). Had he lived, Merton undoubtedly would have developed these intermediary stages of prayer in light of these more recent interests. It is in view of this fact that in the present study these stages are treated only briefly. A more detailed treatment of these intermediary stages from a scholastic viewpoint can be found in *The Ascent to Truth*.

It is clear that those who have progressed a certain distance in the interior life not only do not need to make systematic meditations, but rather profit by abandoning them in favor of a simple and peaceful affective prayer, without fuss, without voice, without much speech, and with no more than one or two favorite ideas or mysteries, to which they return in a more or less general and indistinct manner each time they pray.[47]

Likewise, Merton underscores the crucial importance of the *Dark Night* and the *Prayer of Quiet* in man's progressive opening to God.[48] As man passes through these stages of prayer, the reflexive quality that often marks the beginning of one's life of prayer becomes a source of unrest and dissatisfaction. Man's desire to disappear and to lose himself becomes more pronounced, and yet, at the same time, there is doubt about his own love for God. He feels the need for God; yet, the absence of an awareness of God results in darkness and anguish in which man feels abandoned by God. It is in this absence and abandonment, according to Merton, that man undergoes his real transformation of consciousness. For, it is here that man questions the value of his own life and the meaning of his own existence. It is here that he really loses his self-concern and thus learns to pray earnestly. It is here that man is brought to the "inmost center," the ground of his being, where he can encounter God in the prayer of mystical contemplation.[49]

For Merton, it is this mystical contemplation that is the fruition of a life of prayer that is earnestly lived: "Contemplation," he says, "is the fullness of the Christian vocation, the full flowering of baptismal grace and of the Christ-life in our souls."[50] For, it is in

47. Merton, *What Are These Wounds?*, p. 95.

48. Merton, *The Ascent to Truth*, p. 215.

49. Merton, *No Man Is an Island*, p. 50.

50. Thomas Merton, "Poetry and Contemplation: a Reappraisal," *Selected Poems* (New York: New Directions, 1959), p. 114. Cf. also Thomas Merton "Poetry and the Contemplative Life," *Commonweal*, XLVI (1947), 281, and "The Contemplative Life: Its Meaning and Necessity," p. 29. In *The New Man*, p. 17, Merton says simply: "Contemplation is a mark of a fully mature Christian life." It should be noted that in his writings Merton sometimes refers to this experience of mystical contemplation simply as contemplation or

such contemplation that man, having entered into himself, comes "to pass through the center of his own soul and lose himself in the mystery and secrecy and infinite transcendent reality of God living and working within him."[51] He now realizes himself fully, for he is conscious of his divine sonship and fully aware of his union with God in Christ, not in the sense that he sees or hears God, but rather in the sense that there is a conscious awareness of the inmost reality of his own self as well as an experience of God present within that self. In short, man is now aware that his whole being is permeated with God's presence.[52]

Although, in a certain sense, man becomes more and more aware of God's infinite transcendence as he approaches this experience, at the same time he cannot escape the realization of God's all-prevailing immanence at the intimate center of his own personal being. This Merton points out in *The New Man:* "In mystical experience the spirit of man is indeed aware of the reality of God as the 'Other' immanently present within itself, but the more conscious it becomes

---

simply as mysticism. In general, he seems to prefer the use of contemplation rather than the other two concepts. Likewise, it should be noted that Merton is here talking about *infused* contemplation, which is synonymous with *passive* or *mystical* contemplation, as opposed to *active* or *acquired* contemplation, which prepares a man for infused contemplation in that it disposes man for union with God by trying to bring his whole being into harmony with the will of God. Cf. Merton, "Is Mysticism Normal?", p. 95, where he writes: "The difference between acquired and infused contemplation is not the difference between a contemplation that is entirely active on one hand and one that is entirely passive on the other; it is rather a distinction between a contemplation in which our activity predominates and one in which the activity of the Holy Spirit predominates." Finally, in *What Is Contemplation?*, p. 11, Merton states: "There is really only one kind of contemplation. The word, used properly, in its strict and correct sense signifies infused or mystical contemplation." However, he then continues to say, p. 13: "Passive contemplation is not demanded of all Christians. But at least *some* active contemplation would appear to be, in practice if not in theory, *absolutely essential to a truly Christian life.*"

51. Merton, "Poetry and the Contemplative Life," p. 284.

52. In *The New Man*, p. 18, Merton says: "Contemplation is a mystery in which God reveals Himself to us as the very center of our own intimate self. ... Contemplation is the highest and most paradoxical form of self-realization, attained by apparent self-annihilation."

of His reality and of His 'Otherness' the more also it becomes
conscious of the union and 'sameness' which unite Him to itself."[53]
For this reason, as long as man experiences a sense of separation or of
distance between himself and God, he still has not entered into the
fullness of contemplation which Merton has best described in the
following words:

> Contemplation is the highest expression of man's intellectual and
> spiritual life. . . . It is a vivid realization of the fact that life and
> being in us proceed from an invisible, transcendent and infinitely
> abundant Source. Contemplation is, above all, awareness of the
> reality of that Source. It *knows* the Source, obscurely, inexplic-
> ably, but with a certitude that goes beyond reason and beyond
> simple faith.
> In other words, then, contemplation reaches out to the knowledge
> and even to the experience of the transcendent and inexpressible
> God. . . . Hence contemplation is a sudden gift of awareness, an
> awakening to the Real within all that is real. A vivid awareness of
> infinite Being at the roots of our own limited being. An awareness
> of our contingent reality as received, as a present from God, as a
> free gift of love.
> It is the religious apprehension of God, through my life in God, or
> through "sonship." . . . And so the contemplation of which I
> speak is a religious and transcendent gift. . . . It is the gift of God
> Who, in His mercy, completes the hidden and mysterious work of
> creation in us by enlightening our minds and hearts, by awaken-
> ing in us the awareness that we are words spoken in His One
> Word, and that Creating Spirit . . . dwells in us and we in Him.
> That we are "in Christ" and that Christ lives in us. That the
> natural life in us has been completed, elevated, transformed and
> fulfilled in Christ by the Holy Spirit. Contemplation is the aware-
> ness and realization, even in some sense *experience,* of what each
> Christian obscurely believes: "It is now no longer I that live but
> Christ lives in me."[54]

53. *Ibid.,* p. 98.

54. Merton, *New Seeds of Contemplation,* pp. 1–5 *passim;* also found in his
article, "Notes on Contemplation," pp. 196–98 *passim.* Cf. also his article,
"Community, Politics, and Contemplation," p. 245, where he states:
"Contemplation is the realization of God in our life, . . . the realization that
we belong totally to him and he has given himself totally to us."

In light of this description, one notes the following characteristics of mystical prayer for Merton. First of all, such an experience cannot be a function of the external self, but must take place within the depths of man's inmost self. For, it is there that man transcends his dependence on all sensations and images and concepts, and discovers his true liberty, the freedom that comes from emptying oneself and uniting oneself to God in Christ.[55] In his article, "Contemplation in a World of Action," Merton again speaks of this renunciation and transcendence that are necessary for reaching the true awareness of oneself in God that is part of mystical union.[56]

Second, beyond this awareness of one's inmost self, man must also recognize God as the deepest center of his being: "We do not see God in contemplation—we *know* Him by love: for He is pure love and when we taste the experience of loving God for His own sake alone, we know by experience Who and what He is."[57] Hence, for Merton, contemplation is basically an intuition or intellectual experience of God that is both grounded in love and that terminates in love. "It is itself," he says, "nothing else but an experience of God revealing Himself to us in the intimate embrace of a love so pure that it overwhelms every other affection and

55. It is important to call attention to two factors at this point. First, in *The Climate of Monastic Prayer*, p. 122, Merton calls contemplation "a listening in silence, an expectancy." However, as he then points out in the same paragraph, the listening is not an attentiveness but rather an *emptiness* that has penetrated through all concepts and now "waits to realize the fullness of the message of God within its own apparent void." Second, as is common in the Cistercian Fathers, Merton emphasizes mystical contemplation as the supreme manifestation of one's liberty as a son of God. Cf. Merton, *The New Man*, pp. 13–14; *New Seeds of Contemplation*, pp. 8–9.

56. Cf. Merton's article, "Contemplation in a World of Action," *Contemplation in a World of Action*, pp. 157-165.

57. Merton, *New Seeds of Contemplation*, p. 268. In his most recent book, *The Climate of Monastic Prayer*, p. 104, Merton further describes this knowledge by love involved in contemplation: "The unitive knowledge of God in love is not a knowledge of an object by a subject, but a far different and transcendent kind of knowledge in which the created 'self' which we are seems to disappear in God and to know him alone. In passive purification then the self undergoes a kind of emptying and an apparent destruction, until, reduced to emptiness, it no longer knows itself apart from God."

excludes everything from our souls but the knowledge of Love alone."[58] In saying that love is the source of contemplation, Merton is stating that in contemplation man comes to a supernatural realization of God as He is in Himself. Hence, man recognizes the fact that God is Love and so he loves Him for His own sake. Most simply, in contemplation man becomes one with God in love.[59] In this way, man's knowledge of God becomes inseparable from his experience of love, and thus God, Who is really beyond all knowledge, is known through love.[60]

Four characteristics of this love should be noted. To begin with, because such love transcends all man's natural capacities, it cannot be acquired by his own efforts, but can only be produced in him as a gift from God. Nevertheless, as Merton frequently notes, man must dispose himself and desire this gift through prayer: "Therefore, if anyone should ask, 'Who may desire this gift and pray for it?' the answer is obvious: *everybody*."[61] In addition, there is in contempla-

58. Thomas Merton, "Contemplation in a Rocking Chair," *Integrity*, II (1947–48), 18.

59. Cf. *The Ascent to Truth*, pp. 274–76, where Merton treats *in detail* of this knowledge by love in contemplation. He also expresses it most succinctly in *Faith and Violence*, p. 223, when he says: "God Himself is not only pure being but also pure love, and to know Him is to become one with Him in love." It is important to note that this knowledge "of God as He is in Himself" differs from the knowledge of God which man will achieve in the beatific vision both in its intensity and in its duration in that the knowledge achieved in contemplation in this life is inchoative and transitory. Cf. Merton, *The New Man*, pp. 74, 95. In *The Ascent to Truth*, p. 282, Merton says: "However a distinction must be made between contemplation in this life and in the next. In the Beatific Vision, God is formally and immediately attained and possessed by an act of the intellect. In this life, not so."

60. Merton, *The New Man*, pp. 74–75. One should note that it is here that man also comes to full self-realization, as Merton notes on p. 75: "That is to say we fully 'realize' ourselves when we cease to be conscious of ourselves in separateness and know nothing but the one God Who is above all knowledge."

61. Merton, *What Is Contemplation?*, p. 6. Obviously, such desire cannot obtain contemplation which is basically a gift from God. However, as Merton says in the same book, p. 5: "God often measures His gifts by our desire to receive them, . . ." Cf. *New Seeds of Contemplation*, p. 230, as well as *Bread in the Wilderness*, pp. 17–18, and "The Psalms and Contemplation," p. 342. In all of these writings Merton discusses prayer as a disposition for contemplation.

tive love an *immediacy* of union between man and God. Such perfect love unites man to God without the medium of any created species or ideas or images.[62] Moreover, this love is the witness that the Spirit of Christ lives in man and is intimately united to man's inmost self. Merton underscores this in *No Man Is an Island* when he says: "For to know His love is not merely to know the story of His love, but to experience in our spirit that we are loved by Him, and that in His love the Father manifests His own love for us, through the Spirit poured forth into our hearts."[63] Indeed, it is this Spirit that gives man his new identity; for, it is by Him and through Him that man is fully transformed into Christ. Because of His presence within him, man is and acts as another Christ.[64] Finally, such mystical love implies a recognition of one's own freedom and union of divine sonship with God, as Merton discusses in his article, "The Psalms and Contemplation":

> Contemplation is essentially an experience of our divine sonship. It is an experiential recognition, a "taste," an interior awakening, an intimate and personal appreciation of the truth that God loves us not only as our Creator but as our Father. More, that He is actually present to us as our "Father," that is, as the source of our supernatural life, our charity.[65]

For this reason, man is said to be created for true contemplation, for this life of deep and interior infused prayer: "Contemplation,

---

62. Merton, *The Ascent to Truth*, p. 82. Later in the same book, pp. 279–80, Merton describes the immediacy of this union of love when he says that: "in making us love as He loves, God is said to take the soul entirely to Himself and to give Himself entirely to the soul. When he does this there is no longer any practical or experiential distinction between His activity and the activity of the soul united in one and the same perfect love. This love is God Himself."

63. Merton, *No Man Is an Island*, pp. 77–78.

64. Here one notes Merton's strong Christocentric emphasis in contemplation. Cf. *The Ascent to Truth*, p. 13, where he asserts: "Finally, mystical contemplation comes to us, like every other grace, through Christ. Contemplation is the fullness of the Christ-life in the soul, . . ." Such emphasis is brought out later in the book on pp. 131, 309. In the latter reference Merton shows that there is no contemplation of God except in Christ.

65. Merton, "The Psalms and Contemplation," p. 433.

by which we know and love God as He is in Himself, apprehending Him in a deep and vital experience which is beyond the reach of any natural understanding, is the reason for our creation by God."[66]

It is this recognition of divine sonship that points to the fact that contemplation is not only grounded in love but also terminates in love. For, man's recognition of his union of sonship with God also implies a recognition of his union with all those who live by the same Spirit and are one with him in Christ. As Merton notes: "union with God Who is Love means participation in one of the characteristics of that Love, which is to share itself and pour itself out and communicate itself to others."[67] For Merton, then, true contemplation is essentially communal in that man's union of love with God is inseparable from his union of love with other persons in God. For this reason, contemplation is intimately connected with charity. It is, says Merton, "essentially a union of supernatural charity."[68] In view of this, one can say that man's ultimate purpose in life is to continuously grow in union with the risen Christ

66. Merton, *New Seeds of Contemplation,* p. 225. Such thinking is also expressed in his article, "Can We Survive Nihilism?", p. 16 and in an unpublished manuscript entitled *The School of the Spirit,* p. 17. It is important to recall what was stated earlier regarding mysticism. (Cf. *supra,* pp. 21–23). In Merton's view, all Christians receive a remote call to the mystical life. Such a life, by its very nature, includes at least a latent element of infused prayer, as he points out in his article, "Is Mysticism Normal?" p. 98. Hence, contemplation is both necessary and possible for all Christians, although he admits in *Faith and Violence,* p. 215: "Those who seek it are few and those who find it fewer still." In Merton's view, then, most Christians will never become pure contemplatives, but many do in fact become what he calls "masked contemplatives" or "quasi-contemplatives"—men who live for God and for His love alone in the midst of their activity. Cf. *What Is Contemplation?,* pp. 14–15.

67. Merton, *The School of the Spirit,* unpublished, p. 7. In *New Seeds of Contemplation,* p. 65, Merton says boldly: "For contemplation is not ultimately perfect unless it is shared."

68. Merton, *The Ascent to Truth,* p. 70. Cf., "Is Mysticism Normal?", p. 95 In this same article, p. 94, Merton notes that infused contemplation "consists in the union of the soul with God by perfect charity." Hence, it is charity and not infused contemplation which is of the essence of Christian perfection. Contemplation is but an effective *means* to perfection. Cf. also "The Primacy of Contemplation," p. 5.

towards the complete maturity and perfection that is the full manifestation of Christ in his life, namely, the communication of that Christ-life in and through the Holy Spirit. It is here that one sees the principal fruit of all prayer, including contemplation, in Merton's spirituality. Prayer must lead to a life of more perfect and more fruitful action; contemplation must be supplemented by a life of fraternal and apostolic charity.[69] Indeed such a union of love of man for his fellow man in Christ is highly characteristic of Merton's spirituality.

THE SIGNIFICANCE OF CONTEMPLATIVE PRAYER

A man of prayer, then, cannot live a life of mere individualistic piety. True prayer must lead man outwards to others. This Merton emphasizes when he says: "If we experience God in contemplation, we experience Him not for ourselves alone but also for others."[70] Because the effectiveness of man's intimate union with God should be evidenced in his genuine concern for his fellow man, one's life of prayer should lead to a deeper integration of oneself through Christ into the life of other Christians. It should lead man to seek and to help others discover the true meaning of their lives. In view of this, for Merton it would be a comparatively weak person who would arrive at any degree of prayer in his life and not overflow with a zeal and a love that wants to communicate what it knows

69. This, for Merton, is the highest vocation in the life of a Christian. Cf. *New Seeds of Contemplation*, pp. 270–71, where he says: "The highest vocation in the Kingdom of God is that of sharing one's contemplation with others and bringing other men to the experimental knowledge of God that is given to those who love Him perfectly. Again in *The Seven Storey Mountain*, p. 407, Merton points out that the sharing of the fruit and the truth of one's contemplation is the highest of all lives. Cf. Thomas Merton, "Active and Contemplative Orders," *Commonweal*, XLVII (1947–48), 194.

70. Merton, *New Seeds of Contemplation*, p. 269. It should be noted that it is not necessary that man be conscious or see how his contemplation overflows to others. It is possible, as Merton says in *New Seeds of Contemplation*, p. 269, to share one's gift of contemplation with someone one will never know until he reaches heaven.

of God and of God's love to other men.[71] For this reason, man's moments of formal contemplative prayer must flow over into an abiding prayerful consciousness or awareness of God in his dedicated action: "Contemplation, at its highest intensity, becomes a reservoir of spiritual vitality that pours itself out in the most telling social action."[72]

One can see, therefore, that there is a very real sense in which for Merton man's whole life can become a prayer when one strives to realize his true self by continuously making God's view of reality his own and by interfusing his life of formalized prayer with the rest of his life. By living as habitually and as constantly as possible on this level of union and love, which proceeds from the depths of his own being where he is united with Christ to God, man sees that his entire life becomes a life of prayer.[73] In view of this, the apparent dichotomy or dialectic between prayer and work, between contemplation and activity, is, according to Merton, largely a pseudo-problem. For him man's life of work has an intrinsic connection to his life of prayer: "Work can help us to pray and be recollected if we work properly. . . . Work brings peace to the soul that has a semblance of order and spiritual understanding. It helps the soul to focus upon its spiritual aims and to achieve them."[74] Thus, man must try to see his work in its proper perspective as an essential part of his imitation of Christ and of Christ's redemptive mission,

71. *Ibid.*, p. 272.

72. Merton, "The Contemplative Life: Its Meaning and Necessity," p. 33. In *A Thomas Merton Reader*, p. 437, Merton says: "In actual fact, true contemplation is inseparable from life and from the dynamism of life—which includes work, creation, production, fruitfulness, and above all *love*. Contemplation is not to be thought of as a separate department of life, cut off from all man's other interests and superseding them. It is the very fullness of a fully integrated life. It is the crown of life and of all life's activities."

73. In the unpublished manuscript of his conference on "Prayer" given at Darjeeling in 1968, Merton notes: "Prayer is not so much an expression of something we do; it is much deeper than that. Prayer is not just part of our life, it is not just something that happens five or six times a day. Prayer is an expression of who we are; our very being expresses itself with prayer because prayer flows from our relation to God, and other people."

74. Merton, *No Man Is an Island*, p. 92.

as his personal cooperation with the divine plan of salvation.[75] In addition, he must remember that the apostolate of today, if it is to be authentic, needs people who are experienced in prayer. For, without a personal prayer life a genuine apostolic life cannot mature, nor can one penetrate the deeper value and meaning of his work. As far as Merton is concerned, one simply cannot be a true witness to Christ unless he knows Christ personally; for man gives to his fellow man only in proportion to his own receptiveness to God. Hence, unless one is continually alive to Christ in prayer, it is impossible for him to bring Him to others in his work. "To this end," says Merton, "he will have to look for the same thing in his activity as he finds in his contemplation—contact and union with God."[76]

Because one's external activity is genuinely apostolic only in so far as he permits Christ to work in him and through him, the true Christian does not separate or subordinate his life of prayer from the real world of work and struggle in which he lives.[77] Although they are two distinct aspects in the life of any Christian, they are not mutually opposed or irreconcilable. In fact, as Merton notes in *No Man Is an Island:*

> Action and contemplation now grow together into one life and one unity. They become two aspects of the same thing. Action is charity looking outward to other men, and contemplation is charity drawn inward to its own divine source. Action is the stream, and contemplation is the spring. The spring remains more important than the stream, for the only thing that really

75. In *New Seeds of Contemplation*, p. 19, Merton writes: "When I act as His instrument my labor cannot become an obstacle to contemplation, even though it may temporarily so occupy my mind that I cannot engage in it while I am actually doing my job. Yet my work itself will purify and pacify my mind and dispose me for contemplation."

76. *Ibid.*, p. 192.

77. In *The Climate of Monastic Prayer*, p. 73, Merton notes that "the active life which is germane to the present existence of man in the world always demands the attention even of those called to contemplation. . . . Both are, in fact, demanded by charity, since man is commanded to love both God and his neighbor. Both necessarily must be combined in any earthly vocation, . . ."

matters is for love to spring up inexhaustibly from the infinite abyss of Christ and of God.[78]

Man's activity, therefore, must always be born of his prayer and must resemble it. Hence, although it is his function in life to divinize the world in Christ Jesus, his first and essential duty and desire is to be united in personal contact with God in Christ. And so, the Christian of today, in Merton's view, must keep in mind that before he can truly give himself to others, he must himself become imbued with the Spirit of Christ. For, unless he is continuously renewing his intimacy with Christ and receptive to His love in prayer, his effectiveness in giving that love to his fellow man in his apostolic work will be minimal. Merton writes: "The more fruitful and healthy are our lives as members of Christ, the more we are able to communicate the Christ-life to others, in and through the Holy Spirit."[79] For Merton, then, man will never reach a deep and full integration of charity towards others, unless he first finds himself in God through the direct experience of God in prayer. For union with God in action demands a strong union with Him in prayer. This Merton emphasized again in his last book:

> There is no contradiction between action and contemplation when Christian apostolic activity is raised to the level of pure charity. On that level, action and contemplation are fused into one

78. Merton, *No Man Is an Island,* p. 65. In *New Seeds of Contemplation,* p. 192, he says simply: "Far from being essentially opposed to each other, interior contemplation and external activity are two aspects of the same love of God." Again, the relationship is emphasized in several of his earlier articles, such as, "The Primacy of Contemplation," p. 14, where he says: "Contemplation and action are not two distinct ends of the apostolic life, of which the first is the means to the second. On the contrary, there is one end only: a contemplation so superabundant that it overflows in apostolic action." Cf. also "Active and Contemplative Orders," p. 195, where he states: "This means, in practice, that there is only one vocation . . . no matter who you are or what you are, you are called to the summit of perfection: you are called to be a contemplative and to pass the fruits of your contemplation on to others." This is similarly expressed in *The Seven Storey Mountain,* p. 408. Here one is referred to *supra,* p. 5, footnote 16.

79. Merton, *Life and Holiness,* pp. 86–87.

G

entity by the love of God and of our brother in Christ. But the trouble is that if prayer itself is not deep, powerful and pure and filled at all times with spirit of contemplation, Christian action can never really reach this high level.[80]

Only if this presence of God is all-pervading in his life, can man escape a two-fold danger present in society today. He will avoid either prolonging isolated and artificial prayer by occupying himself with God and forgetting the sensibility of God's people, or, what Merton feels is more prevalent today, abandoning prayer and losing oneself in external activity to such an extent that man no longer notices that there is little or nothing in him of a truly personal relationship with God.

It is in light of this teaching on prayer and its relationship to man's activity that one must understand Merton's tendency in his more recent writings to emphasize man's life of service, as for instance in *Life and Holiness*, where he asserts: "There is no genuine holiness without this dimension of human and social concern. . . . We are obliged to take an active part in the solution of urgent problems affecting the whole of society and of our world."[81] Hence, it is only when man's actions bear witness to his own communion with God that one can say, according to Merton, that he is living a full and authentic spiritual life. For the mature Christian is one who is marked both with a sense of apostolicity as well as with the continuing presence of Christ. He is a person who has come to a deeper understanding of the totality of his own person as one who receives from God in prayer and gives to others in his work. As Merton noted recently: "To say that a man is a person is to say, ultimately, that he has a vocation to contemplate God and to share that contemplation with his fellow man."[82] Such a man sees himself as a person who must live a life dedicated

80. Merton, *The Climate of Monastic Prayer*, p. 153.

81. Merton, *Life and Holiness*, p. 100. Cf. *The New Man*, p. 114, where Merton tells us that as Christians we must let people know "by the spirituality and purity and strength of our own lives that God is love, and that He loves them all as He loves His own Son, and that He wants all men to recover their true identity as His sons."

82. Merton, *Redeeming the Time*, p. 63.

and united to God, yet also dedicated and united to his fellow man. Merton himself sums it up well in *Faith and Violence*?

> Hence I want to say that the highest form of life is this "spiritual life" in which the infinitely "fontal" (source-like) creativity of our being in Being is somehow attained, and becomes in its turn a source of action and creativity in the world around us.[83]

Because there is an insufficiency in a spirituality which arrives at a sense of individual and personal fulfillment in Christ and yet does not have a vital connection with other members of the Mystical Body of Christ, the effectiveness of a balanced life of contemplative prayer must be evidenced also in man's communal prayer, in his public and universal sharing of the Liturgy.[84] "It is," says Merton, "a law of man's nature, written into his very essence, . . . that he should want to stand together with other men in order to acknowledge their common dependence on God, their Father and Creator."[85] There is, then, in Merton's spirituality, an intimate relationship

83. Merton, *Faith and Violence*, p. 115; similarly expressed by Merton in his comments in *War Within Man*, p. 47. In "Christ the Way," p. 147, Merton earlier expressed a similar view when he said that the Christian life is "a life in which drawn to union with God in Christ by the Holy Spirit, we strive to express our love and our new being by acts of virtue."

84. It should be noted at the beginning of this discussion on the Liturgy that Merton does not seem to allow as much scope for the Liturgy as appears to be indicated by Vatican II in its Constitution on the Sacred Liturgy (no. 10) when it states: "Nevertheless the liturgy is the summit toward which the activity of the Church is directed." According to Merton, infused contemplation is the end to which all liturgical and personal prayer should be directed (cf. *Waters of Siloe*, p. 318; *The Climate of Monastic Prayer*, p. 66). For Merton, the Liturgy is a work of the active life and prepares man for contemplation which he sees as the final perfection of Christian personalism, as he notes in *Seasons of Celebration*, p. 26. Notwithstanding this, two points will be discussed in the following pages in order to complete the treatment on the significance of contemplative prayer: (1) the intimate relationship in Merton's spirituality between liturgical and personal prayer; (2) the importance of liturgical worship in his spirituality.

85. Merton, *The Seven Storey Mountain*, p. 19. It is important to note here Merton's use of the word *Liturgy*. In *The Waters of Siloe*, p. 385, he describes the liturgy as: "The system of prayers and sacred texts and ceremonies established by the Church as the official vehicle of her public worship of God

between private prayer and public worship in that he sees the value and the necessity of both to form the individual into God, to express his inner self-commitment to Christ, and to transform him into the likeness of Christ.[86] In both the Christian participates in the mysteries of Christ's death and resurrection. For this reason they presuppose and complement each other as Merton himself admits:

> Indeed the superficial opposition so often created between liturgical prayer and "personal" prayer—an opposition which has no basis in reality—makes all genuine understanding of either liturgy or meditation practically impossible: as if liturgy were thinkable without some meditation, and as if meditation did not presuppose and complement the liturgical celebration of the mysteries of our redemption.[87]

precisely as a group, or better, as the Mystical Body of Christ." As such, it includes for Merton both the Divine Office and the Eucharistic Sacrifice. The latter, he held, was the core of the liturgy. Cf. Merton, *Basic Principles of Monastic Spirituality*, p. 21; Thomas Merton, "Sonship and Espousals," *Sponsa Regis*, XXVIII (1956–57), 170; *Bread in the Wilderness*, p. 79. In the present discussion, the term *liturgy* is used in the latter sense of referring exclusively to the Eucharistic Sacrifice of the Mass in view of the fact that the present discussion is centered upon the significance of contemplative prayer in the life of *all Christians* and not merely in the life of those called to a contemplative religious order. The present writer has been careful to avoid any reference to a work where it is obvious from the context that Merton is referring exclusively to the Divine Office and not to the Mass.

86. Cf. Merton, *Spiritual Direction and Meditation*, p. 86. In *The Climate of Monastic Prayer*, p. 65, Merton after noting that any conflict between "public" and "private" prayer is a pseudo-problem, goes on to say: "Liturgy by its very nature tends to prolong itself in individual contemplative prayer, and mental prayer in its turn disposes us for and seeks fulfillment in liturgical worship." Cf. also *Basic Principles of Monastic Spirituality*, pp. 23–24, and "Sonship and Espousals," p. 173. In a letter to Dan Walsh, quoted by Rev. Daniel Walsh in "Thomas Merton: The Sense of Mystery," *Saint John's*, IX (1969), 15, Merton deals specifically with the question of the relationship between liturgy and contemplation and says: "I know a lot of people over here in America are . . . so scared that there really is a conflict between the liturgy and contemplation . . . and are so desperately anxious for liturgy unqualified to be 'the highest contemplation' so that then there will be nothing to fear. Isn't it all too pitiable! I have not entered into the controversy at all but hope I have gone beyond and above it."

87. Merton, *Seasons of Celebration*, p. 4. Cf. Thomas Merton, "Liturgy and Spiritual Personalism," *Worship* XXXIV (1960), 494. In an unpublished

Frequently throughout his writings, therefore, Merton emphasizes that the contemplative orientation of man's prayer life must be nourished and formed by the Liturgy.[88] "The Liturgy," he says, "is supposed to form and spiritualize man's consciousness, to give him a tone and a maturity without which his prayer cannot normally be either very deep or very wide or very pure."[89] At the same time, in Merton's view, personal and interior forms of prayer tend to complete man's liturgical piety.[90] For, no matter how enthusiastic may be one's engagement in the Liturgy, unless it is prompted and supplemented by an interior and contemplative union with God, which comes from habitual personal prayer of the heart, it tends to become superficial and routine, and to result in plain babbling. In fact, if man tries to live by the Liturgy alone, without any personal and interior prayer, there will result nothing but a degradation of the Liturgy itself. For, in such a case, the Liturgy would become merely the expression of a collective and formalistic ritual participation with no personal or inner confrontation with God.[91] Hence, the importance of understanding the essentially spiritual values of the Liturgy in Merton's spirituality.

Although every man, both as an individual and as a member of society, is instinctively impelled to worship God and to have a many-sided life of prayer, Merton nonetheless notes that the Liturgy is the very heart of man's life of prayer in that it is the most

----

manuscript entitled "Aids to Mental Prayer," Merton also stresses this relationship between liturgy and meditation by showing the necessity of a meditative attitude during the Liturgy.

88. Merton, "Time and the Liturgy," p. 9.

89. Merton, *No Man Is an Island*, pp. 41–42. Cf. also *A Balanced Life of Prayer*, p. 12, where Merton points out: "The foundation of the life of prayer is *active* participation in the Holy Sacrifice of the Mass."

90. *The New Man*, p. 133, where Merton says: "But this growth and development will never be complete unless they prolong these liturgical contacts by private prayer, meditation, asceticism and works of charity."

91. Cf. Merton's unpublished manuscript, *Prayer as Worship and Experience*, pp. 41–42, where he shows how liturgical prayer and personal contemplation supplement and inspire each other."

direct way to an awareness of his union in Christ.[92] For this reason the Liturgy should not be looked upon merely as the fulfillment of a natural duty nor merely as a *corporate* expression which man as a social being owes to God. To assert such a view results only in the individual trying to divest himself of all individuality and personality.[93] The Liturgy is a deeper mystery in which *individual* men as members of society are transformed in the very depths of their beings through a mystical participation in Christ's death and resurrection. This Merton notes in *The New Man* when he says: "The divinizing and transforming action of God is exercised upon our souls in a very special way in the Liturgy."[94] To reach this transformation, man must, as he does in his personal prayer, empty himself of his superficial and private self in order that he might be led to a discovery of his deeper self in Christ.[95] For Merton, however, liturgical worship *of its very nature* takes man out of himself and elevates him to this deeper level of union with God in Christ in that it is a living and visible expression of man's union with God in love.[96]

92. Cf. Merton, *The Living Bread*, pp. xix–xx.

93. Cf. Merton, *Seasons of Celebration*, p. 9; also *Prayer as Worship and Experience*, p. 42.

94. Merton, *The New Man*, p. 132. In "Time and the Liturgy," p. 5, Merton calls the Liturgy "the great school of Christian living and the great transforming force which reshapes our souls and our characters in the likeness of Christ."

95. Merton, *The Climate of Monastic Prayer*, pp. 142–43. Later in the same book, Merton discusses the need for emptiness in liturgical worship. In an earlier writing, *Basic Principles of Monastic Spirituality*, p. 23, Merton points out the need for sacrifice in liturgical worship: "Liturgy demands of us the sacrifice of what is merely individualistic and eccentric in our lives, that we may rise above ourselves to the supra-personal level of the Bride of Christ. In the Liturgy we must sacrifice and lose something of ourselves in order to find ourselves again on a higher level. But the Liturgy can never make us mere automatons praising God like machines. On the contrary, Liturgical praise is the *collective interior prayer* of persons who are fully conscious of themselves as members of Christ."

96. Merton, *Prayer as Worship and Experience*, p. 43. In *The Living Bread*, pp. 53–54, Merton further comments on this union of love in the Liturgy as follows: "What we behold at Mass is the very reality of God's own love. And we enter into that reality. . . . We become able to unite ourselves with the

In addition to its mystical significance of uniting man to Christ by involving him in a deeper sharing in the life and mind and prayer of Christ Himself, Merton also views an active participation in the Liturgy as a more significant awakening of man's consciousness of his true identity, namely, his freedom as a son of God. For, in the Liturgy man is enabled to discover and to express the deepest meaning of his Christian person by discovering the person of Christ Himself and by affirming his own divine sonship.[97] This Merton notes in *What is Contemplation?* when he states: "We become contemplatives to the extent that we participate in Christ's Divine Sonship, and that participation is granted to us in a special way in Holy Mass."[98] It is in light of this full acknowledgement of man's true identity as a son of God that Merton feels the Liturgy has a deeply human value. For, only if the Liturgy is the activity of free persons offering their own contributions yet participating together, can it hope to achieve a real spiritual meaning.

Furthermore, because it is a collaboration of free and responsible persons, the Liturgy, according to Merton, is a deeper expression, not only of man's own inmost self, but also of the inmost self of his neighbor, in the unity of the mystery of Christ. "It is," he says, "recognition of the fact that in reality we cannot be without Him, that we are centered in Him, that He dwells in us, and that because

---

Word in the great act of sacrificial love by which He bore witness on the Cross to His love for the Father and for us. And at the same time we unite ourselves—in the very heart of the mystery—with the eternal love by which, as Word, He offers His endless 'sacrifice' of praise to the Father in the depths of the Holy Trinity."

97. Cf. Merton, *Seasons of Celebration*, pp. 22–23. It is in this sense that Merton acknowledges the "political" significance of liturgical worship. The liturgy affords man an opportunity to exercise his true freedom through active participation. Cf. his article, "Liturgy and Spiritual Personalism," for a more complete discussion of the "political" significance.

98. Merton, *What Is Contemplation?*, p. 13. Cf. *The Living Bread*, p. 96, where Merton stresses the relationship between the Mass and man's freedom as a son of God. This is also brought out in *Prayer as Worship and Experience*, p. 46, where he shows how man can live up to his destiny as a son of God in liturgical worship.

He is in us, and we in Him, we are one with one another in Him."[99]
Man does not go to Christ as an isolated individual but rather
as a member of a community, namely, of Christ's Mystical Body.
It is this expression of brotherhood or community that is implicit
in the following words from *Seasons of Celebration:*

> Now it is precisely in the Liturgy, the *public* prayer of the Christian
> Assembly that the Christian best discovers the secret of his own
> inviolable solitude, and learns to respect the solitude of his brother
> while at the same time sharing it. . . . The Christian person finds
> himself and his brother in the *communal celebration of the mystery of
> Christ.*[100]

Such an expression of unity and solidarity of all the members in
Christ is an important quality in Merton's consideration of the
Liturgy. Indeed, a lack of involvement in the Liturgy can cause a
diminishment in modern man in that it is in the Liturgy that man
principally gains an awareness of how he can fulfill his vocation as a
community, as a communion of men united to one another in the
Spirit of Christ. For, it is the Liturgy that gives man the solitude
he needs to be united to Christ and through Christ to one another.[101]

Finally, in showing men how to fulfill their vocation as a
community of men united in the Spirit, the Liturgy also urges them
to carry out that work of the Spirit in the world. Merton alludes
to this cosmic significance of liturgical worship when he says:

99. Thomas Merton, "Symbolism: Communication or Communion" in
New Directions in Prose and Poetry 20, ed. by J. Laughlin (New York: New
Directions, 1968), pp. 12–13. In an earlier article, "Christianity and Mass
Movements," *Cross Currents,* IX (1959), 209, Merton says: "The supreme
manifestation of Christian unity is always the relatively small group that
gathers around the altar for Mass." Finally, cf. Merton, *Disputed Questions,*
p. 145.

100. Merton, *Seasons of Celebration,* p. 22; "Liturgy and Spiritual Personalism," p. 504.

101. Cf. Merton, *The Sign of Jonas,* p. 262, where he notes: "Solitude and
society are formed and perfected in the Sacrifice of the Mass." Previously in
the same book, p. 198, Merton asserts this point in his own life by saying: "It
is at Mass, by the way, that I am deepest in solitude and at the same time mean
most to the rest of the universe."

"We meet Christ in the Liturgy in order to be Christ, and with Him save the world."[102] For this reason, the Liturgy cannot be an evasion from life nor a negation of reality. Rather, it is the total commitment of man to the Kingdom of God. It is a work that affords him the opportunity to cooperate and to collaborate with the divine Redeemer by uniting him with Christ the High Priest in His work of redeeming and sanctifying the cosmos. It is in this way that the Liturgy expresses more fully the highest personal and spiritual dignity of the Christian, namely, his participation in the priesthood and sonship of Christ.[103] Hence, one can conclude that, as far as Merton is concerned, the Liturgy is the highest expression of the Christian's personal dedication in that it expresses more vividly what is implicit in all contemplative prayer, namely: "The more fruitful and healthy are our lives as members of Christ, the more we are able to communicate the Christ-life to others, in and through the Holy Spirit."[104] Therefore, the love of Christ that man receives in prayer and more expressly in the Liturgy must somehow reach out to others in charity. If it fails to do so, then man's own *apparent* love for Christ is simply a fiction.

In summary, then, the principal characteristic of contemplative prayer meant for all Christians, lies in its submission or emptiness or what Merton calls its "apparently useless element":

> If the contemplative orientation of prayer is its emptiness, its "uselessness," its purity, then we can say that prayer tends to lose its true character in so far as it becomes busy, full of ulterior purposes, and committed to programs that are beneath its own level.[105]

It is precisely through such a contemplative orientation to his prayer that man can come to realize the necessity of surrendering

102. Merton, "Time and the Liturgy," p. 7; cf. also *Seasons of Celebration*, p. 55. In *The Living Bread*, p. 119, Merton, speaking of the Eucharist in the context of liturgical worship, says: "This Sacrament is not given to us merely in order that we do something but that we may *be* someone: that we may be Christ. That we may be perfectly identified with Him."

103. Merton, *Seasons of Celebration*, p. 15.

104. Merton, *Life and Holiness*, pp. 86–87.

105. Merton, *The Climate of Monastic Prayer*, p. 152.

and losing himself in order to find and gain the true and deeper self that is the perfect Image of God within him, namely, his capacity and freedom as a son of God to love like God, Who is love.

It is the deepening of this realization in love and the awakening to a new awareness of ourselves in Christ that constitutes the real purpose of prayer according to Merton.[106] Hence, "prayer of the heart" and contemplation must be seen in the light of the double movement of man's entering into the deepest center of himself and then passing through that center and going out of himself to God. It is there in the very roots of his own being that man is brought from emptiness to self-transcendence, to a fullness in nothingness, to a conscious and total awareness of the Christ-life in his being. He is no longer conscious of himself; rather, having been transformed, he now sees himself as a dependent being,—a being who exists in God. There is, says Merton, "a transcendent union of consciousness in which man and God become, according to the expression of St Paul, "one spirit."[107]

Such an experience of one's union with God is not meant for man alone. It is meant to be shared with others. This is evident in Merton's teaching. For him the effectiveness of contemplative prayer must be evidenced both in man's charity and concern for his fellow man as well as in his participation in the communal and public prayer of the Church, the Liturgy. However, man must always remember that:

> He who attempts to act and do things for others or for the world without deepening his own self-understanding, freedom, integrity and capacity to love, will not have anything to give others. He will communicate to them nothing but the contagion of his own obsessions, his aggressivity, his ego-centered ambitions, his delusions about ends and means.[108]

106. Merton, "Contemplation in a World of Action," p. 161.
107. Merton, *Faith and Violence*, p. 222.
108. Merton, "Contemplation in a World of Action," p. 5.

Hence, the love of God must remain the source of all living and authentic love for other men.

For Merton, therefore, the whole mystery of "contemplative prayer" is basically a mystery of love, of personal vocation and of free gift. Although each man will find his relationship with God in his own way, one can say that the goal which is to be ultimately achieved by all Christians in their life of prayer involves both the unitive knowledge of God in loving contemplation together with selfless good will and charity towards other men in the world. It is in this sense that Merton says: "every Christian is potentially a contemplative."[109] His life of prayer becomes a continuous searching for God and finding Him and sharing Him with others. Such a search is accomplished principally in love: "As we grow in love . . . with those who are loved by Christ (that is to say, all men), we become more and more capable of apprehending and obscurely grasping something of the tremendous reality of Christ in the world, Christ in ourselves, and Christ in our fellow man."[110]

However, as Merton notes, this perfect love or charity is fed by God not only in prayer but also in sacrifice. For, in contemplation there are always two aspects: "the positive one, by which we are united to God in love, and the negative one, by which we are detached and separated from everything that is not God. Without both these elements there is no real contemplation."[111] Hence, man's life of prayer must always, at the same time, be a life of sacrifice. It will be the purpose of the following chapter to consider this "negative" aspect showing the relationship and necessity of asceticism for man's entering his inmost depths and experiencing the awakening of the true self that is the Image of God within him. In this way there will be presented a complete view of Merton's teaching on the theology of prayer in his spirituality.

---

109. Merton, "Is Mysticism Normal?," p. 95.
110. Merton, *Disputed Questions*, p. 123.
111. Merton, *The Waters of Siloe*, p. 51. Cf. also *Disputed Questions*, p. 222.

CHAPTER IV

ASCETICISM AND CONTEMPLATIVE PRAYER

A S WAS SHOWN in the preceding chapter, contemplative
prayer, according to Merton, is primarily intended to open
man's heart to God and to deepen his awareness of the
intimate presence of God within him. This it accomplishes through
the double movement of man's entering into the deepest center of
himself, and then, after passing through that center, transcending
himself in God. It is in this way that man finds out who he really is,
and having made such a discovery, is thus ready for a full life of
love and service to other men. Because such prayer is personal and
dictated by man's own particular needs for reaching communion
with God, Merton places great emphasis on it as *the* means for
union with God in Christ.

If man is to reach his real or true self, then he must be delivered
from the illusory and false self which he has created by his habits of
selfishness and self-centeredness. While prayer in itself enables man
to surrender his inmost depths to God's presence within him, in its
full context, contemplative prayer is a movement of renunciation
as well as of self-transcendence. Hence, according to Merton's
spirituality, self-discipline and asceticism must be considered
important elements for achieving union with God: "And to achieve
this union with Him, this freedom based on true values and firm
adhesion to God's will, we must necessarily purge out of our hearts
all attachment to false ego-centered values and all reliance on our

own will."[1] But these, Merton admits, must always be viewed in their relation to man's life of prayer since they are part of the renunciation involved in contemplative prayer and cannot be understood apart from it.[2] In that they are necessary to re-establish the proper conditions for the awakening of what is inmost in man, his spiritual "I," they too can be said to have as their primary objective the awakening of man's inner self and the disposing of this self for conscious communion with God.[3] Interior peace, which leads to union with God and which one might call the proximate goal of the spiritual life according to Merton, necessarily involves some form of asceticism in that man must separate himself from everything that is not God if he is to reach the transforming or mystical union of contemplation. This Merton notes in *No Man Is an Island:*

> Christian self-denial is only the beginning of a divine fulfillment. It is inseparable from the inward conversion of our whole being from ourselves to God. It is the denial of our unfulfillment, the renunciation of our own poverty, that we may be able to plunge freely into the plenitude and the riches of God and of his creation without looking back upon our own nothingness. . . . It is the first step toward a transformation of our entire being in which, according to the plan of God, even our bodies will live in the light of His divine glory and be transformed in Him together with our souls.[4]

1. Merton, *Seasons of Celebration,* p. 127. See also "Self-Denial and the Christian," p. 649.

2. Thomas Merton, "Solitude," *Spiritual Life,* XIV (1968), 173. Cf. *The Climate of Monastic Prayer,* p. 99, where Merton asserts: "Without trying to make of the Christian life a cult of suffering for its own sake, we must frankly admit that self-denial and sacrifice are absolutely essential to the life of prayer."

3. In *The Silent Life,* p. 3, Merton writes: "Asceticism itself does not produce divine union as its direct result. It only disposes the soul for union." In "Renewal and Discipline," Merton further brings out the intimate relationship between prayer and asceticism in man's life when he points out that the objective of discipline is to deepen man's awareness of his authentic life in Christ and to help him towards a self-transcendence and transformation in Christ, *Contemplation in a World of Action,* pp. 98–116.

4. Merton, *No Man Is an Island,* p. 89.

Hence, in Merton's spirituality, man's life of "contemplative prayer," if it is lived fully and sincerely, must be accompanied by a life of asceticism.[5] In view of this, the present chapter will examine certain fundamental ascetical themes in Merton's writings showing their relation and necessity to man's entering his inmost depths and experiencing the awakening of the true self that is the Image of God within him. In addition, it will be both necessary and beneficial to study briefly Merton's own basic attitude and relation to the world, as well as the apparent paradox of solitude and communion in his own life. Both are logical developments of his essential teaching on asceticism, and together with it, are necessary for perfecting a Christian's life of prayer.

ASCETICISM IN MERTON'S SPIRITUALITY

According to Merton, it would certainly be a misunderstanding of Christian life to base one's asceticism on some cult of suffering and pain or to view it as a destruction or annihilation of one's body.[6] Although always opposed to such exaggerated yet restricted concepts of asceticism in that asceticism should lead man to a growth in interior charity and not to slavery, Merton nonetheless viewed a balanced asceticism as unavoidable in Christian

5. Thomas Merton, "Contemplation and Ecumenism," *Season*, III (1965), 133. Speaking of contemplation, he says: "This direct awareness is a gift, but it also normally presupposes the knowledge and practice of certain traditional disciplines. Thus we can say that contemplation is both a 'gift' (a 'grace') and an 'art.' " This is later found in *Mystics and Zen Masters*, pp. 203–204.

6. Merton throughout his life had little attraction for the narrow seventeenth-century spirituality of most Cistercian manuals and openly opposed the rigid teaching of many Trappist writers who followed the de Rancé school of asceticism. Abbé de Rancé, commonly known as the Reformer of La Trappe, was a Trappist of the seventeenth century, who, although highly respected in many ways, was nonetheless noted for an exaggerated asceticism where merit and value were measured in terms of self-inflicted pain and austerities as well as extraordinary penances and mortifications. Cf. Merton, *The Waters of Siloe*, pp. 72–83.

life.[7] Without it, man cannot become detached from all the illusions
he holds about himself, nor can he completely empty himself of his
false self. However, this asceticism must be rightly understood in
Merton's spirituality. It is not something negative such as the mere
negation or crushing of all spontaneous and instinctive reactions in
human nature. For Merton, it is the positive element of Christian
asceticism that is the more important. Asceticism must enable man
to grow in his existential communion with God in Christ, as he
says in *The Basic Principles of Monastic Spirituality:* "What matters
most is not so much that we deny ourselves and give up (the flesh),
but the new life which develops in us in proportion as we are
emptied of self (the life of the Holy Spirit)."[8] Hence, Merton
describes asceticism as "the recovery of our true self, man's true
'nature,' created for union with God. It is the purification, and
liberation of the divine image in man, hidden under layers of
'unlikeness.' "[9] Early in his writings he states its purpose when he
says:

> The real function of asceticism is, then, to liberate us from desires
> that debase and enslave our souls made for union with God in
> pure love and even in contemplation. The real purpose of self-
> denial is to turn over the faculties of our soul and body to the

7. In *Seasons of Celebration,* pp. 131–32, Merton asserts: "Christian asceticism
is remarkable above all for its balance, its sense of proportion. It does not
overstress the negative side of the ascetic life, nor does it tend to flatter the ego
by diminishing responsibilities or watering down the truth. It shows us clearly
that while we can do nothing without grace, we must nevertheless cooperate
with grace." See also, "Self-Denial and the Christian," p. 650.

8. Merton, *Basic Principles of Monastic Spirituality,* p. 20; "Sonship and
Espousals," p. 169. In *Seasons of Celebration,* p. 142, Merton further brings out
the importance of the positive element in asceticism when he says: "The true
self-denial of the Christian is not a conquest of himself by himself, but a
dying to self in order to live to God in Christ."

9. Merton, *The Silent Life,* p. 22. In *The Ascent of Truth,* p. 158, a similar
though more generic definition is found: "First of all, what do I mean by
asceticism? I mean the active self-purification by which the soul, inspired and
fortified by grace, takes itself in hand and makes itself undergo a rigorous
spiritual training in self-denial and in the practice of virtue."

Holy Spirit in order that He may work in us the work of trans-formation. . . .[10]

Because of this close connection with the process of man's liberating himself from all narrow and superficial egoism, Merton views all ascetical practices as the first step in man's real inner transformation. Together with the compunction and dread which man experiences in his "prayer of the heart," asceticism is part of man's self-emptying.[11] Ultimately, however, like prayer, it must lead to man's freedom as a son of God and to his union with God in charity. This Merton emphasizes in *No Man Is an Island:* "It is the first movement of a liberty which escapes the boundaries of all that is finite and natural and contingent, enters into a contact of charity with the infinite goodness of God, and then goes forth from God to reach all that He loves."[12] It is here that one notes the intimate relationship between asceticism and prayer in Merton's spirituality. Ascetical discipline must bear fruit in a deep life of prayer which, in turn, leads to works of active charity.

In discussing the necessity and the importance of asceticism,

10. Merton, "Self-Denial and the Christian," p. 652. In *The Waters of Siloe*, p. 381, Merton notes simply: "The acquisition of detachment is the proximate end of all asceticism." Indeed, without such detachment, it is difficult to conceive how man can enter his inmost depths and experience the "awakening" of that inner self that is the Image of God within him.

11. In *Zen and the Birds of Appetite*, p. 76, Merton points out that "in all these higher religions the path to transcendent realization is a path of ascetic self-emptying and 'self-naughting'. . . ." Likewise, in *Faith and Violence*, p. 113, he notes the importance of discipline in assisting man to transcend his empirical self and find his true self. See also Merton's Comments in *War Within Man* p. 46.

12. Merton, *No Man Is an Island*, p. 89; also p. 94, where Merton asserts: "It is true that discipline is supposed to bring us, eventually, to spiritual liberty." In his last conference, "Marxist Theory and Monastic Theoria," delivered in Bangkok, December 10, 1968, the day of his death, Merton again made reference, in speaking of the Monastic view of reality, to the fact that ascetical discipline must lead to freedom: "It is the view that if you once penetrate by detachment and purity of heart to the inner secret of the ground of one's ordinary experience, you attain to a liberty which nobody can touch, which nobody can affect, . . ."

Merton inevitably relates it to several other concepts. Among them, one finds penance as well as self-denial, abnegation and mortification, suffering as well as sacrifice, renunciation and detachment. While each one carries its own nuance, the fullness of the ascetical dimension in Merton's spirituality can be grasped by examining two of the concepts, which, more frequently than the others, are singled out by Merton in his writings. First is his emphasis on the importance of *sacrifice,* which Merton says must complement man's life of prayer and renunciation: "A life entirely given to prayer is made possible by the renunciation of those things which impede prayer, and such a life becomes, in its entirety, a sacrifice of praise to God."[13] For Merton, sacrifice is really the culmination of man's life of asceticism. He writes: "One of the chief tasks of Christian asceticism is to make our life and our body valuable enough to be offered to God in sacrifice."[14] One can say, then, that it is sacrifice that really effects the divine and religious transformation in man

13. Merton, *Monastic Peace,* p. 30. The importance of sacrifice in one's prayer life is also brought out in *A Balanced Life of Prayer,* pp. 8–9, as well as in *The Climate of Monastic Prayer,* p. 102. In the latter Merton says: "Our ability to sacrifice ourselves in a mature and generous spirit may well prove to be one of the tests of our interior prayer. Prayer and sacrifice work together. Where there is no sacrifice, there will eventually turn out to be no prayer, and vice versa. When sacrifice is an infantile self-dramatization, prayer will also be false and operatic self-display, or maudlin self-pitying introspection." In the same book, p. 101, Merton further brings out the complementarity by showing the importance of prayer for man's sacrifice: "Such exercises as fasting cannot have their proper effect unless our motives for practicing them spring from personal meditation. We have to think what we are doing, and the reasons for our action must spring from the depths of our freedom and be enlivened by the transforming power of Christian love. Otherwise, our self-imposed sacrifices are likely to be pretenses, symbolic gestures without real interior meaning."

14. Merton, *No Man Is an Island,* p. 89. It should be noted here that strictly speaking there is a difference in Merton's spirituality between asceticism and sacrifice. Earlier in the same book, p. 87, Merton says: "Asceticism is content systematically to mortify and control our nature. Sacrifice does something more: it offers our nature and all its faculties to God. A self-denial that is truly supernatural must aspire to offer God what we have renounced ourselves. The perfection of Christian renunciation is the total offering of ourselves to God in union with the sacrifice of Christ." Hence, asceticism strictly speaking is the first step in man's inner transformation.

H

and thus consecrates and unites him more closely to God. However, man cannot begin to realize this union with God that results from emptiness unless he is detached from his own selfish interests and concerns.

This brings us to the second important element stressed by Merton in his writings on asceticism, namely, his emphasis on renunciation or detachment which he describes as the proximate end of all asceticism.[15] For Merton, two characteristics should be noted as regards renunciation. First of all, such renunciation is not something negative such as the denunciation or despising of creatures. Rather, there is a positive fulfillment in that through detachment man begins to value created things as they really should be valued. He realizes the true value of creatures in their relation to God and learns to love them as God loves them.[16] In addition, because such detachment (or renunciation) must reach into the depths of man's own being, to renounce oneself in the fullest sense, man must detach himself not merely from what he has but also from what he is: "We do not detach ourselves from things in order to attach ourselves to God, but rather we become detached *FROM OURSELVES* in order to see and use all things in and for God."[17] In this way, man becomes liberated from any fixation upon himself and is able to discover his transcendence in God. Both characteristics must be kept in mind in assessing Merton's concept of renunciation, especially as it is evidenced in his own attitude and relationship to the contemporary world. For, in speaking of Christian asceticism Merton says:

> It warns us that we must make an uncompromising break with the world and all that it stands for, but it keeps encouraging us to

15. Merton, *The Waters of Siloe*, p. 381.

16. It is in light of this that Merton can say in *New Seeds of Contemplation*, p. 268: "True mystical experience of God and supreme renunciation of everything outside of God coincide. They are two aspects of the same thing. For when our minds and wills are perfectly free from every created attachment, they are immediately perfectly filled with the gift of God's love: . . ."

17. *Ibid.*, p. 21. Cf. also *Life and Holiness*, p. 109, and "Growth in Christ," p. 202.

understand that our existence in "the world" and in time becomes fruitful and meaningful in proportion as we are able to assume spiritual and Christian responsibility for our life, our work, and even for the world we live in.[18]

MERTON'S ATTITUDE TOWARD "THE WORLD"

Perhaps nowhere has Merton been more criticized than as regards his attitude toward the world. Many authors have taken issue with his pessimistic outlook and his apparent denunciation of the contemporary world, especially as it is manifested in his early writings.[19] More recent authors have commented on the complete change in his attitude and his responsibility toward the world, citing his earlier attitude of escape, of separation, and of abandonment from the bewildered and confused world as somewhat excessive.[20] In their view it would appear that Merton, by pushing

18. Merton, *Seasons of Celebration*, p. 132. See also "Self-Denial and the Christian," p. 650.

19. Cf. James M. Gillis, "Action and Contemplation," *Cross and Crown*, I (1949), 257; Graham, "Thomas Merton/A Modern Man in Reverse," p. 74; Shaddy, "Thomas Merton and *No Man Is an Island*," p. 54; F. Dell'Isola, "The Conversion and Growth of Thomas Merton," p. 57. Frequently the authors cite or allude to the passage in *Seeds of Contemplation*, p. 60, as evidence of their position: "Do everything you can to avoid the amusements and the noise and the business of men. . . . Do not read their newspapers, if you can help it. . . . Be glad if you can keep beyond the reach of their radios. . . . Do not smoke their cigarettes or drink the things they drink or share their preoccupation with different kinds of food. Do not complicate your life by looking at the pictures in their magazines." However, as Sister T. Lentfoehr notes in her Introductory Comments to "Thomas Merton on Renunciation," p. 421, such a passage must be interpreted in the context of the chapter's emphasis on interior solitude in man's spiritual life, as well as in the context of the chapter's final paragraph, p. 61, which balances such a remark: "And yet remember, if you seek escape for its own sake and run away from the world only because it is (as it must be) intensely unpleasant, you will not find peace and you will not find solitude. If you seek solitude merely because it is what you prefer, you will never escape from the world and its selfishness; you will never have the interior freedom that will keep you really alone."

20. Cf. Charles Dumont, "Père Louis-Thomas Merton," *Collectanea Cisterciensia*, XXXI (1969), 4, who says: "L'abrupt refus du monde évoluera

the ideal of renunciation to its extreme, has despised the world with a little too much enthusiasm to be entirely convincing. Finally, there are those authors who underscore the early Merton's profound contempt for the modern world and criticize him for an attitude that is both limited and inadequate, if not completely inhuman.[21] According to these critics, Merton, as a young monk, cared only about the spiritual salvation of men and not about their earthly condition and hence, offered no analysis nor suggested any solution to the problems of the world.[22]

In general, one could say that Merton himself, in his writings, would admit that his initial complaints about the world were

---

jusqu'à un desir réfléchi d'ouverture au monde; le *contempus mundi* est devenu, dans les derniers écrits, 'un sentiment de compassion pour ce monde qui passe'." A similar thought is found in his article, "A Contemplative at the Heart of the World–Thomas Merton," p. 639. Also, Baker, "The Social Catalyst," p. 258ff. traces the change between the cloister and the world from one of spiritual isolationism to social involvement in which prayer and social action are given equal importance in the achievement of Christian perfection. Such an opinion, this writer feels, is false and contrary to Merton's own words as cited on pp. xiv–xv of this study: "Whatever I may have written, I think it all can be reduced in the end to this one root truth: that God calls human persons to union with Himself and with one another in Christ, . . . But if I have written about interracial justice, or thermonuclear weapons, it is because these issues are terribly relevant to one great truth: that man is called to live as a son of God." Cf. "Concerning the Collection in Bellarmine College Library," pp. 3–4.

21. Cf. Baker, *ibid.*, esp. pp. 256–58. Clifford Stevens, "Thomas Merton: an Appraisal," *American Benedictine Review*, XVIII (1967), 255, speaks of Merton's early writing as being "immature in its judgment of 'the world'."

22. Cf. James Baker, "The Two Cities of Thomas Merton," *Catholic World*, CCXI (1970), 151. In the same paragraph the author describes Merton's change of attitude and notes that for the early Merton, there were two distinct worlds: the world outside the monastery and the Church, and God's society, which included the Church and especially the monastery. For the later Merton, the two cities became intertwined and became synonymous with selfishness and goodness, both of which can exist outside of and even within the monastery and the Church. The former, Merton called "The City," while the latter he called "The Community." According to Merton, says Baker, p. 152, they are distinguished principally "by their participation in or neglect of God's love as received primarily through contemplation, . . ."

carried to an extreme.[23] Likewise, the change and growing expansiveness in his own attitude towards the world were obvious to him.[24] As he found a certain peace within himself through his life of prayer, his own vision expanded and his compassion grew with the result that he himself became more receptive to the world, for prayer transformed his vision of the world and made him see it in the light of God.[25] On the other hand, Merton never admits in

23. Merton, *The Sign of Jonas*, p. 163. Earlier in the book, p. 97, Merton says: "Perhaps the things I had resented about the world when I left it were defects of my own that I had projected upon it." Interestingly, Merton attributes his earlier criticism of the world to defects within himself. This shall be discussed in more detail later in the chapter. In *Conjectures of a Guilty Bystander* he says: "As far as I can see, what I abandoned when I left the world and came to the monastery was the *understanding of myself* that I had developed in the context of civil society—my identification with what appeared to me to be its aims." Cf. "As Man to Man," p. 92, where Merton further describes this point when speaking of his attitude at the time of entering the monastery: "It is true that when I came to this monastery where I am, I came in revolt against the meaningless confusion of a life in which there was so much activity, so much movement, so much useless talk, so much superficial and needless stimulation, that I could not remember who I was." See also, "Dieu n'est pas un problème," pp. 20–21.

24. Merton, *The Sign of Jonas*, pp. 97–98, where he says: "Now, on the contrary, I found that everything stirred me with a deep and mute sense of compassion. . . . I seemed to have lost an eye for merely exterior detail and to have discovered, instead, a deep sense of respect and love and pity for the souls that such details never fully reveal." Cf. p. 312 for a similar acknowledgment of his change of attitude. In his article, "Introducing a Book," p. 9, Merton describing his decision of renunciation from society says: "Yet the attitude and the assumption behind this decision have perhaps changed in many ways. For one thing, when I wrote this book, the fact uppermost in my mind was that I had seceded from the world of my time in all clarity and with total freedom. The break and the secession were, to me, matters of the greatest importance. Hence, the somewhat negative tone of so many parts of this book. Since that time, I have learned, I believe, to look back into that world with greater compassion, seeing those in it not as alien to myself, not as peculiar and deluded strangers, but as identified with myself. In breaking from 'their world,' I have strangely not broken from them. In freeing myself from their delusions and preoccupations, I have identified myself, none the less, with their struggles and their blind, desperate hope of happiness."

25. Cf. *Conjectures of a Guilty Bystander*, pp. 156–57, where Merton describes an experience of his visit to Louisville in which he reveals his love and concern for people.

his writings to any kind of open denunciation of the world of his time nor to any rejection or contempt of reality.[26] Instead, he |has found a reality which most men today have missed, and he has discovered this without ever really altering his pessimistic analysis of the condition of the contemporary world.[27] Moreover, he always maintained: "The job of giving ourselves to God and renouncing the world is deeply serious, admitting of no compromise."[28] However, in keeping with the two basic characteristics

26. In his article, "As Man to Man," p. 92, ("Dieu n'est pas un problème," p. 26), Merton says: "and I have no right to repudiate the world in a purely negative fashion, because if I do that my flight will have taken me not to truth and to God but to a private, though doubtless pious, illusion." In *Mystics and Zen Masters*, p. 114, he asserts: "Certainly it has never been Christian to reject 'the world' in the sense of the cosmos created by God, dwelt in by the Incarnate Word, sanctified by the presence and action of the Mystical Christ, and destined to be transformed with man in a new eschatological creation." Cf. also Thomas Merton, "Virginity and Humanism in the Latin Fathers," *Sponsa Regis*, XXXIV (1963), 131. In *Life and Holiness*, p. 78, he clarifies his own meaning of rejecting the world (not reality) by saying: "To reject the 'world' is not to reject people, society, the creatures of God or the works of man, but to reject the perverted standards which make men misuse and spoil a good creation." This is also found in, "The Life of Faith," p. 171.

27. Thomas Merton, "Is the World a Problem?" *Commonweal*, LXXXIV (1966), 307. After asserting that it is an evasion of choice to reject or show contempt for the world, Merton goes on to say: "On the other hand the stereotype of world-rejection is now being firmly replaced by a collection of equally empty stereotypes of world affirmation in which I, for one, have very little confidence." Further examples of Merton's pessimism towards the conditions of contemporary society can be found in an earlier article, "We Have to Make Ourselves Heard," *Catholic Worker*, XXVIII (1962), 5, and in his essay, "Peace: A Religious Responsibility," in *Breakthrough to Peace*, ed. by Merton, pp. 102–103, as well as in his book, *Faith and Violence*, pp. 116–16, where he asserts: "I think we have to recognize the hollowness . . . of the kind of material and depersonalized abundance which we presently enjoy in the United States. Not only does this tend to stifle and corrupt the real spiritual depths of man's being, not only does it imprison him in every possible kind of spiritual delusion, but I think the very frustration and self-contradictions of materialistic affluence, coupled with frantic and useless activism, do much to explain the death-wish of our warfare economy and culture." This is also found in his Comments in *War Within Man*, p. 48.

28. Merton, *Life and Holiness*, p. 51.

of his renunciation enumerated above, Merton advocated a renunciation of the world that was essentially an unmasking or a
dispelling of all illusions and pretenses.[29] Because of it, man could
realize the true value of creatures in their relation to God. For, by
leaving the world, he is sufficiently purified to take the world to
his heart.[30] In addition, because of such renunciation, man can
achieve the full liberation that is his as a son of God on earth, and
without which, any question of love for the people in the world
would be completely irrelevant.[31]

For Merton, then, renunciation of the world must be considered
essentially as an unmasking of an illusion, namely, the unmasking
of man's own alienated and false self.[32] Therefore, man's flight from

29. Cf. "Introducing a Book," p. 9, where Merton discusses this point at
length.

30. This idea of renunciation of the world enabling man to see and respect
creatures for their true value can be found in *Basic Principles of Monastic
Spirituality*, pp. 10–11 and similarly in "Seeking God," p. 120. In an earlier
article entitled "September, 1949," *Month*, III (1950), 110–111, Merton after
speaking about his detachment from created things, goes on to discuss his
reverence for the holiness of all created things in that they belong to God.
Finally, in *The Living Bread*, p. 92, he says: "This life in spirit and in truth, this
life in God, which we live while remaining in the world, does not diminish
our appreciation for the reality of the creation with which God has surrounded
us. It makes it more real for us, because we now see all ordinary created
things in a new light. We see them and know them and love them in Christ."
It is in light of this that Merton can make such a remark as the following in
The Secular Journal of Thomas Merton, p. 222: "Also anyone who believes in
the Mystical Body of Christ realizes I could do more for the Church and for
my brothers in the world, if I were a Trappist at Gethsemani than if I were a
staff worker at Friendship House."

31. In *The Waters of Siloe*, pp. 358–59, Merton shows the relationship
between this renunciation and freedom: "It is relatively easy to renounce a
world whose pleasures are boring and whose ambitions are a waste of time
and effort. It is not too hard to give up licit satisfactions when the sacrifice
soon finds more ample compensation in the delights of interior freedom and
the taste of supernatural things."

32. It is in this sense that Merton, in his article, "Christian Freedom and
Monastic Formation," p. 294, speaks of contempt of the world as "the
beginning of our return to ourselves and to God." Cf. "Is the World a
Problem?", p. 309, where Merton says: "The world itself is no problem, but
we are a problem to ourselves because we are alienated from ourselves."

the world becomes in reality a flight from the selfishness of his own empirical self.[33] It is in this sense that Merton primarily uses the expression, "the world." For him, it signifies not the cosmos but those people who love the transient and unimportant things of this life, who are self-seeking and ego-centered, and who have rejected God's love. "To renounce the world," he says, "means not only to leave the world physically and to live apart from it, to follow ways that differ from those of the world and to devote oneself to life of ascesis and prayer which has as its end the glory of God in all things: it is above all the renunciation of one's own will."[34] In light of this, only the man who is detached from his false self and who discovers the freedom of his true self can come to love fully the world in which he lives. This Merton emphasized in an unpublished article entitled, "Seven Words":

> The man who was able to contemn the world, that is to affirm his own independence of servitude to the "given," was proclaiming his respect for the free person. This in its turn redounded to the world's advantage in the long run because the free person, instead of submitting blindly to stereotyped patterns and familiar

33. Cf. *New Seeds of Contemplation*, p. 79, where Merton asserts: "For the flight from the world is nothing else but the flight from self-concern."

34. Thomas Merton, "Conversatio Morum," *Cistercian Studies*, I (1966), 143. Cf. also *Seasons of Celebration*, p. 170, where he admits: "Created things stand as obstacles between man and God only when man himself is an obstacle, when his will has darkened the light of truth." Cf. Thomas Merton, "A Homily on Light and on the Virgin Mother," *Worship*, XXXVII (1963), 578. Merton himself admits to the New Testament usage of the world, in this sense, in *No Man Is an Island*, p. 139, when he says that "the world in the New Testament is the collective name for all those subjected to the desire of temporal and carnal things as ends in themselves." Cf. also *Monastic Peace*, p. 4, where he shows the New Testament usage of "the world" as referring to "the division in God's creation brought about by man's spirit of selfishness and dissension." In light of this, one could almost say that Merton's criticism of the world is really a criticism of an attitude of worldliness. However, one should note that for Merton, the term, "worldliness" refers merely to an over-involvement or over-concern with what is in vogue at present, *Conjectures of a Guilty Bystander*, p. 284. In conclusion, one can say, as Merton does in his article, "Is the World a Problem?" esp. pp. 306, 308–309, that man discovers his own attitude toward the world by discovering himself.

ways, felt himself called to develop new ways and new attitudes, and eventually to make new discoveries which changed the world. Contempt for the world was in reality the first beginning of love for the world. . . .[35]

Because technological power and automation threaten the realization of this true freedom within man by enhancing the illusions of his false self and by leading to the superficiality of the "mass man," Merton is strongly critical of such processes in contemporary society.[36] In the end, such power structures lead only to the dehumanization of man in that they either enslave him or destroy him by forcing him to become a frustrated and unidentified cog in a huge impersonal machine. Man becomes confused about who he really is and the effect of prayer and contemplation, which reveals his true identity, is destroyed. Having lost his personal identity and dignity, he then becomes submerged in a life that is easily reduced to mere empty routine. Consequently, he yields to the falsities and to the illusions of the massive organization with the result that his spiritual creativity and freedom become dried up. He loses his point of contact with God and so becomes a depersonalized man incapable of authenticity. His only hope in such a crisis, says Merton, "is to respond to his inner need for truth, with a struggle to recover his spiritual freedom."[37]

Merton himself foresaw the dangers of an age that would set such a high price upon technology and such a small price upon authentic human values, and early in his writings he openly

35. Merton, unpublished manuscript entitled "Seven Words."

36. First of all, it is important to note here that Merton in no way maintains that technology is intrinsically evil. Cf. *Conjectures of a Guilty Bystander*, p. 222; "Peace: a Religious Responsibility," in *Breakthrough to Peace*, pp. 102–103; "We Have to Make Ourselves Heard," p. 5. On the contrary, it can and should be a very great good. In actual fact, however, it has become too autonomous, and hence, will only destroy man by forcing him to become part of a mass—"mass man." This he notes in *Conjectures of a Guilty Bystander* pp. 72–73, 76.

37. Merton, *Faith and Violence*, p. 52. See also Merton's Introduction to *The Prison Meditations of Father Alfred Delp*, p. xii.

expressed his concern over this spiritual inadequacy in man.[38] Indeed, it was to this tragedy of modern man, who has lost his creativity, his spirituality, and his contemplative independence, that Merton responded especially in his more recent writings on the contemplative life and on his own life of solitude as a hermit. This is clear from his recent book, *The Climate of Monastic Prayer*, in which he says:

> For the monk searches not only his own heart: he plunges deep into the heart of that world of which he remains a part although he seems to have "left" it. In reality the monk abandons the world only in order to listen more intently to the deepest and most neglected voices that proceed from its inner depth.[39]

The contemplative life, he felt, should be a matter of the greatest importance to modern man in that it is basically an affirmation of the absolute value of human life and of the person who is a transcendent being. "It is," he recently said, "the peculiar office of the monk in the modern world to keep alive the contemplative experience and to keep the way open for modern technological man to recover the integrity of his own inner depths."[40] In order to find this inner center of his life, the contemplative must separate himself to some extent by a certain detachment from the ordinary concerns of man. This, for Merton, is not an escape or a flight from reality but a thrust into a new kind of reality. "The monk is a man who withdraws deliberately to the margins of society with a view to deepening fundamental human experience."[41] This experience is seen principally in terms of a new freedom. Hence, the contemplative's withdrawal from the world is simply a

38. Cf. "The Contemplative Life: Its Meaning and Necessity," p. 27, where Merton says: "Generation after generation of men have so lost the sense of an interior life, have so isolated themselves from their own spiritual depths by an exteriorization that has at last ended in complete superficiality, that now we are scarcely capable of enjoying any interior peace and quiet and stability."

39. Merton, *The Climate of Monastic Prayer*, p. 35.

40. Cf. his unpublished manuscript, "Monastic Experience and East-West Dialogue," (1968).

41. *Ibid.*

movement toward liberation, toward the freedom that is his as a son of God.[42] And it is this freedom that gives him the new and higher perspective with which he views the realities of life.[43]

Because of this detachment from the external compulsions of contemporary society, the contemplative is able to penetrate more deeply into this process of liberating himself than most other men, and thus he is able to have a much more spiritual grasp of what is real and authentic in his own being. Furthermore, in liberating himself as a complete and whole man, he also strives to further this wholeness in others by showing them the same freedom. In this way, says Merton, he becomes "a sign of freedom, a sign of truth, a witness to that inner liberty of the sons of God with which Christ has come to endow us."[44] Because of this search for true freedom, the contemplative can be said to love the world with a greater depth and a more profound understanding than many of his fellow men.[45] Also because he desires to further that freedom in others, he

42. In his article, "Is the 'Contemplative Life' Finished?" p. 40, Merton emphasizes this point when he asserts: "in the contemplative and monastic life we have sought out a certain kind of solitude and separation from the world for the sake of *freedom.*" Later, in the same article, p. 60, he describes this freedom as follows: "The freedom that we seek in the cloister is the freedom to be open to the new life which comes from Christ, the freedom to follow His Spirit." In an article entitled "Monastic Renewal: Problems and Prospects," (1967), Merton also discusses this freedom of the contemplative: "This is the secret of monastic 'renunciation of the world.' Not a *denunciation,* not a denigration, not a precipitous flight, a resentful withdrawal, but a liberation, a kind of permanent 'vacation' in the original sense of 'emptying'. . . ."

43. In *Seeds of Destruction,* p. xiv, he says: "The freedom of the Christian contemplative is not freedom *from* time, but freedom *in* time."

44. Cf. Merton's article, "The Monk Today," *Contemplation in a World of Action,* p. 230. It should be noted that it is in this way, as Merton writes in *Seeds of Destruction,* p. 210, that the contemplative's "separation from the world constitutes the basis, indeed the only valid basis, for his dialogue with the world." Cf. also *Redeeming the Time,* p. 112; Thomas Merton, "The Monk in the Diaspora," *Commonweal,* LXXIX (1963), 744, and *Blackfriars,* XLV (1964), 300.

45. In *Seeds of Destruction,* p. 220, Merton says: "The monk retains his own perspective and his own horizons which are those of the desert and of exile. But this in itself should enable him to have a special understanding of his fellow man in an age of alienation." *Redeeming the Time,* p. 119.

can be said to meet his fellow man at the deepest level of being—
the level of transcendence, the level of his own closeness to God. It
is this Merton hints at when he says:

> It would perhaps be more truly monastic to say that the monk
> who is effectively liberated from the servitudes and confusions of
> "the world" in its negative and sterile sense, ought to be enabled
> by that very fact to be more truly present to his world and to his
> time by love, by compassion, by understanding, by tolerance, by
> a deep and Christlike hope.[46]

In addition to this deepening of the personal dimension of one's
liberty, the contemplative, insofar as he is a man who is trying to
renew some kind of contact with his inner depths, at the same time
strives to deepen the clarity and the truth of his own inner awareness
and thus live a life in which he can more readily and more simply
and more naturally live in an awareness of his direct dependence
upon God.[47] For, it is this sense and recognition of one's dependence
on God that gives man's life its basic authenticity.[48] This is the

46. Cf. Thomas Merton, "Dialogue and Renewal in the Contemplative
Life," *Spiritual Life,* XIV (1968), 49. The article is also found as "Monastic
Attitudes: a Matter of Choice," *Cistercian Studies,* II (1967), 3–14.

47. In his article, published posthumously as "The Contemplative and the
Atheist," *Schema XIII,* I (1970), 11, Merton, after noting the importance of
the contemplative's sharing his experience with others and of his need to listen
to others, says: "But above all he seeks to go deeper into that divine source
from which all life springs, and to understand the destinies of man in the light
of God." In an earlier unpublished writing, "Monastic Renewal: Problems
and Prospects," Merton also points out the importance of this *awareness* in the
contemplative's life. He says: "monasticism aims at the cultivation of a certain
quality of life, a level of awareness, a depth of consciousness, an area of
transcendence and of adoration which are not usually possible in an active
secular existence." All this, in turn, is but a re-echo of what he said in *The
Seven Storey Mountain,* p. 365: "That is the meaning of the contemplative
life, . . .—that we may get sick of the sight of ourselves and turn to Him:
and in the end, we will find Him in ourselves, in our own purified natures
which have become the mirror of His tremendous Goodness and of His
endless love."

48. Interestingly enough, it is this authenticity that is the real witness value
of the contemplative's life and makes his life truly apostolic. This Merton

reality of life, the fruit of his own sense of prayer and detachment, that the contemplative shares with others. It is in this way that he is "in the world of his time as a sign of hope for the most authentic values to which his time aspires."[49] Merton summarized it well in some comments written the year before his death and later published under the title. "As Man to Man." He said:

> The message of hope the contemplative offers you, then, brother, is . . . that whether you understand or not, God loves you, is present to you, lives in you, dwells in you, calls you, saves you, and offers you an understanding and light. . . . The contemplative has (sic) nothing to tell you except to reassure you and say that if you dare to penetrate your own silence and dare to advance without fear into the solitude of your own heart, and risk the sharing of that solitude with the lonely other who seeks God through you and with you, then you will truly recover the light and the capacity to understand what is beyond words and beyond explanations because it is too close to be explained: it is the intimate union in the depths of your own heart, of God's spirit and your own secret inmost self, so that you and He are in all truth One Spirit.[50]

SOLITUDE AND COMMUNION IN MERTON'S LIFE

Within the context of such a contemplative life, Merton gave meaning to his own life in a rather unique way. While a sense of concern and compassion for all men characterized his entire life, it seems to come through very strongly in his later writings in which he manifests a profound understanding of the peculiarly con-

---

brought out in a taped conference to Novices on "The Contemplative and the Apostolate," which this writer listened to while at the Abbey of Gethsemani. Cf. also Thomas Merton, "The Council and Religious Life," *New Blackfriars*, XLVII (1965–66), 12: "The authenticity of the religious commitment is what makes all religious life (even that which is contemplative and cloistered) apostolic, . . ." This is similarly found in "The Council and Monasticism," in *The Impact of Vatican II*, ed. by J. P. Dougherty (St. Louis: B. Herder Book Co., 1966), p. 54.

49. Merton, "Dialogue and Renewal in the Contemplative Life," p. 49.
50. Merton, "As Man to Man," p. 94; Dieu n'est pas un problème," p. 23.

temporary problems of peace, of personal fulfillment, and of communion with one's fellow man—all of which demand an authentic Christian answer.[51] Because of an increasing sensitivity towards these problems, Merton was ultimately led to a life of complete withdrawal from the excitement and confusion of society, yet paradoxically, to a life that was marked by a complete openness and by a participation in the anguish of man that was most genuine. For, it was here in his life of solitude that Merton grew in an awareness of his own unwavering love for man, and thus found his true communion with his fellow man. And it was here that he could see more clearly than ever before that all human reality is

---

51. In his more recent writings, Merton has openly expressed such concern for contemporary man. Two clear examples can be cited. First, his article, "The Monk Today," where he says: "I feel myself involved in the same problems, and I need to work out the problems of the world with other men because they are also my problems." *Contemplation in a World of Action*, p. 231. Second, "Is The World a Problem?" p. 305, where he cites one of his most beautiful passages concerning his identification with his fellow man: "This is simply the voice of a self-questioning human person who like all his brothers, struggles to cope with turbulent, mysterious, demanding, exciting, frustrating, confused existence . . . in which people suffer together and are sometimes utterly beautiful, at other times impossibly pathetic. In which there is much that is frightening, in which almost everything public is patently phony, and in which there is at the same time an immense ground of personal authenticity that is right there and so obvious that no one can talk about it and most cannot even believe it is there." Although such an attitude is not as evident in his earlier writings, one is still reminded of the presence of this concern in his early monastic life from the words of *The Secular Journal of Thomas Merton*, p. 222: "Also anyone who believes in the Mystical Body of Christ realizes I, could do more for the Church and for my brothers in the world, if I were a Trappist at Gethsemani than if I were a staff-worker at Friendship House." This is brought out well by one of his critics, Illtud Evans in "Elected Speech. Thomas Merton and the American Conscience," *The Tablet*, CCXX (1966) 1270, who says: "but even in his angriest denunciations of 'the world' there were the signs of a tenderness, a loving concern for the human condition, which the enthusiastic rhetoric of a first fervour only partly concealed." Basil De Pinto, "In Memoriam: Thomas Merton, 1915–1968," in *The Cistercian Spirit: A Symposium*, ed. by M. Basil Pennington, (Spencer, Mass.: Cistercian Publications, 1969), p. viii, says in commenting on Merton's critical concern for modern man, "And yet his relentless realism never turned bitter and he retained a basic optimism in the power of man to be converted and live: . . ."

"life in Christ." For this life of solitude would provide him with the distance and the perspective he knew was a prerequisite for the communion he sought with God, and in opening himself to God, he knew he could not help opening himself to his fellow man through a life of perfect authenticity. As he himself remarked: "We do not go into the desert to escape people but to learn how to find them; we do not leave them in order to have nothing more to do with them but to find out the way to do them the most good."[52]

For Merton, then, as for any Christian who aspires toward union with God, *solitude* holds an extremely important place in life in that it is a prerequisite for the *communion* one must seek both with God and with other men. In *The Sign of Jonas,* Merton points this out in reference to his own life: "Meanwhile, for myself, I have only one desire and that is the desire for solitude—to disappear into God, . . ."; and still later when he says: "It is clear to me that solitude is my vocation, not as a flight from the world but as my place in the world, . . ."[53]

For himself Merton knew that the truest solitude could not be something that was necessarily outside of himself—the mere physical state of aloneness apart from noise and other men. Rather, it must be primarily something within you—"an abyss opening up in the center of your own soul," where you can come face to face with yourself in the lonely ground of your own being.[54] Here Merton would be stripped of any illusory image of himself and would realize the true inner dimension of his being—the self that is created in the Image of God.[55] By discovering this sense of his

52. Merton, *Seeds of Contemplation*, p. 58.

53. Merton, *The Sign of Jonas*, pp. 26, 251.

54. Merton, *New Seeds of Contemplation*, p. 80. Thomas Merton, "Love and Solitude," *Critic*, XXV (1966), 36, where he says that in true solitude man is at the root of existence.

55. Thomas Merton, "Franciscan Eremitism," *Cord*, XVI (1966), 364. Here Merton notes that the gift of solitude is ordered principally to the recovery of one's deep self and to the renewal of authenticity. In *Disputed Questions*, p. 180, Merton speaks of one of the first essentials of interior solitude being man's discovery of his own mystery and the mystery of God as one reality, namely, the discovery that God lives in him and he in God.

own personal integrity and of his true reality, he would then be more ready for the gift of himself to others. Hence, this true interior solitude that Merton sought in his own life is best described as "simply the solitude of pure detachment—a solitude which empties our hearts and isolates us from the desires and ambitions and conflicts and troubles and lusts common to all the children of this world."[56] As such, this solitude does not necessarily mean a withdrawal or separation from one's union with other men, but rather, a renunciation of all the deceptive myths and falsities that can only alienate a man from God, from himself, from others, and thus prevent him finding them in the truest sense. For this reason, Christian solitude, according to Merton, is never a solitude *from* people but a solitude *for* people. Because of it, man can reach a new relation with his fellow man, one that is on a higher and more spiritual level, namely, the mystical level of the Body of Christ. Merton hints at this in his early writings:

> I had left all my friends and the ruins that remained of my family; but I already knew that in Christ I had them all, and loved them all far more perfectly and effectively than I could by any human affection. . . . My human affection for all the people I ever loved has lost none of its reality in the monastery, but it is submerged in a higher and more vital reality, in the unity of a vaster and deeper and more incomprehensible love, the love of God, in Whom I love them, and in Whom, paradoxically, I am more closely

56. Merton, *The Waters of Siloe*, p. 362. Here, it is important to note that Merton is not proposing any kind of escape from the anguish of the world. He is speaking about an interior solitude which he describes in *No Man Is an Island*, p. 171, as something more than either the desire or the fact of being alone. In the passage quoted from *The Waters of Siloe*, Merton is proposing that man withdraw or separate himself, at least in spirit, from the artificial and fictional level of being that men have constructed for themselves. Such solitude is more one of attitude than of fact, although it certainly can include the latter. Merton implies this in *The Sign of Jonas*, p. 59, when he says: "Today I seemed to be very much assured that solitude is indeed His will for me and that it is truly God Who is calling me into the desert. But this desert is not necessarily a geographical one. It is a solitude of heart in which created joys are consumed and reborn in God."

united to them than I could be if I had stayed in the world, pre-
ferring their company to His.[57]

For Merton, this relation is a union of love in which man shares
the true self that comes to maturity in his solitude. In this way, he
is *really* united with other men, not on the superficial level of
intimacy which is often called "togetherness," but in the true
relationship which God intends to exist between men. This new
level of union Merton called *"communion."*

And it is this that is the paradox of true solitude, not only in
Merton's life, but in the life of any Christian. His solitude must lead
to unity, to a unity of love, to a *communion.* This Merton notes in
The Living Bread: "The life of every man is a mystery of solitude
and communion: solitude in the secrecy of his own soul, where
he is alone with God; communion with his brethren, who share
the same nature, who reproduce in themselves his solitude, who
are his 'other selves' isolated from him and yet one with him."[58]
Merton also describes this communion as implying an awareness,
not only of a participation in a natural love for one's brothers
through direct activity, but also of a participation in God's love for
them through a purifying of one's own heart.[59] Hence, it is not
something that can be reduced to mere communication, to a simple

57. Cf. *A Thomas Merton Reader*, pp. 153–54. It is for this reason that Merton
calls real solitude a love. Cf. Thomas Merton, "Solitude and Love," in *The
Spirit of Man*, ed. by Whit Burnett (New York: Hawthorne Books, Inc.,
1958), p. 119. In *The Sign of Jonas*, p. 70, he says simply: "His love is my
solitude." In light of this, man's union of love with his fellow man is founded
in God Who is Love. Merton experienced this union of love in his own life,
as he brings out in *The Sign of Jonas*, p. 261: "It is in deep solitude that I find
the gentleness with which I can truly love my brothers. . . . Solitude and
silence teach me to love my brothers for what they are, not for what they say."

58. Merton, *The Living Bread*, p. 141.

59. Merton, "Symbolism: Communication or Communion?" in *New
Directions in Prose and Poetry 20*, p. 10, defines communion as "the awareness
of participation in an ontological or religious reality: in the mystery of being,
of human love, of redemptive mystery, of contemplative truth." In *New
Seeds of Contemplation*, pp. 54–55. Merton shows how it is genuine solitude
and not mere togetherness that leads to this communion.

sharing of ideas, or of knowledge, or of truth.[60] To live in communion with others, man must come to respect his fellow man in
his own authentic personal reality. And this he cannot do, unless
he himself has attained a basic self-respect and a mature identity by
means of interior solitude. For, it is in solitude that he establishes
the union with Christ which is the foundation of his communion
with others.[61] It is this that Merton implied when he said simply:
"It is because I want to be more to them than a friend that I become
to all of them, a stranger."[62]

While the solitude necessary for this communion is above all an
interior solitude, Merton does not deny that physical or exterior
solitude is also important for anyone who wants to lead a con-

60. Cf. *Disputed Questions*, p. 205, where he refers to the "wordless communion of genuine love." In recent years, Merton became more and more
interested in this meaning of communion. In "Monastic Experience and
East-West Dialogue," (1968), he says that among monks the only true
communication is this true communion which is beyond the level of words.
It is shared both on a pre-verbal level and a post-verbal level which he then
describes as follows: "The *pre-verbal* level is that of the unspoken and in-
definable preparation, the *pre-disposition* of mind and heart, . . . This demands
among other things a *freedom from automatisms and routines*, a candid liberation
from external social dictates, from conventions, limitations and mechanisms
which restrict understanding and inhibit experience of the new, the un-
expected. . . . The *post-verbal* level will then, at least ideally, be that on which
they both meet beyond their own words and their own understanding in the silence
of an ultimate experience which might conceivably not have occurred if they
had not met and spoken." Here one finds the full implication of a remark
made in an extemporaneous talk delivered at the Spiritual Summit Conference in Calcutta, October 22–26, 1968, and later published as "Merton's
View of Monasticism: Seeking God through Total Love is Goal," *Washington
Post* (January 18, 1969), C9: "And the deepest level of communication is not
communication, but communion. It is wordless. It is beyond words and it is
beyond speech and it is beyond concepts."

61. Cf. *New Seeds of Contemplation*, p. 65, where Merton says: "Therefore
when you and I become what we are really meant to be, we will discover not
only that we love one another perfectly but that we are both living in Christ
and Christ in us, and we are all One Christ. We will see that it is He Who
loves in us." Also *No Man Is an Island*, p. 131, where such a thought is similarly
expressed when Merton says: "We cannot find them in God without first
perfectly finding ourselves in Him."

62. Merton, "Introducing a Book," p. 9.

templative Christian life.[63] In fact, says Merton, "You will never find interior solitude unless you make some conscious effort to deliver yourself from the desires and the cares and the interests of an existence in time and in the world."[64] Indeed, such withdrawal can be a special sign of love for one's fellow man.[65]

Since each man, therefore, must seek the degree of exterior solitude which is commensurate with his own spiritual maturity, it was not surprising that Merton should have responded to the world through his own life of solitude and communion in a creative and unique way by seeking the fullness of the contemplative life in a life of eremitism.[66] Thus it was that during the latter years of his

63. In *Disputed Questions*, p. 166, Merton says: "For without the efficacious desire of exterior solitude, interior solitude will always remain a fantasy or an illusion." Cf. Thomas Merton, Preface to *Alone with God*, by Dom J. Leclercq, tr. by E. McCabe (New York: Farrar, Straus and Cudahy, 1961), p. xv, for a similar view. (The book is a translation of Leclercq's *Seul avec Dieu: La Vie Érémitique*). Merton, however, is still emphatic in maintaining the primacy of interior solitude. This is why he says in *New Seeds of Contemplation*, p. 56: "There is no true solitude except interior solitude."

64. Merton, *New Seeds of Contemplation*, p. 84.

65. In speaking of solitude in the sense of withdrawal from one's society, Merton says in *The Solitary Life*, pp. 2–3: "It can be in him a sign of love for his fellow man to leave the company of others and live alone." Merton himself experienced this in his own life as he writes in *The Sign of Jonas*, p. 261: "It is in deep solitude that I find the gentleness with which I can truly love my brothers. The more solitary I am, the more affection I have for them. It is pure affection, and filled with reverence for the solitude of others. Solitude and silence teach me to love my brothers for what they are, not for what they say."

66. Continuously throughout his writings, Merton considers eremitical solitude the ideal of the monastic life and hence of the Christian life in that the hermit aspires more than any other person to perfect union with Christ. Cf. *Disputed Questions*, p. 171. This thought has become the focal point of several articles written in recent years by Thomas Merton: "The Council and Religious Life," p. 9; "The Council and Monasticism," p. 49; "For a Renewal of Eremitism in the Monastic State," *Collectanea Ordinis Cisterciensium Reformatorum*, XXVII (1865), 121, 123, 124, 147–18. In another article entitled "Day of a Stranger," *Hudson Review*, XX (1967), 213, Merton contrasts the calm of a hermit's life with the turbulence of the monastic life. However, Merton is realistic enough to realize that man must first find God in community living before he can seek him as a hermit. Cf. *Thoughts in Solitude*, p. 110: "Do not flee to solitude from the community. Find God first in the community, then He will lead you to solitude."

life he found the life of solitude for which he had always longed and which he knew he needed in order to grow and to be himself.[67] Here in the authentic inner quiet of his hermitage he knew he could live alone with God in an atmosphere which was most propitious for deep interior prayer. For in the confrontation with such solitude, he would have the opportunity to empty himself of all falsity.[68] In addition, he knew that his complete and total dedication to God as a hermit would also lead to a recognition of his oneness with others and to a greater communion of genuine love with his fellow men. He once wrote: "My solitude, however, is not my own, for I see now how much it belongs to them—and that I have a responsibility for it in their regard, not just in my own. It is because I am one with them that I owe it to them to be alone, and when I am alone they are not 'they' but my own self. They are no strangers!"[69]

67. First, it should be noted that the attraction to the eremitical life was always a part of Merton. He himself admitted this in *The Sign of Jonas*, p. 20: "I have always felt a great attraction to the life of perfect solitude. It is an attraction I shall probably never entirely lose." Cf. "Introducing a Book," p. 10, where he said: "I have never had any doubt whatever of my monastic vocation. If I have ever had any desire for change, it has been for a more solitary, more 'monastic' way." In *A Controversy of Poets: an Anthology of Contemporary Poetry*, ed. by Paris Leary and Robert Kelly (Garden City, N.Y.: Doubleday, 1965), p. 542, Merton writes: "And I have been here since, and have never questioned my vocation to the monastic life, but have needed more and more solitude." Second, it is here that one sees the primary reason for his own life of eremitism, namely, his need to grow and to realize his true self, the person who has found the freedom of a son of God. In "Christian Solitude: Notes on an Experiment," *The Current*, VII (1967), 20, Merton notes that: "If after fifteen or twenty years in the common life a monk can go to a hermitage, he can there create a new personal pattern which will fulfill his own special needs for growth." Later, in the same article, p. 23, he continues: "The hermitage then provides the monk with something that a mature person needs: the chance to explore, to risk, to abandon himself sagaciously to untried possibilities." Cf. his letter, "On the Future of Monasticism," published in *L'Osservatore Romano*, IV (January 23, 1969), 5, where he says simply: "some of us must be alone in order to be ourselves."

68. In "Love and Solitude," p. 32, Merton says: "The true solitary does not seek himself but loses himself."

69. Merton, *Conjectures of a Guilty Bystander*, p. 158. This second reason for his life of eremitism, namely, the awareness of his own deeper communion

Such communion Merton did achieve. Somehow, although living the solitary life of a hermit removed from the cares of the world, he nonetheless was able to show his deepening concern and to be more open to contemporary America than many others who lived in the midst of it. This double tendency manifested simultaneously in his life, however paradoxical or ironical it may appear presented no contradiction to Merton. He simply realized that since he belonged to God, he needed seclusion; since he belonged to man, he needed to give himself to people. As a hermit he knew that, by going deeper into the process of liberating himself and realizing his Transcendent Self, he would find the freedom that was his as a son of God. Thus, in his seclusion, he would re-discover the ground of unity that would enable him to meet men in solidarity and communion at the deepest level of their being.[70] And in this way, Merton realized that he could make a unique contribution to present-day society; he could become involved at a level that others could never know. For, as a Christian hermit, he would have a special function in the Mystical Body of Christ, and that would be to give witness to the transcendent, by showing men the need for values such as solitude, communion, authenticity, and contemplation.[71] Likewise, as a hermit, he would bring the resources

---

with others, is brought out often in his writings, as for instance, when he says in *New Seeds of Contemplation*, p. 53, "Go into the desert not to escape other men but in order to find them in God." Cf. "Solitude," p. 177, where in speaking of the hermit's life, Merton says: "His isolation in solitude unites him more closely in love with all the rest of his brothers in the world."

70. For Merton, it is important that the man of true solitude first find himself and see his oneness with other men before he can fully give himself to them. This he points out in *No Man Is an Island*, p. 185: "If I cannot distinguish myself from the mass of other men, I will never be able to love and respect other men as I ought. If I do not separate myself from them enough to know what is mine and what is theirs, I will never discover what I have to give them, and never allow them the opportunity to give me what they ought." Cf. "Solitude and Love," in *The Spirit of Man*, p. 115.

71. Cf. *Disputed Questions*, p. 191, where Merton writes of the solitary's life: "On the contrary, his function in the Christian community is the paradoxical one of living outwardly separated from the community. And this, whether he is conscious of it or not, is a witness to the completely

of his own deep prayer to bear on the serious wrongs of the present day by unmasking the illusions of his fellow men, as he had unmasked his own. In this way, he would be offering a unique answer to the manifold problems of society. This Merton notes of the life of any solitary when he says:

> He may perhaps do more good to the human race by being a solitary than he ever could have done by remaining the prisoner of the society where he was living. For anyone who breaks the chains of falsity and strives, even unsuccessfully, to be true to God and to his inner self, is doing more for the world than can be done even by a saint in politics.

> The hermit has a very real place in a world like ours that has degraded the human person and lost all respect for solitude.[72]

This, then, is the full dimension of Merton's asceticism. Ascetical practices are really the first step in bringing man to the inner detachment and the emptiness where he will find the true freedom that is his as a person created in the Image of God. Because of this there is an intrinsic connection, according to Merton, between asceticism and contemplative prayer.

---

transcendental character of the Christian mystery of our unity in Christ . . . he testifies to the essentially mystical bond of unity which binds Christians together in the Holy Spirit. Whether he is seen or not, he bears witness to the unity of Christ by possessing in himself the fullness of Christian charity." Earlier in the same book, p. 182, Merton notes that the solitary is not called to leave or withdraw from society but rather to *transcend* society.

72. Merton, *The Solitary Life*, p. 8. Cf. *Disputed Questions*, pp. 186, 188, 193–94, where Merton also speaks of this renunciation of illusion on the— part of the solitary as a means of helping others to regain a clearer vision of Christian truth. It is here that one sees the third reason for Merton's choosing the eremitical life, namely, that in a unique way, the hermit has something to contribute to society. Finally, in his article, "Love and Solitude," p. 37, Merton says: "But we must learn to know and accept this ground of our being. . . . Only when our activity proceeds out of the ground in which we have consented to be dissolved does it have the divine fruitfulness of love and grace. Only then does it really reach others in true communion. . . . It is in solitude that illusions finally dissolve."

Although Merton uses many concepts in discussing asceticism, he relates it especially to sacrifice and to renunciation. The former is considered the culmination of asceticism in that it offers to God that which man himself has renounced. However, it is renunciation, which Merton calls the proximate end of asceticism, that enables man to detach himself from all false illusions about himself. Thus liberated from any fixation upon himself, he is able to discover his transcendence in God in contemplative prayer.

In relation to his teaching on renunciation there is Merton's personal attitude and relationship to the contemporary world. Merton, far from rejecting or denouncing the reality surrounding him, proposes a renunciation of the world that is essentially an unmasking or dispelling of all illusions and pretenses of man's alienated or false self. It is ultimately a renunciation that should lead to a new freedom. It is because technology threatens this freedom that Merton is highly critical of such processes in contemporary society.

In light of this renunciation and freedom the contemplative of today has a very positive value to offer human society. In that he is striving to recover the authenticity of his own true self by a deep penetration into the process of liberation, he is capable of fulfilling the highest destiny for which man is created. Within the context of such a life, Merton himself gave meaning to his own life in a rather unique way. Through a life of eremitism, he found the necessary solitude in which he could explore the ground of his own being in prayer. And it was this that ultimately led to the even deeper level of involvement with other men that he called "communion"—a level that Merton almost prophetically knew would one day be realized in his own life. For years earlier he imagined God saying to him:

And when you have been praised a little and loved a little I will take away all your gifts and all your love and all your praise and you will be utterly forgotten and abandoned and you will be nothing, a dead thing, a rejection. And in that day you shall begin to possess the solitude you have so long desired. And your solitude will bear immense fruit in the souls of men you will never see on earth.

Do not ask when it will be or where it will be or how it will be: . . . It does not matter. So do not ask me, because I am not going to tell you. You will not know until you are in it.

But you shall taste the true solitude of my anguish and my poverty and I shall lead you into the high places of my joy and you shall die in Me. . . .[73]

---

73. Merton, *The Seven Storey Mountain*, pp. 411–12.

CHAPTER V

A CRITICAL EVALUATION

IN VIEW OF the preceding chapters which presented a comprehensive view of Merton's teaching on contemplative prayer, there can be little doubt of the centrality of prayer in Thomas Merton's spirituality and of his personal high regard for its real influence in his own life and in the life of every Christian. There now remains to offer a critical evaluation of Merton's theology of contemplative prayer. This will be done, first, by presenting a critique of Merton's ideas concerning contemplative prayer in light of their originality and contemporaneity for today's Christians, and second, by offering an evaluation of his theology of contemplative prayer in light of its value for providing a suitable and positive solution to some of the problems confronting contemporary man.

Merton's whole theology of prayer, which is grounded in his own personal experience of searching for God, has but one function and that is to bring man into an awareness of his personal union with God in Christ. It is this for which man was created. For this reason, every man has a fundamental duty to orient his entire being and life to God and to strive after this intimate union with God. Ultimately, however, man will achieve this communion when he discovers his true self, since it is there that he awakens to the presence of the God-man in the core of his own existence. As noted previously, this awareness or awakening to the presence of God within man, which is essentially the meaning of contemplative prayer for Merton, is not merely a mental exercise, but the gradual result of man's total submission of his being to God. As such, it involves a two-fold movement: man entering into the deepest center of himself where he discovers his complete emptiness, and then passing through that center to his true self where he discovers the freedom that is his as a son of God who is seeking to recover his perfect likeness to God in Christ and by the Spirit of Christ. Here, he is no longer conscious of "self" but, having transformed his consciousness, he recognizes himself as a dependent being, a "self in God." Finally, as was noted, for man to achieve this transcendent self, there is need for renunciation and sacrifice in his life of prayer. For, it is such ascetical discipline that will give him the detachment he needs, not only to recognize his own freedom as a son of God, but also to become aware of all others who share that sonship in Christ.

THE ORIGINALITY OF MERTON'S CONTEMPLATIVE PRAYER

The uniqueness of such a teaching on prayer lies, first of all, in the relevant significance of its *contemplative* approach in which man's being takes precedence over his doing. As such, it offers a theological foundation which implies that the life and the integrity of the person are of much greater value than any activity to which the person might dedicate himself. Such a focus should result in man's prayer becoming a more integral part of his spiritual life. For, along with pointing out the shallowness and the superficiality which underlie much of the feverish activity prevalent in today's society, Merton's contemplative approach to prayer stresses the need for creative silence and solitude, for interior peace and spiritual freedom, for authenticity and personal integrity, as the true way for all men to achieve an intimate union with God. These are the elements that are especially necessary today if man is to maintain his human and Christian dignity and grow interiorly toward the full development of a personal self-realization in which he finds himself as a spiritual or self-transcending being. Hence, they *must* be a part of man's Christian experience. And yet, such values are often inaccessible to him, although in recent years society has begun to realize more and more that to be a truly social being, a "person" who lives his human life fully, there must be this contemplative dimension to man's existence in which he senses the presence of God within him. Otherwise, the "person" that man brings to any encounter will be somewhat unreal.

In a society, then, where man's true personality is often either obscured by a false personalism, which identifies the person with the external or empirical self, or dissolved into a non-entity as a result of his own technological achievement, Merton's theology of contemplative prayer, with its primary objective on the awakening of man's interior self, offers a somewhat unique response for the man who is intent on discovering the true value and the spiritual dignity of his personality. For, in recovering the integrity of his own inner depths, man discovers the real or true self that has realized its freedom as a son of God. To this extent, man's basic hope in his very capacity to be a person is restored, and thus his prayer life can enrich his "person." In fact, for Merton, it is the *only real* means of bringing the human personality to a mature fruition, namely, to the recovery of man's likeness to God, in Christ, by the Spirit.

It is this sound anthropological foundation to Merton's theology of prayer, that principally heightens the originality of his teaching on prayer. For, not only does Merton view man as the image of God recreated in the divine likeness through Christ, he even sees this image as grounded in man's very nature, thus giving him a radical potentiality for divine union and making him humanly capable of God's love. While such a theology maintains a clear distinction between nature and grace, in emphasizing the essential goodness of human nature as well as man's natural capacity for union with God, it strongly upholds their interdependence and inter-relatedness.[1] And man today, in searching for his authentic personality, is in dire need of being reminded of this capacity for the

1. Throughout his writings, Merton continually emphasizes that an outstanding call to human dignity lies in man's call to communion with God. It may be well to recall here that in asserting the doctrine of man's union with God, Merton makes clear that man's natural capacity for union with God (i.e., in so far as he is created in the image of God) can be actualized only through man's spiritual union or supernatural union in grace (i.e., the image is turned into a likeness through Christ). This is perfected, in turn, in man's

infinite within him. Only in this way can he hope to avoid the despair rampant in human society. Hence, one can say that Merton's contemplative approach to prayer, because of its affirmation of the goodness of man, explicitly shows man that even in his *apparent* incapacity for any kind of genuine spiritual experience, a response to God in prayer is still possible on the part of man.

Such an anthropological foundation also saves Merton's theology of contemplative prayer from becoming sheer self-introspection. For this image of God within man continually urges him to "let go" of himself and to transcend himself. Otherwise, he will contradict the image within him by becoming selfish and self-centered. This is why Merton can suggest that contemplative prayer must not only be a listening and a searching for one's deepest center, but an awakening of the depths of man's being in the presence of God. In this way, man not only comes to grips with the superficiality of his own existence, but he sees himself more clearly as he really is in the eyes of God. Aware of how little he can do by himself, he recognizes his need for and complete dependence upon God. Such abandonment of the self-centered and self-sufficient ego by a total surrender to God ultimately brings about the new and liberated self who acts in the Spirit. For, as this prayer develops, man is no longer conscious of himself as a subject, nor of concentrating on self nor even on God as an object of reflection, but sees only God as the source of his own existence and subjectivity. To realize this he concerns himself with penetrating the inner meaning of his life in Christ and with losing himself in Christ Who alone can restore to his human person a true divine likeness. To the extent that he achieves this likeness of the Word of God within him, he will be truly himself. His personhood will be fulfilled; for, the divine image within him will have been realized and restored to a divine likeness.

---

mystical or transforming union (i.e., the perfect possession of God through love in Christ, a communion or oneness in charity) which can be realized inchoatively in this life. Hence, in no way is the supernatural life destructive of man's natural life; rather, it is its supreme fulfillment. And so, for Merton, the supernatural man is the perfected natural man with all his obediential potentialities fulfilled. Throughout Merton's teaching on "union with God, one is reminded of Rahner's teaching on the *supernatural existential*.

This restoration of the divine image in man leads, not only to a discovery of one's own inmost self in the mystery of Christ, but also to a consciousness and an opening out to the inmost self of all other men who bear within themselves this same image of God. Although Merton himself does not specify exactly how one is to relate or transfer his life of prayer into his real life, his theology of contemplative prayer does bring into question, not only the value of man's existence as a person, but also the reality of his commitments and the authenticity of his every day life. For this reason, man's prayer cannot be divorced from reality. In fact, Merton's primary concern is to show that the importance of such prayer lies in the fact that man cannot really give himself in perfect charity to his fellow man until he himself has become transformed in Christ and has developed a rich interior life of union with God.[2] Once man is imbued with this Spirit of Christ and recognizes his own sonship in Christ, then his life of prayer should overflow into a life of union and genuine concern for other men in order that they too may be able to penetrate the mystery of God's love in their lives. For this reason, in contemplative prayer, man should become more and not less aware of his solidarity with other men. Finally, it is in light of such thinking about man that it becomes perfectly understandable why Merton should view contemplation—man's immediate intuition of his perfect union with God—as the traditional perfection and summit of the Christian life.

THE CONTEMPORANEITY OF MERTON'S CONTEMPLATIVE PRAYER

In reflecting upon the contemporaneity of such inner meditative prayer for the life of Americans, the present writer feels that it must

2. This is the uniquely Cistercian element in Merton's theology of prayer, which, one must remember, is the result of a spirituality of being and of doing. However, it should be noted that it does not follow from such a spirituality that contemplative prayer is merely intrapersonal and not interpersonal. Such a criticism is sometimes leveled against it. Because of its Christological dimension, such prayer must lead outward to others; for, in discovering Christ in his own life, man simultaneously comes to recognize Him as already present in his fellow man.

somehow be centered around an understanding of man's religious experience. Men today are pragmatic at least to the extent that they are immersed in a practical and activist way of life. They want a type of spirituality that will be applicable to their every day lives and they want to see the relevancy and the importance of their life of prayer in helping them face the modern world. In light of this one may rightly wonder at the actual practicality of Merton's teaching on contemplative prayer. For, rather than issuing some specially planned technique for discovering or awakening one's inner self in prayer, Merton is intent mainly on issuing a call for such prayer. Yet, such a theology can be quite realistic. For not merely contemplatives but all Christians can effectively practice it in their every day lives provided they are willing to admit the necessity for moments of solitude and personal reflection. Inasmuch as such an approach to prayer in itself is habitual and intensely personal, it appears to be more relevant and meaningful for today's Christians than other types of prayer. In addition, its unique and perhaps more accurate perspective affords a firmer grasp on reality itself and leads towards a deeper penetration of the fundamental truths of human existence. Because of this, man becomes more capable of discovering both the religious and the human meaning of existence in a world that tends to be confused and meaningless, not because of its formal unbelief, but because of the confusion and the inability to think on the part of many well-meaning people.

A clear example of this realism can be seen in Merton's concept of *dread* as a necessary starting-point in contemplative prayer. Because of it, man is immediately brought to an experience of his own wretchedness and helplessness in the presence of God. Although Merton is somewhat unique in presenting such a pessimistic picture of man, he is quick to underscore the fact that the purpose of this dread is to disturb and unsettle man and thus force him to become aware of the necessity for communion with God in his life. It is because of such dread that man's focus in prayer becomes one of praise and of loving attention to the presence of God within him rather than one of mere asking for things.

Such realism is likewise evidenced in man's *transformation of consciousness* (sometimes referred to as a *deepening of consciousness* or simply as an *inner transformation*) whereby man, rather than focusing directly on self in prayer, realizes himself as a person to be dissolved and lost in God. Such a realization is not a discovery in the more active and strict sense of the term; rather, it is man's creative and personal realization of having been found and loved and possessed by God in the inmost depths of his being. As such, it demands a personal response of listening and surrendering to God Who is present within man. It is in light of this that Merton's theological teaching on prayer cannot become a systematic search for God resulting in certain guidelines and formulas. Merton is a spiritual teacher who is intent on pointing out the need for personal submission to a God Who communicates Himself in man's heart (the ground of his being).

It is this overwhelming urge in man to lose himself in God (or to be found by Him) that prompted Merton's interest in the Eastern religions and especially in Zen Buddhism, which he saw as an enrichment to Christianity. In his view Zen sought enlightenment as to the ground of its own being, not primarily as a religion, but as a way of life. And so, a Christian, Merton felt, could enter such thought without compromising his own beliefs. He recognized that both his own teaching on contemplative prayer as well as the teaching of Zen brought man into an authentic confrontation with himself, with reality and with his fellow man. Both, in turn, offered man a more contemplative approach to life with their strong reaction to technology and Cartesianism (in that they sought an awareness of pure being beyond subject and object), as well as in their emphasis on personal spontaneity and on a desire for the deep things of God.[3]

Again, even here, one is confronted with the realism of Merton's contemplative orientation to prayer. A man who was always responsive to new ideas that might increase his awareness of life and

3. In spite of the fact that Zen Buddhism is a metaphysical intuition (or awareness or consciousness) of the ground of being and the Christian religion (and hence, Merton's spirituality) is essentially a revelation, the influence of Zen Buddhism on Merton's Christian approach to contemplative prayer is manifold.

his understanding of reality, Merton continually presents his teaching on prayer in a language that is thoroughly contemporary to modern Americans in its articulation of ideas. Although even his final book, *The Climate of Monastic Prayer,* does not offer a complete synthesis on prayer, its presentation in terms of his interest in Christian Existentialism and Eastern Mysticism is clearly in evidence over the scholastic terminology of his earlier book on contemplation, *The Ascent to Truth.*

And yet, despite this developmental approach, there is still a basic continuity between his latest work and what had been written in his earlier writings. This is indicated in the wholeness and balance of his teaching on prayer, as shown, first of all, in the intimate relationship that always existed in his spirituality between asceticism and prayer. For Merton, both are specifically related to man's spiritual freedom —to liberating his true self and to letting him, so to speak, out of himself from the inside. Through both, man acquires the detachment and the personal discernment necessary to transcend his empirical self and to allow his "person" to develop supernaturally in its deepest and most vital capacities with the result that man becomes capable of loving others as God loves them.[4] In showing those who want to be free where their freedom really lies, Merton, it would seem, is offering the man of today a profound style of Christian living. For man today needs to realize that it is possible to find God in society, not only through involvement, but also by separating oneself, to a degree, from one's ordinary concerns. In fact, the more *detached* man becomes from the world in a real and deep sense, the more *attached* he can become to it, since he will then be capable of loving the world all the more freely and purely at the deepest level of its being.

4. According to Merton, *freedom* is basically a spiritual reality which is principally exercised in *love.* Since *God is Love,* man exercises his freedom fully when he loves others as God loves them. In light of this, man's freedom, which makes him the image of God, is a participation in the freedom of God. He is free insofar as he is like God. Hence, such a spiritual liberation consists both in a self-renunciation of man's false and illusory autonomy as well as in a self-recovery beyond self, namely, self-transcendence. For Merton, this is real freedom.

Such wholeness and balance are also brought out by Merton in his teaching on the continuity of all prayer as a way of resting in God, as well as in the close unity that must exist between liturgical and personal prayer, and finally, in the apostolic leanings of all contemplative prayer. These topics already have been discussed at length in Chapter Three, and hence, there is no need to dwell on them here.

In conclusion, then, one can say that it is elements such as these that underscore the realism of prayer in the spirituality of Thomas Merton and thus show that contemplative prayer should have a place in the life of the contemporary Christian who is desirous of living his life authentically. While holiness can never be sought in prayer alone, Merton's teaching is primarily intent on underscoring the fact that man must also remember that true holiness is nourished by prayer. Only in this way can the vitality and the energy of man's action be guided by the Holy Spirit and not end up as the pseudo-spirituality of activism. Such, then, is the contemporaneity of prayer in Merton's spirituality. There now remains to show its vitality and its value for today's Christians as a resolution to some of their basic uncertainties and hesitations.

THE VALUE OF MERTON'S THEOLOGY OF PRAYER

At a time when almost every conceivable human effort has been brought to bear on the problems of the present time and with apparently little success, Merton, it would appear, has re-discovered and developed a theology of prayer that can be acceptable to contemporary man at least to the extent that it takes into account some of the difficulties confronting the secular-minded times of today and attempts to offer a solution to them. Indeed, no contemporary spiritual writer seems more aware and yet more sensitive and sympathetic to the troubled climate facing man today than Thomas Merton, who was himself immersed in the world in a deeply profound and creative way. Although his theology of prayer, as noted above, tends to be somewhat theoretical and not practical, it can

K

certainly be said to be *pragmatic* in the sense that it addresses itself to some of the contemporary questions that agitate present-day society.

Undoubtedly, the primary value of such prayer lies in the fact that, at a time when God is being denied or even declared to be "dead" in the sense of being obsolete and meaningless to men who feel that an experience of His reality and of His relevence to life is fraudulent and illusory, there is in a contemplative type of prayer a sharp and an explicit refocusing of man on the ultimate reason for his existence, namely, the contemplation of God in which his being is fulfilled and perfected. Although Merton underscores the infinite transcendence of God in his thinking about the "beyond," his stronger emphasis on the direct and personal presence of God within the very ground of man's being clearly shows man that even in his blindness and apparent incapacity for God, God is still with him and that an encounter with Him in this life is still possible. In fact, man's very geniune need to pray—to listen, to be attentive, to be open—is a mysterious expression of this presence of God in man's being.

Because of this explicit acknowledgment of the presence of God within man, there is in Merton's contemplative prayer more stress on the necessity of the individual's responsibility of surrendering to God and of experiencing His love. For this reason, there appears to be in this type of prayer a more *personal* seeking and acceptance of God. God is not "given" by someone else or accepted in a set, stereotyped manner on somebody else's word. Hence, there is less danger of God becoming a matter of mere conformism or expediency in man's life. Such a more personal and existential approach to man's relationship with God is especially worth considering in light of the challenges of the "Diaspora Situation," which Merton refers to in his more recent writings as a situation in which Christians will become more and more marginal persons—a dispersed community existing in a secular and non-believing society, as well as the challenges of a "Death of God Movement," which deny the need of God and of His relevancy for contemporary man.[5]

5. For an explanation of Merton's "Diaspora Situation," see above, p. xxiii, footnote 25. For a further clarification of exactly how a contemplative approach

Secondly, man today, in a very definite sense, has become too self-reliant. In trying to give meaning to his life, he has been led to depend too much on himself and too little on God, the Source of his existence. Such a loss of contact with God, has, in turn, created an identity crisis in man. Having lost sight of Christ in his life, man has become a depersonalized being incapable of authenticity in his being. Confused and alienated, he is no longer capable of full and personal self-realization. Merton's theology of contemplative prayer emphasizing man's discovery of his true self created in the image and likeness of God, shows man that he can recover his identity and authenticity by realizing himself and giving himself fully and maturely to God. Against the alienating pressures of commercialism and technology with its deification of man's external self, Merton repeatedly stresses contemplative prayer as a way of becoming detached from all illusions about oneself and of recovering the integrity of one's being. In such prayer, man must continually "let go" of himself, knowing full well that such self-surrender leads not only to a death of selfishness and self-centeredness, but to a death that will also be Christ's glorification in him.

It is this search for an authentic identity that became one of Merton's fundamental concerns throughout his writings and might well serve as a key to an understanding of his entire spirituality. In fact, if man is not willing to attempt this search within the ground of his own being through the self-renunciation involved in contemplative prayer, then it seems that either he will submit to the pretense and sham of a limited and egotistical self, a false identity, or he will seek the false solution of psychedelic drugs and hallucinogens as an attempt to satisfy this desire for authenticity or to short-cut his way to the true self-transcendence that can only come from a contact between his inmost reality and the infinite reality of God.

---

to prayer offers a more personal and existential resolution to the "Death of God Movement," one need only recall the discussion on the "meaning of consciousness" in Chapter II, esp. p. 31, footnote 20. In addition, a contemplative approach to prayer, such as Merton's, with its emphasis on "transformation of consciousness," can pave the way for a common meeting point with the hippie movement and their cult of "transcendental meditation."

PROBLEM OF DIVINE AND HUMAN LOVE

Thirdly, this search for authenticity within the ground of one's being necessarily involves man in the question of love. Because he is created in the image and likeness of God, the measure of man's identity is really the amount of his love for God in Whom he realizes his own identity as a person by becoming perfectly free and therefore loving without limit. Hence, the man who has discovered his true self in Christ and who is united to God in the depths of his own being as a son of God is the man who loves perfectly as God Himself loves. For Merton such love or charity is acquired more readily in a contemplative spirit of prayer where the principal purpose is to educate man to the discovery of the freedom of the Spirit, which is the likeness of Christ in his very being.

Here one sees a unique contribution on the part of Merton's theology of contemplative prayer for resolving one of the paramount problems confronting contemporary Christians. At a time when man too often seeks his perfection almost exclusively in terms of a love for his fellow man, Merton's contemplative prayer interiorizes that love by reminding man of the importance and the necessity of recognizing that he is first loved by God and hence must love Him. Granted that neither love is possible without the other, Merton, without compromising or opposing them, shows in his teaching on contemplative prayer that it is possible for man to love his fellow man and to grow in his capacity for loving him by first loving God.[6] Indeed, it is this union of love with God, which can only result from man's direct experience of God as Someone and of himself as a person who is grounded in His love, that can bring about

6. For every spiritual writer, charity is always *twofold* although it has but one object, namely, God. Man can reach Him both directly in Himself, which is essentially "love of God," and indirectly through others, which is basically "love of man." To this extent the two loves are, in fact, one, and hence, should not, in any way, be obstacles to each other. Unless there is a continual and vital contact with God through both approaches in one's life, man's spiritual life will die. This applies, even in a contemplative spirituality, such as Merton's, where the emphasis is on the vertical and direct relationship with God rather than on the horizontal relationship of man with man.

the perfect union of love of man for man in Christ that is characteristic of Merton's spirituality, as well as the dominating force
throughout his own life, as was shown in the discussion on solitude
and communion. For him, solitude meant to live with Christ, and
so, although set apart from other men, Merton knew that he did
have a love for them. It was in the love of Christ which he nurtured
in his prayer where he entered deeply into the mystery of God's love
for his fellow man.

Finally, without in any way minimizing the eschatological dimension of contemplative prayer, one notices that there is something
uniquely incarnational about this type of prayer which offers a
challenging solution to the sacred-secular problem current in today's
culture. Rather than rejecting the material universe or renouncing a
particle of what is genuinely real in today's secular culture or even
denying that one can live in reality and find God—all of which
might be expected in a contemplative orientation to prayer, Merton
actually enables secular culture to become more fully human. In
underscoring the Christological dimension in contemplative prayer
by stressing the importance of the Incarnation among the mysteries
of Christ's life, Merton helps man to appreciate and to value more
highly the reality of the creation with which God has surrounded
him.

For Merton conceives Christ as being at the center of the universe
and hence, it is in Christ and only in him that the world can truly
make sense. Because everything converges on Him, the person most
closely related to Christ in contemplative prayer is, in Merton's
view, the person who is most deeply embedded in the world. For
such a person is no longer limited by narrow provincial views nor
involved in the superficial confusion which most men today assume
to be reality. Rather, detached from such superficiality because of
his own closeness to Christ, he is most deeply concerned with the
world and with dedicating himself fully to the service of God, and
thus is able to find a truly incarnational involvement that will bring
him into the deepest contact with reality.[7] In light of this, it would

7. Earlier in the discussion, it was noted that Merton's teaching on contemplative prayer tended to be more theoretical than practical in that Merton

seem that men today need the kind of inner meditative prayer that Merton advocates if they are to accept fully their responsibility as Christians both to God and to their fellow man.

In conclusion, it can be said that Thomas Merton in his teaching on contemplative prayer, offers a real note of hope and encouragement to contemporary man by reminding him of his true capacity for inner spiritual freedom. In a world where fear and distrust can be seen as overpowering forces and where men seek to rely on human force and strategy, he has injected into his writings the true Christian call to hope and to trust, namely, a reliance on divine love. Men today must seek to give God a greater place in their lives and must strive to meet the demands of divine love with a generous response of true Christian charity.

Merton, throughout his writings, is insistent in his appeal for a return to this genuine Christian charity. However, one must remember that in his spirituality, it is, above all, a charity that is nourished, not by mere human enthusiasm nor by the inspiration of natural ambitions, but by a deep interior union with God in prayer. Such charity, he continually reminds man, manifests itself, not so much in material works, as in a true love for man. As Merton himself asserted: "What hope can there be of men living at peace together when they do not love one another? And how can they love one another as brothers if they do not love God, their Common Father?"[8]

Such, then, is the uniqueness, the contemporaneity, and the value

---

does not specify *how* man is to bring his prayer into his real life. It seems that, for all Christians, the ultimate answer is to be found somewhere in the question of man's detachment from superficialities in life and to his attachment to Christ Whom he recognizes to be at the center of all life. Certainly it is this that leads to the deeper and more authentic involvement of the contemplative in today's world. He becomes, quite simply, a witness to a God Who is really Someone.

8. Merton, *The Last of the Fathers*, p. 83. A similar sentiment is expressed in his unpublished manuscript, *Prayer as Worship and Experience*, pp. 23–24, when he points out that there can be no love in today's world unless there is prayer; for, it is in prayer that man brings his being into direct and living contact with the living God Who is the Source of all love.

of contemplative prayer in the spirituality of Thomas Merton. For him, although times have changed and although man must in a certain sense change with them, nonetheless, he is still man—the Image of God—and so he is capable of using his freedom and his love in the highest experience of God, namely, *contemplation*.[9] It is this contemplation of God that must be the objective of the spiritual life. It was in view of this that prayer and learning about prayer became the central preoccupation of Merton's own life as a Cistercian.[10] Because such prayer ultimately led to a union with God in which Merton recognized himself as the Image of God, it also led him to a union with all other men who bear in themselves this same Image. This, he once reminded his friends when he told them: "I shall continue to feel bound to all of you in the silence of prayer. Our real journey in life is interior: it is a matter of growth, deepening, and of an ever greater surrender to the creative action of love and grace in our hearts. Never was it more necessary for us to respond to that action."[11]

It is for this reason that Merton's theology of prayer is appreciated most fully only when understood within the context of the central message of his spirituality, namely, life is a seeking of God and finding Him by love and sharing that love with others. Only in a life such as this can man satisfy both his desire to be himself with the fullest possible freedom that is his as a son of God, and his desire for

9. In *Faith and Violence*, p. 215, Merton notes that "since the direct and pure experience of reality in its ultimate root is man's deepest need, contemplation must be possible if man is to remain human." This is not to deny that contemplation is still essentially a gift from God.

10. It is appropriate that Merton's last book, which he completed shortly before he departed for his Asian trip, should have been on prayer. In *The Climate of Monastic Prayer*, pp. 146–47, he said that prayer had no place in the margins of life but belonged at the very heart of life: "It would consequently be a serious error to ignore the true meaning of inner meditative prayer and its crucial importance for the whole Christian life, . . . The prayer of the heart must penetrate every aspect and every activity of Christian existence." See also, p. 143, where he adds: "Prayer must penetrate and enliven every department of our life, including that which is most temporal and transient."

11. Thomas Merton, "Letter to Friends," (Fall, 1968); later published as "A Letter from Thomas Merton," *Sewanee Review*, LXXVII (1969), 556.

unity, peace, and love with his fellow men. For, it is in prayer that man realizes that he can no longer live for himself but that he must live for others. However, to live for others, he must, first of all, live in God and with God Who is present within the ground of his own being.[12] This is why, for Merton, prayer was simply a search for God, a continued effort to realize God and to become aware of the reality of His presence in Christ within the depths of his own soul. Merton himself searched for this awareness of God, and having found Him within himself, then searched for ways to manifest Him to others, always remembering that it was his continued life of prayer that kept God and him in communion with one another.

12. Merton himself was always conscious of this presence of God within him and of his call to live in communion with God. Indeed, this basic relationship of man to God is evidenced early in his writings. Cf. *New Seeds of Contemplation*, p. 37, where he says: "God utters me like a word containing a thought of himself. . . . A word will never be able to comprehend the voice that utters it. . . . But if I am true to the concept that God utters in me, if I am true to the thought of him I was meant to embody, I shall be full of his actuality and find him everywhere in myself, and find myself nowhere. I shall be lost in him: . . ." This thought was recently expressed by Fr Flavian Burns in his "Homily at the Mass for Father M. Louis (Thomas Merton.... *Cistercian Studies*, III (1968), 280) who said: "We are men of God only insofar as we are seeking God, and God will only be found by us insofar as we find him in the truth about ourselves." This is also found in *Collectanea Cisterciensia*, XXXI (1969), 8.

CONCLUSION

THOMAS MERTON has been hailed as a spiritual writer of unique significance for the present times—a man who could achieve the distinction of making the present world more aware than ever before of the value of prayer.[1] Much of his appeal, no doubt, is due to the fact that he wrote from a rather unique point of view, that of a contemplative monk. A man of uncommon perception and complete sincerity, as a monk he was a witness to a remarkable Christian authenticity in today's world—a person who really knew Christ and bore witness to His reality among his fellow men.

In speaking of the Christian's life in an article for *The Current*, a literary magazine published at Harvard University, he remarked:

> The Christian life is to be seen dialectically, not only as a communal effort from which solitude is ostracized nor as a lonely pilgrimage without fraternal solidarity, but as a growth in one "Mystical Person," one Christ, in whom the solitude and independence of the person develop together with his capacity for love and commitment.[2]

1. One has only to review the large number of tributes written at the time of Merton's death for proof of this statement. Of special note is the article by Stevens, "Thomas Merton 1968: A Profile in Memoriam," p. 7, who says: "No spiritual writer in modern times has had an impact upon the contemporary Catholic like Thomas Merton . . . his writings will stand beside the great spiritual literature of all time."

2. Merton, "Christian Solitude: Notes on an Experiment," pp. 14–15.

Merton's own life was a fulfillment of this dialectic. It was a life that involved both a continuous search and struggle to effect the closest possible union with God in the solitude of prayer as well as the search for new ways to bind men together in love by implicating himself in the crises and problems of the world in which he lived. Yet, such love and widening concern for others never led him to compromise his loyalty to the contemplative life nor did it make him less truly a solitary. Merton knew that only the person who is completely rooted and grounded in God's love is sincerely capable of loving his fellow man.

Moreover, the disillusionment, which he often felt about man's ability to establish unity, peace, and love, did not force him to reject or to abandon the world of his fellow men. He looked candidly and without any illusion at that world and, although he saw much darkness in it, his ultimate answer was one of deep Christian hope. It was a hope that first led him to seek a change of heart in his own conversion where he discovered that the only way to live is to live in a world that is charged with the presence and the reality of God. It was a hope that ultimately led him deeper and deeper into complete solitude where he discovered that the full growth of man's life lies in helping others to become aware of how much they are capable of loving God or of how much they already love Him without realizing it. And so, Merton, the hermit, ever conscious of living in the presence of God, became a unique sign of hope for the most authentic value to which contemporary man can aspire—the revivification of his true self through union with God. This Merton notes in *New Seeds of Contemplation* where he says: "The only true joy on earth is to escape from the prison of our own false self, and enter by love into union with the Life Who dwells and sings within the essence of every creature and in the core of our own souls."[3]

In addition to his own life, Merton's writings also point the way toward a more hopeful and a more challenging horizon in Christian spirituality for the man of today. His is a spirituality that has much to offer to the person interested in learning the meaning of life and

3. Merton, *New Seeds of Contemplation*, p. 25.

of trying to live accordingly. For Merton was aware, as few others have been, of the inward crisis of the present age and of the acute need for the dimension of contemplation. He once remarked "that the best thing for all of us to do is to vanish and try, each one as honestly and sincerely as he can, to discover himself on some other, more vital, more unofficial level: the level of real, not legal solitude, and the level of real, not legal contemplation."[4] He recognized that the real problem confronting contemporary man is basically a spiritual problem: "The moral evil in the world is due to man's alienation from the deepest truth, from the springs of spiritual life within himself, to his alienation from God."[5] Merton addressed himself specifically to that problem by showing that the only value to man's life is that it is a gift from God. Again and again in his writings he points out: "There is no true love except in God."[6] Only in Him can man discover the real meaning of love, of life, of true communion with his fellow man. It is this type of spirituality that is sorely needed today to put man in the fullest possible contact with reality. For, to be absorbed in God is to be conscious of humanity in the most sublime way of all. Man is then able once again to see God living in His world.

This, then, is the vitality and the relevancy of the spirituality of Thomas Merton. It is a spirituality which deeply penetrates the inner meaning of one's life in Christ and sees the full significance of its demands, namely, that all Christians, who are called in some way or other to an intimate union with God in Christ, "must play a constructive and positive part in the world of our time."[7] But this

4. Thomas Merton, "Monk and Hunters," *Commonweal*, LIV (1951), 40; similarly found as "Le moine et le chasseur," *Dieu Vivant*, XVII (1949–51), 93–98.

5. Merton, "Christian Action in World Crisis," p. 259. In light of this, he goes on to say later in the same article, p. 266: "The present world crisis is . . . a crisis of man's spirit," He then says, p. 266: "The real problem of our time is basically spiritual." Cf. also "Christian Morality and Nuclear War," pp. 12–22.

6. Merton, *No Man Is an Island*, p. 131.

7. Merton, *Life and Holiness*, p. 107. In *No Man Is an Island*, p. 122, Merton writes: "All vocations are intended by God to manifest His love in the world. For each special calling gives a man some particular place in the Mystery of

they will do only if they remember "that the love of man is insecure and elusive unless it proceeds from the hidden action of God's love and grace. The love of God is the source of all living and authentic love for other men."[8] This message came from a man who found such love within a Cistercian monastery where he lived his life in search of his true freedom as a son of God completely aware of his total dependence on that God. But that man, in spite of his distance and solitude, was also completely aware of the state of things in the world and knew that each man must discover for himself the kind of environment in which he can best find such love and thus lead a full spiritual life.[9] Nonetheless, he realized that what he found in his life could be meaningful for the lives of others. This he once remarked:

> Actually, I have come to the monastery to find my place in the world, and if I fail to find this place in the world I will be wasting my time in the monastery.

> Coming to the monastery has been for me exactly the right kind of withdrawal. It has given me perspective. It has taught me how to live. And now I owe everyone else in the world a share in that life.[10]

His untimely death on December 10, 1968, did not mark the end of Merton's sharing of his life with others. Years earlier, at the time

---

Christ, gives him something to do for the salvation of all mankind. The difference between the various vocations lies in the different ways in which each one enables men to discover God's love, appreciate it, respond to it, and share it with other men. Each vocation has for its aim the propagation of divine life in the world."

     8. Merton, *Faith and Violence*, p. 283.

     9. Cf. *No Man Is an Island*, p. 91. In *Faith and Violence*, p. 149, he also brings out the awareness of his openness to others' vocations: "Though there are certainly more ways than one of preserving the freedom of the sons of God, the way to which I was called and which I have chosen is that of the monastic life." Cf. also *What Are These Wounds?*, p. 190, where he says: "Whoever we are, whatever may be our state of life, we are all called to the glory and freedom of the sons of God. Our vocation is union with Christ. We are coheirs with Him of His own divine glory. We share His divine Sonship."

     10. Merton, *The Sign of Jonas*, p. 312.

of his ordination, he had written on a card announcing the event: "He walked with God and was seen no more because God took him."[11] In a paradoxical way, his priesthood was indeed a fulfillment of this. He found the solitude he needed to be alone with God; and yet, this solitude led to a deep communion with his fellow men. By a strange coincidence, it has been noted that he concluded his last conference in Bangkok with the words: "so I will disappear."[12] In a sense, his death later that day saw the fulfillment of those words; and yet, even in death, there can be "an *absence* that is a *presence*."[13] Indeed, Merton lived his entire life as a contemplative in the presence of such a life-beyond-death, a life in which he knew that he would one day achieve a true oneness with the God-man, Christ—a oneness that would unite him most closely with all other men in Christ. For, in Christ every man is one man. No person is more deserving of the words written in a long narrative poem entitled "The Legacy of Herakleitos," than the man who wrote them. Thomas Merton said:

> There await men when they die
> such things as they look not for,
>   nor dream of!
>
> Greater deaths
> win greater portions. . . .
>
> . . . They (who die great deaths)
> rise up and become the wakeful
>   guardians
> of the living and the dead.[14]

11. Cf. Rice, "Thomas Merton," p. 35, who notes this fact.

12. Cf. "Marxist Theory and Monastic Theoria." This has been noted by Dumont, "A Contemplative at the Heart of the World—Thomas Merton," p. 639.

13. Merton himself spoke of such a presence in a letter to a group of students at Mount St Paul College during a display of his manuscripts which he could not attend. Cf. Sr M. Thérèse Lentfoehr, "The Spiritual Writer," *Continuum*, VII (1969), 254. In *Conjectures of a Guilty Bystander*, p. 225, Merton says regarding his own death: "My life and my death are not purely and simply my own business. I live by and for others, and my death involves others."

14. Thomas Merton, *The Behavior of Titans* (New York: New Directions, 1961), p. 106.

BIBLIOGRAPHY

I. *Works by Thomas Merton*

Books and Pamphlets

The Ascent to Truth. New York: Harcourt, Brace, 1951.

A Balanced Life of Prayer. Trappist, Kentucky: Gethsemani Abbey, 1951.

Basic Principles of Monastic Spirituality. Bardstown, Kentucky: Abbey of Gethsemani, 1957.

The Behavior of Titans. New York: New Directions, 1961.

Bread in the Wilderness. New York: New Directions, 1953.

Cables to the Ace; or Familiar Liturgies of Misunderstanding. New York: New Directions, 1968.

Cistercian Contemplatives: a Guide to Trappist Life. Trappist, Kentucky: Gethsemani Abbey, 1948.

The Climate of Monastic Prayer. Cistercian Studies Series, no. 1. Spencer, Mass.: Cistercian Publications, 1969.

Conjectures of a Guilty Bystander. New York: Image Books, 1968.

Contemplation in a World of Action. New York: Doubleday, 1971.

Contemplative Prayer. New York: Herder and Herder, 1969.

Disputed Questions. New York: Farrar, Straus and Cudahy, 1960.

Early Poems/1940–42. Lexington, Kentucky: The Anvil Press, 1971.

Emblems of a Season of Fury. Norfolk, Conn.: New Directions, 1963.

Exile Ends in Glory; the Life of a Trappistine, Mother M. Berchmans, o.c.s.o. Milwaukee: Bruce, 1948.

Faith and Violence: Christian Teaching and Christian Practice. Notre Dame, Indiana: University of Notre Dame Press, 1968.

Figures for an Apocalypse. Norfolk, Conn.: New Directions, 1947.

The Geography of Lograire. New York: New Directions, 1969.

Gethsemani—a Life of Praise. Trappist, Kentucky: Abbey of Gethsemani, 1966.

Gethsemani Magnificat—Centenary of Gethsemani Abbey. Trappist, Kentucky: Gethsemani Abbey, 1949.

Guide to Cistercian Life. Trappist, Kentucky: Gethsemani Abbey, 1948.

Hagia Sophia. Lexington, Kentucky: Stamperia del Santuccio, 1962.

The Last of the Fathers; Saint Bernard of Clairvaux and the encyclical letter, Doctor Mellifluus. New York: Harcourt, Brace, 1954.

Life and Holiness. New York: Image Books, 1964.

The Living Bread. New York: Farrar, Straus and Cudahy, 1956.

A Man in the Divided Sea. Norfolk, Conn.: New Directions, 1946.

Marthe, Marie et Lazare. Translated by J. Charles-DuBos. Paris: Desclée de Brouwer, 1956.

Monastic Peace. Trappist, Kentucky: Abbey of Gethsemani, 1958.

My Argument with the Gestapo: a macaronic journal. New York: Doubleday, 1969.

Mystics and Zen Masters. New York: Farrar, Straus and Giroux, 1967.

Nativity Kerygma. Trappist, Kentucky: Abbey of Gethsemani, 1958.

The New Man. New York: Mentor-Omega Books, 1961.

New Seeds of Contemplation. Norfolk, Conn.: New Directions, 1961.

No Man is an Island. New York: Image Books, 1967.

Opening the Bible. Collegeville, Minn.: Liturgical Press, 1970.

Original Child Bomb: Points for Meditation to be scratched on the walls of a cave. New York: New Directions, 1962.

Praying the Psalms. Collegeville, Minnesota: Liturgical Press, 1956.

Prometheus, a Meditation. Lexington, Kentucky: Margaret I. King Library Press of University of Kentucky, 1958.

Raids on the Unspeakable. New York: New Directions, 1966.

Redeeming the Time. London: Burns and Oates, 1966.

La révolution noire. Translated by M. Tadié. Paris: Casterman, 1964.

Seasons of Celebration. New York: Farrar, Straus and Giroux, 1964.

The Secular Journal of Thomas Merton. New York: Dell Publishing Co., 1959.

Seeds of Contemplation. Norfolk, Conn.: New Directions, 1949.

Seeds of Destruction. New York: Farrar, Straus and Giroux, 1964.

Selected Poems. New York: New Directions, 1959.

The Seven Storey Mountain. New York: Signet Books, 1952.

The Sign of Jonas. New York: Image Books, 1956.

Silence in Heaven: a book of the monastic life. New York: Studio Publications in association with Thomas Y. Crowell, 1956.

The Silent Life. New York: Farrar, Straus and Cudahy, 1957.

The Solitary Life. Lexington, Kentucky: Stamperia del Santuccio, 1960.

Spiritual Direction and Meditation. Collegeville, Minnesota: Liturgical Press, 1960.

The Strange Islands. New York: New Directions, 1957.

The Tears of the Blind Lions. New York: New Directions, 1949.

Thirty Poems. Norfolk, Conn.: New Directions, 1944.

Thomas Merton on Peace. Edited and with an Introduction by Gordon C. Zahn. New York: McCall Publishing Co., 1971.

A Thomas Merton Reader. Edited by T. McDonnell. New York: Harcourt, Brace and World, 1962.

Thoughts in Solitude. New York: Image Books, 1968.

The Tower of Babel. Norfolk, Conn.: New Directions, 1958.

The True Solitude. Selections from Thomas Merton's writings by Dean Walley. Kansas City, Missouri: Hallmark Productions, 1969.

The Waters of Siloe. New York: Image Books, 1962.

The Way of Chuang Tzu. New York: New Directions, 1965.

What Are These Wounds? The Life of a Cistercian Mystic, Saint Lutgarde of Aywières. Milwaukee: Bruce, 1950.
What Is Contemplation? London: Burns, Oates and Washbourne, 1950.
Zen and the Birds of Appetite. New York: New Directions, 1968.

Articles in Periodicals[1]

"Absurdity in Sacred Decoration." *Worship*, XXXIV (1959–60), 248–55.
"Action and Contemplation in St. Bernard." *Collectanea Ordinis Cisterciensium Reformatorum*, XV (1953), 26–31, 203–216; XVI (1954), 105–21.
"Active and Contemplative Orders." *Commonweal*, XLVII (1947–48), 192–96.
"The Advent Mystery." *Worship*, XXXVIII (1963–64), 17–25.
"Albert Camus and the Church." *Catholic Worker*, XXXIII (December, 1966), 1, 4–5, 8.
"Answers on Art and Freedom." *The Lugano Review*, I (1965), 43–45.
"An anti-poem: Plessy vs. Ferguson: Theme and Variations." *Commonweal*, LXXXIX (1968–69), 592–93.
"Art and Worship." *Sponsa Regis*, XXXI (1959–60), 114–17.
"As Man to Man." *Cistercian Studies*, IV (1969), 90–94.
"The Ascent to Truth." *Thought*, XXVI (1951–52), 361–83.
"Ash Wednesday." *Worship*, XXXIII (1958–59), 165–70.
"Asian Letter I." *Cistercian Studies*, III (1968), 272–76.
"Auschwitz: A Family Camp." *Catholic Worker*, XXXIII (November, 1967), 4–5, 8.
"Baptism in the Forest: Wisdom and Initiation in William Faulkner." *Catholic World*, CCVII (1968), 124–30.
"Barth's Dream and Other Conjectures." *Sewanee Review*, LXXIII (1965), 1–18.
"The Benedictines." *Monastic Studies*, I (1963), 137–41.
"Bernard of Clairvaux." *Jubilee*, I (1953–54), 33.
"Beyond the Sacred—a Letter to Editors." *Commonweal*, LXXXVII (1967–68), 479.
"The Black Revolution." *Ramparts*, II (1963–64), 4–23.
"Blake and the New Theology." *Sewanee Review*, LXXVI (1968), 673–82.
"*Book Review of Giuseppe Turbessi's Ascetismo e Monachesimo Prebenedittino.*" *Monastic Studies*, III (1965), 269–71.
"Boris Pasternak." *Jubilee*, VII (1959–60), 17–31.
"Buddhism and the Modern World." *Cross Currents*, XVI (1966), 495–99.
"Building Community on God's Love." Edited by Naomi Burton Stone. *Sisters Today*, XLII (1970), 185–93.
"A Buyer's Market for Love." *Ave Maria*, CIV (December 24, 1966), 7–10, 27.
"Called Out of Darkness." *Sponsa Regis*, XXXIII (1961–62), 61–71.

---

[1] In this section of the bibliography the writer includes, in addition to Merton's prose articles, the various book reviews and excerpts from his writings published in periodicals.

L

"Camus: Journals of the Plague Years." *Sewanee Review*, LXXV (1967), 717–30.

"Can We Survive Nihilism?" *The Saturday Review of Literature*, L (April 15, 1967), 16–19.

"The Catholic and Creativity: Theology of Creativity." *American Benedictine Review*, XI (1960), 197–213.

"The Cause of Our Joy." *Catholic World*, CLXVII (1948), 364–65.

"The Challenge of Responsibility." *The Saturday Review of Literature*, XLVIII (February 13, 1965), 28–30.

"Christ Suffers Again." *Action Now*, V (March, 1952), 13.

"Christ, the Way." *Sponsa Regis*, XXXIII (1961–62), 144–53.

"Christian Action in World Crisis." *Blackfriars*, XLIII (1962), 256–68.

"The Christian as Peacemaker." *Fellowship*, XXIX (March, 1963), 7–9.

"Christian Culture Needs Oriental Wisdom." *Catholic World*, CXCV (1962), 72–79.

"Christian Ethics and Nuclear War." *Catholic Worker*, XXVIII (March, 1962), 2, 7.

"Christian Freedom and Monastic Formation." *American Benedictine Review*, XIII (1962), 289–313.

"Christian Humanism." *Spiritual Life*, XIII (1967), 219–30.

"Christian Morality and Nuclear War." *Way*, XIX (June, 1963), 12–22.

"Christian Solitude: Notes on an Experiment." *The Current*, VII (Feb., 1967), 14–28.

"Christianity and Mass Movements." *Cross Currents*, IX (1959), 201–11.

"A Christmas Devotion." *Commonweal*, XLVII (1947–48), 270–72.

"The Christmas Sermons of Bl. Guerric." *Collectanea Ordinis Cisterciensium Reformatorum*, XVII (1955), 229–44.

"Church and Bishop." *Worship*, XXXVII (1962–63), 110–20.

"Classic Chinese Thought." *Jubilee*, VIII (1960–61), 26–32.

"The Climate of Mercy." *Cord*, XV (1965), 89–96.

"The Climate of Monastic Prayer." *Collectanea Ordinis Cisterciensium Reformatorum*, XXVII (1965), 273–87.

"Community, Politics, and Contemplation." Edited by Naomi Burton Stone. *Sisters Today*, XLII (1971), 241–46.

"Concerning the Collection in the Bellarmine College Library—a Statement, November 10. 1963." *Merton Studies Center*, I (1971), 13–15.

"A Conference on Prayer." *Sisters Today*, XLI (1970), 449–56.

"Conquistador, Tourist and Indian." *Good Work*, XXV (1962), 90–94.

"Contemplation and Ecumenism." *Season*, III (1965), 133–42.

"Contemplation in a Rocking Chair." *Integrity*, II (1947–48), 15–23.

"Contemplation in a World of Action." *Bloominewman—Newsletter of Newman Club of University of Louisville*, II (April, 1968), 1–5.

"Contemplation in a World of Action." Edited by Naomi Burton Stone. *Sisters Today*, XLII (1971), 345–51.

"The Contemplative and the Atheist." *Schema XIII*, I (1970), 11–18.

"The Contemplative Life: Its Meaning and Necessity." *Dublin Review*, CCXXIII (1949), 26–35.

"Conversatio Morum." *Cistercian Studies*, I (1966), 130–44.

"The Council and Religious Life." *New Blackfriars*, XLVII (1965–66), 5–17.

"Creative Silence." *The Baptist Student*, XLVIII (February, 1969), 18–22.

"The Cross Fighters—Notes on a Race War." *Unicorn Journal*, (1968), 26–40.

"Dans le désert de Dieu." *Témoignages*, XLVIII (1955), 132–36.

"Day of a Stranger." *Hudson Review*, XX (1967–68), 211–18.

"The Death of God, I: The Death of God and the End of History." *Theoria to Theory*, II (1967), 3–16.

"The Death of a Holy Terror: The Strange Story of Frère Pascal." *Jubilee*, XV (1967–68), 35–38.

"Death of a Trappist." *Integrity*, II (1947–48), 3–8.

"Dialogue and Renewal in the Contemplative Life." *Spiritual Life*, XIV (1968), 41–52.

"Dieu n'est pas un problème." *Collectanea Cisterciensia*, XXXI (1969), 19–23.

"Easter: The New Life." *Worship*, XXXIII (1958–59), 276–84.

"Ecumenism and Monastic Renewal." *Journal of Ecumenical Studies*, V (1968), 268–83.

"Elected Silence: passages from *Seven Storey Mountain*." *Month*, I (1949), 158–79, 221–40.

"Elias: Variations on a Theme." *Thought*, XXXI (1956), 245–50.

"The English Mystics." *Collectanea Ordinis Cisterciensium Reformatorum*, XXIII (1961), 362–67.

"The English Mystics: review of Knowles' *The English Mystical Tradition*." *Jubilee*, IX (1961–62), 36–40.

"Ethics and War—a Footnote." *Catholic Worker*, XXVIII (April, 1962), 2.

"Examination of Conscience and Conversatio Morum." *Collectanea Ordinis Cisterciensium Reformatorum*, XXV (1963), 355–59.

"Excerpts from *Conjectures of a Guilty Bystander*." *Life*, LXI (August 5, 1966), 60–73.

"Excerpts from a Letter from Father Thomas Merton." *The Center Letter*, III (1968), 7; IV (1968), 7.

"Few Questions and Fewer Answers." *Harper's Magazine*, CCXXXI (November, 1965), 79–81.

"Final Integration: Toward a 'Monastic Therapy.'" *Monastic Studies*, VI (1968), 87–99.

"First Christmas at Gethsemani," Unpublished material from original manuscript of *Seven Storey Mountain* with introductory comment by Sr M. Thérèse Lentfoehr, S.D.S. *Catholic World*, CLXX (1949–50), 166–73.

"Flannery O'Connor." *Jubilee*, XII (1964–65), 49–53.

"For a Renewal of Eremitism in the Monastic State." *Collectanea Ordinis Cisterciensium Reformatorum*, XXVII (1965), 121–49.

"La formation monastique selon Adam de Perseigne." Translated by C. Dumont. *Collectanea Ordinis Cisterciensium Reformatorum*, XIX (1957), 1–17.

"Franciscan Eremitism." *Cord*, XVI (1966), 356–64.

"From Pilgrimage to Crusade." *Cithara*, IV (1964), 3–21.

"The Function of a Monastic Review." *Collectanea Ordinis Cisterciensium Reformatorum*, XXVII (1965), 9–12.

"The General Dance." *Jubilee*, IX (1961–62), 8–11.

"The Gentle Revolutionary." *Ramparts*, III (1964–65), 28–32.

"Gethsemani (chronique de nos Abbayes: Annual Report—Gethsemani, written in French). N. D. de Gethsemani." *Collectanea Ordinis Cisterciensium Reformatorum*, XII (1950), 132–34; XIII (1951), 141–42; XIV (1952), 143–44; XV (1953), 223; XVI (1954), 145.

"Ghandi and the One-Eyed Giant." *Jubilee*, XII (1964–65), 12–17.

"The Gift of Understanding." *The Tiger's Eye*, I (1948), 41–45.

"The Good News of the Nativity: A Monastic Reading of the Christmas Gospels." *Bible Today*, XXI (1965–66), 1367–1375.

"Grace at Work; excerpt from *Seven Storey Mountain*." *Catholic Mission Digest*, VI (November, 1948), 8–10.

"Growth in Christ." *Sponsa Regis*, XXXIII (1961–62), 197–210.

"Hagia Sophia: prose poem." *Ramparts*, I (1962–63), 65–71.

"Herakleitos the Obscure." *Jubilee*, VIII (1960–61), 24–31.

"Heyschasm." *Diakonia*, II (1967), 380–85.

"The Historical Consciousness." *Contemplative Review*, I (May, 1968), 2–3.

"A Homily on Light and on the Virgin Mother." *Worship*, XXXVII (1962–63), 572–80.

"The 'Honest to God' Debate." *Commonweal*, LXXX (1964), 573–78.

"How It Is—Apologies to an Unbeliever." *Harper's Magazine*, CCXXXIII (1966), 36–39.

"How to Believe in God—excerpt from *The Ascent to Truth*." *Catholic Digest*, XVI (1951–52), 41–44.

"The Humanity of Christ in Monastic Prayer." *Monastic Studies*, II (1964), 1–27.

"Huxley's Pantheon." *Catholic World*, CLII (1940–41), 206–209.

"I Begin to Meditate—excerpt from *Seven Storey Mountain*." *Catholic Digest*, XIII (1948–49), 116–20.

"I Have Chosen You." *Sponsa Regis*, XXX (1958–59), 1–6.

"I Will Be Your Monk." Unpublished material from original manuscript of *Seven Storey Mountain* with introductory comment by Sr M. Thérèse Lentfoehr, S.D.S. *Catholic World*, CLXXI (May, 1950), 86–93.

"Introducing a Book: Introduction to Japanese Edition of *Seven Storey Mountain*." *Queens Work*, LVI (1964), 9–10.

"Is Mysticism Normal?" *Commonweal*, LI (1949–50), 94–98.

"Is the 'Contemplative Life' Finished?" *Monastic Studies*, VII (1969), 11–62.

"Is the World a Problem?" *Commonweal*, LXXXIV (1966), 305–309.

"Isaac of Stella—an Introduction to Selections from His Sermons." *Cistercian Studies*, II (1967), 243–51.

"ISHI—a Meditation." *Catholic Worker*, XXXIII (March-April, 1967), 5–6.

"Itinerary to Christ." *Liturgical Arts*, XXX–XXXII (1961–64), 60.

"The Japanese Tea Ceremony." *Good Work*, XXXII (1969), 6–7.

"The Jesuits in China." *Jubilee*, X (1962–63), 34–39.

"The Ladder of Divine Ascent." *Jubilee*, VII (1959–60), 37–40.

"Let the Poor Man Speak." *Catholic Mind*, LX (1962), 47–52.

"Let the Poor Man Speak." *Jubilee*, VIII (1960–61), 18–21.

"A Letter from Thomas Merton." *Sewanee Review*, LXXVII (1969), 555-56.
"Letter to a Bishop—August, 1968." *Peace*, III (1968-69), 11-12.
"A Letter to Pablo Antonio Cuadra concerning Giants." *Blackfriars*, XLIII (1962), 69-81.
"Letters to a White Liberal." *Blackfriars*, XLIV (1963), 464-77, 503-16.
"Lettre d'Asie." *Collectanea Cisterciensia*, XXXI (1969), 14-18.
"A Life Free from Care." *Cistercian Studies*, V (1970), 217-27.
"The Life of Faith." *Sponsa Regis*, XXXIII (1961-62), 167-71.
"The Life that Unifies." Edited by Naomi Burton Stone. *Sisters Today*, XLII (1970), 65-73.
"Liturgical Renewal: The Open Approach." *Critic*, XXIII (1964-65), 10-15.
"Liturgy and Spiritual Personalism." *Worship*, XXXIV (1959-60), 494-507.
"Love and Maturity." *Sponsa Regis*, XXXII (1960-61), 44-53.
"Love and Person." *Sponsa Regis*, XXXII (1960-61), 6-11.
"Love and Solitude." *Critic*, XXV (L966-67), 30-37.
"Man Is a Gorilla with a Gun: Reflections on an American Best Seller." *New Blackfriars*, XLVI (1964-65), 452-57.
"Manifestation of Conscience and Spiritual Direction." *Sponsa Regis*, XXX (1959), 277-82.
"Marcel and Buddha: a Metaphysics of Enlightenment (foreword by Thomas Merton)." *Journal of Religious Thought*, XXIV (1967-68), 51-57.
"Martyr to the Nazis: excerpts from Introduction to the *Prison Meditations of Father Delp*." *Jubilee*, X (1962-63), 32-35.
"The Meaning of Malcolm X." *Continuum*, V (1967), 432-35.
"Meditation." *L'Osservatore Romano*, XL (October 2, 1969), 6.
"Meditation—Action and Union." *Sponsa Regis*, XXXI (1959-60), 191-98.
"Meditation in the Woods." *Catholic Digest*, XXXII (1968), 20-24.
"Merton: Regain the Old Monastic Charism—Letter to Editors." *The National Catholic Reporter*, IV (January 11, 1968), 11.
"Merton: View of Monasticism. Seeking God through Total Love Is Goal." Extemporaneous talk delivered at Spiritual Summit Conference in Calcutta, October 22-26, 1968. *Washington Post* (January 18, 1969), C9.
"Message to Poets from Thomas Merton (Mensaje de Thomas Merton)." *Americas*, XVI (May, 1964), 29.
"Le moine dans la Diaspora." *Bulletin de Liaison des Monasteres d'Afrique*, III (1965), 23-31.
"Le moine et le chasseur." Translated by C. Burdo. *Dieu Vivant*, XVII (1949-51), 93-98.
"Moines et spirituels non chretiens II." *Collectanea Ordinis Cisterciensium Reformatorum*, XXIX (1967), 179-94.
"Monachesimo del futuro: quale?" *Vita Monastica*, XCVI (1969), 3-15.
"Monachisme bouddhique: Le Zen." *Collectanea Ordinis Cisterciensium Reformatorum*, XXIX (1967), 132-50.
"Monastery at Midnight—excerpt from *Sign of Jonas*." *Catholic Digest*, XVII (May, 1953), 112-16.
"Monastic Attitudes: a Matter of Choice." *Cistercian Studies*, II (1967), 3-14.
"Monastic Vocation and Modern Thought." *Monastic Studies*, IV (1966), 17-54.

"Monk and Hunters." *Commonweal*, LIV (1951), 39–40.
"The Monk and Sacred Art." *Sponsa Regis*, XXVIII (1956–57), 231–34.
"The Monk in the Diaspora." *Blackfriars*, XLV (1964), 290–302.
"The Monk in the Diaspora." *Commonweal*, LXXIX (1963–64), 741–45.
"The Monk Today." *Latitudes*, II (1968).
"Morte d'Urban: Two Celebrations." *Worship*, XXXVI (1961–62), 645–50.
"Mount Athos." *Jubilee*, VII (1959–60), 8–16.
"A Mountain of Monks." *Catholic Digest*, XXV (December, 1960), 100–103.
"Mystics and Zen Masters." *Chinese Culture*, VI (1965), 1–18.
"The Name of the Lord." *Worship*, XXXVIII (1963–64), 142–51.
"Nativity Kerygma." *Worship*, XXXIV (1959–60), 2–9.
"The Negro Revolt." *Jubilee*, XI (1963–64), 39–43.
"Negro Violence and White Non Violence." *The National Catholic Reporter*, III (September 6, 1967), 8.
"The New Man—excerpts from *The New Man*." *Tablet*, CCXVI (1962), 79–80, 102–103, 127–28, 151–52.
"News of the Joyce Industry." *Sewanee Review*, LXXVII (1969), 543–54.
"The Night Spirit and the Dawn Air." *New Blackfriars*, XLVI (1964–65), 687–93.
"Nonviolence Does Not—Cannot Mean Passivity." *Ave Maria*, CVIII (September 7, 1968), 9–10.
"Note on the New Church at Gethsemani." *Liturgical Arts*, XXXVI (1967–68), 100–101.
"Notes on Contemplation." *Spiritual Life*, VII (1961), 196–204.
"Notes on Love." *Frontier*, X (1967–68), 211–14.
"Notes on Sacred and Profane Art." *Jubilee*, IV (1956–57), 25–32.
"Notes on Spiritual Direction." *Sponsa Regis*, XXXI (1959–60), 86–94.
"Notes on the Future of Monasticism." *Monastic Exchange*, I (1969), 9–13.
"Nuclear War and Christian Responsibility." *Commonweal*, LXXV (1961–62), 509–13; LXXVI (1962), 84–85.
"One Sunday in New York—excerpt from *Seven Storey Mountain*." *Information*, LXII (1948), 437–41.
"Opening the Bible." *The Bible Today*, L (1970), 104–113.
"Openness and Cloister." *Spiritual Life*, XV (1969), 26–36.
"Openness and Cloister." *Cistercian Studies*, II (1967), 312–23.
"Orthodoxy and the World." *Monastic Studies*, IV (1966), 105–115.
"The Other Side of Despair: Notes on Christian Existentialism." *Critic*, XXIV (1965–66), 12–23.
"Ouverture et cloture." *Collectanea Cisterciensia*, XXXI (1969), 24–35.
"The Ox Mountain Parable of Meng Tzu." *Commonweal*, LXXIV (1961), 174.
"Pâques, une vie nouvelle." *La Vie Spirituelle*, C (1959), 345–59.
"The Pasternak Affair in Perspective." *Thought*, XXXIV (1959–60), 485–517.
"Peace and Protest." *Continuum*, III (1966), 509–12.
"Peace and Revolution: a Footnote from Ulysses." *Peace*, III (1968–69), 5–10.
"Peace That Is War—excerpt from *Seeds of Contemplation*." *The Ligourian*, XXXVII (1949), 431.

"La place de l'obéisance dans le renouveau monastique." *Lettre de Ligugé*, CXIX (1966), 8–19.

"The place of Obedience in Monastic Renewal." *American Benedictine Review*, XVI (1965), 359–68.

"Poetry and Contemplation: a Reappraisal." *Commonweal*, LXIX (1958–59), 87–92.

"Poetry and the Contemplative Life." *Commonweal*, XLVI (1947), 280–86.

"The Poorer Means." *Cord*, XV (1965), 243–47.

"The Pope of the Virgin Mary." *Marian Literary Studies*, LXII (1958), 1–15.

"Poverty—excerpt from *Seeds of Contemplation*." *Catholic Worker*, XV (April, 1949), 3.

"Prayer and Conscience." Edited by Naomi Burton Stone. *Sisters Today*. XLII (1971), 409–18.

"Prayer for Guidance." *Liturgical Arts*, XXVII (1959), 64.

"Prayer, Personalism, and the Spirit." Edited by Naomi Burton Stone. *Sisters Today*, XLII (1970), 129–36.

"Prayer, Tradition, and Experience." Edited by Naomi Burton Stone. *Sisters Today*, XLII (1971), 285–93.

"Praying the Psalms." *Worship*, XXIX (1954–55), 481–83.

"Presuppositions to Meditation." *Sponsa Regis*, XXXI (1959–60), 231–40.

"The Primacy of Contemplation." *Cross and Crown*, II (1950), 3–16.

"The Psalms and Contemplation." *Orate Fratres*, XXIV (1950), 341–47, 385–91, 433–40.

"The Psalms as Poetry—excerpt from *Bread in the Wilderness*." *Commonweal*, LIX (1953–54), 79–81.

"Rafael Alberti and His Angels." *Continuum*, V (1967–68), 175–79.

"Raids on the Unspeakable—A Devout Meditation in Memory of Adolf Eichmann." *Ramparts*, V (1966–67), 8–9.

"Raids on the Unspeakable—A Meditation on Adolf Eichmann." *Catholic Digest*, XXXI (1966), 18–20.

"Rain and the Rhinocerous." *Holiday*, XXXVII (May, 1965), 8–16.

"Raissa Maritain's Poems." *Jubilee*, X (1962–63), 24–27.

"Reality, Art and Prayer—excerpt from *No Man Is an Island*." *Commonweal*, LXI (1955), 658–59.

"Le recueillement—excerpt from *No Man Is an Island*." *Témoignages*, XLVIII (1955), 321–30.

"Reflections on Some Recent Studies of St. Anselm." *Monastic Studies*, III (1965), 221–34.

"Religion and Race in the United States." *New Blackfriars*, XLVI (1964–65), 218–25.

"Religion and the Bomb." *Jubilee*, X (1962–63), 7–13.

"Renewal and Discipline in the Monastic Life." *Cistercian Studies*, V (1970), 3–18.

"Renewal in Monastic Education." *Cistercian Studies*, III (1968), 247–52.

"Renouveau de la formation monastique." *Collectanea Cisterciensia*, XXX (1968), 211–17.

"Rites for the Extrusion of a Leper." *The Kentucky Review*, II (February, 1968), 26–30.

"The Root of War: excerpt from *New Seeds of Contemplation*." *Catholic Worker*, XXVIII (October, 1961), 1, 7–8.

"Ruben Dario." *Continuum*, IV (1966), 469–70.

"Sacred Art and the Spiritual Life." *Sponsa Regis*, XXXI (1959–60), 133–40.

"The Sacred City." *Catholic Worker*, XXXIV (January, 1968), 4–6.

"The Sacred City." *The Center Magazine*, I (March, 1968), 72–77.

"Le Sacrement de l'Avent dans la spiritualité de Saint Bernard." Trans. by P. Bastord, *Dieu Vivant*, XXIII (1953), 21–43.

"Schoolboy in England—excerpt from *Seven Storey Mountain*." *Commonweal*, XLVIII (1948), 469–71.

"Schoolboy's Lament—excerpt from *Seven Storey Mountain*." *Catholic Digest*, XIII (June, 1949), 80–82.

"Second Coming." *Jubilee*, III (1955–56), 6–9.

"The Secular Journals of Thomas Merton: excerpts from the famous Trappist's pre-monastic notebook." *Jubilee*, VI (1958–59), 16–20.

"Seeking God." *Sponsa Regis*, XXVIII (1956–57), 113–21.

"Seeking Our Redeemer." *Sponsa Regis*, XXVIII (1956–57), 141–49.

"Self-Denial and the Christian." *Commonweal*, LI (1949–50), 649–53.

"September, 1949." *Month*, III (1950), 107–13.

"Seven Qualities of the Sacred." *Good Work*, XXVII (1964), 15–20.

"The Shakers." *Jubilee*, XI (1963–64), 36–41.

"The Shelter Ethic," *Catholic Worker*, XXVIII (November, 1961), 1, 5.

"The Shoshoneans." *Catholic Worker*, XXXIII (June, 1967), 5–6.

"The Sign of Jonas—excerpts." *This Week Magazine, New York Herald Tribune* (March 8, 1953), 18, 30, 43, 50)

"Sincerity in Art and Life: from a letter of Owen Merton." *Good Work*, XXX (1967), 58–59.

"The Solitary Life." *Cistercian Studies*, IV (1969), 213–17.

"Solitude." *Spiritual Life*, XIV (1968), 171–78.

"Sonship and Espousals." *Sponsa Regis*, XXVIII (1956–57), 169–78.

"The Sounds Are Furrows." *Critic*, XXV (April-May, 1967), 76–80.

"Spiritual Direction." *Sponsa Regis*, XXX (1958–59), 249–54.

"The Spiritual Father in the Desert Tradition." *Monastic Studies*, V (1968), 87–111.

"The Spiritual Father in the Desert Tradition." *Cistercian Studies*, III (1968), 3–23.

"Spirituality for the Age of Overkill." *Continuum*, I (1963), 9–21.

"St Anselm and His Argument." *American Benedictine Review*, XVII (1966), 238–62.

"St Bernard, Monk and Apostle." *Cross and Crown*, V (1953), 251–63.

"St Bernard: Monk and Apostle." *Tablet*, CCI (1953), 438–39, 466–67.

"St John of the Cross." *Perspectives U.S.A.*, IV (1953), 52–61.

"St Peter Damien and the Medieval Monk." *Jubilee*, VIII (1960–61), 39–44.

"The Street Is for Celebration." *The Mediator*, XX ,Summer, 1969), 2–4.

"The Subject of Meditation." *Sponsa Regis*, XXXI (1959–60), 268–74.

"Sweet Savor of Liberty—excerpt from *Seven Storey Mountain*." *Commonweal*; XLVIII (1948), 514–44.

"Teilhard's Gamble: Betting on the Whole Human Species." *Commonweal*, LXXXVII (1967–68), 109–11.

"Temperament and Meditation." *Sponsa Regis*, XXXI (1959–60), 296–99.

"Terror and the Absurd: Violence and Nonviolence in Albert Camus." *Motive*, XXIX (February, 1969), 5–15.

"The Testing of Ideals." *Sponsa Regis*, XXXIII (1961–62), 95–100.

"The True Legendary Sound." *Sewanee Review*, LXXV (1967), 317–24.

"Thich Nhat Hanh Is My Brother." *Jubilee*, XIV (1966–67), 11.

"This Is God's Work." *Sisters Today*, XLII (1970), 1–7.

"Thomas Merton 1915–1968: Excerpts from *Commonweal*." *Commonweal*, LXXXIX (1968–69), 435–37.

"Thomas Merton on Renunciation." Unpublished material from original manuscript of *Seven Storey Mountain* with introductory comment by Sister M. Thérèse Lentfoehr, S.D.S. *Catholic World*, CLXXI (1950), 420–29.

"Thomas Merton on the Strike—letter." *Catholic Worker*, XXVIII (February, 1962), 7.

"Thomas Merton Replies to a Perceptive Critic." *The National Catholic Reporter*, III (January 18, 1967), 4.

"Three Saviors in Camus." *Thought*, XLIII (1968), 5–23.

"Time and the Liturgy." *Worship*, XXXI (1956–57), 2–10.

"To Each His Darkness." *Charlatan*, I (Spring, 1964), unpaged.

"Todo y Nada, Writing and Contemplation." Unpublished material from original manuscript of *Seven Storey Mountain* with introductory comment by Sister M. Thérèse Lentfoehr, S.D.S. *Renascence*, II (1950), 87–101.

"The Tower of Babel." *Jubilee*, III (1955–56), 20–35.

"The Transforming Union in St. Bernard and St. John of the Cross." *Collectanea Ordinis Cisterciensium Reformatorum*, X (1948), 107–17, 210–23; XI (1949), 41–52, 353–61; XII (1950), 25–38.

"A Trappist Speaks on People, Priests and Prayer." *Messenger of the Sacred Heart*, LXXXIII (April, 1948), 58–61, 89–90.

"The Trappists Go to Utah." *Commonweal*, XLVI (1947), 470–73.

"Trappists Make Silent Martyrs—excerpt from *Waters of Siloe*." *Catholic Digest*, XIV (November, 1949), 29–36.

"A Tribute to Flannery O'Connor; reprint from *Jubilee*." *Catholic Mind*, LXIII (March, 1965), 43–45.

"Truth and Violence." *Continuum*, II (1964), 268–81.

"Two Letters of the Late Thomas Merton: On the Future of Monasticism; Buddhist Monasticism and Meditation." *L'Osservatore Romano*, IV (January 23, 1969), 5, 10.

"The Vietnam War: An Overwhelming Atrocity." *Catholic Worker*, XXXIV (March, 1968), 1, 6–7.

"Virginity and Humanism in the Latin Fathers." *Sponsa Regis*, XXXIV (1962–63), 131–44.

"Visions of Peace: some reflections on the monastic way of life." *Jubilee*, VI (1958–59), 24–27.

"War and Vision: the Autobiography of a Crow Indian." *Catholic Worker*, XXXIII (December, 1967), 4, 6.

"We Have to Make Ourselves Heard," *Catholic Worker*, XXVIII (May, 1962), 4–6; (June, 1962), 4–5.

"What Is Meditation?" *Sponsa Regis*, XXXI (1959–60), 180–87.

"The White Pebble." *Sign*, XXIX (July, 1950), 26–28, 69.

"Why Some Look up to Planets and Heroes—Poem with Commentary; excerpt from *Emblems of a Season of Fury*." *America*, CVIII (1963), 433.

"The Wild Places." *Catholic Worker*, XXXIV (June, 1968), 4, 6.

"The Wild Places." *The Center Magazine*, I (1968), 40–44.

"Wilderness and Paradise." *Cistercian Studies*, II (1967), 83–89.

"Writing as Temperature." *Sewanee Review*, LXXVII (1969), 535–42.

"You and I (a brief excerpt: *No Man Is an Island*)." *Books on Trial*, XIII (1954–55), 311.

"Zen in Japanese Art." *Catholic Worker*, XXXIII (July–August, 1967), 8.

"The Zen Koan." *The Lugano Review*, I (1966), 126–39.

"The Zen Revival." *Continuum*, I (1964), 523–38.

"Zen: Sense and Sensibility." *America*, CVIII (1963), 752–54.

Articles Appearing in Books.[2]

"Albert Camus and the Church," in *A Penny a Copy*. Edited by Thomas C. Cornell and James H. Forest. New York: Macmillan, 1968, pp. 254–71.

"Art Speaks to the Soul (excerpt: *The Seven Storey Mountain*)," in *The Consolations of Catholicism*. Edited by Ralph L. Woods. New York: Appleton–Century–Crofts, Inc., 1954, pp. 106–107.

"Atlas Watches Every Evening," in *New Directions in Prose and Poetry* 18. Edited by J. Laughlin. New York: New Directions, 1964, pp. 10–15.

"August Seventh (excerpt: *What Are These Wounds?*)," in *Christian Conversation* (Catholic Thought for Every Day in the Year). Edited by Ann Freemantle. New York: Stephen Daye Press, 1953, unpaged.

"Baptism in the Forest: Wisdom and Initiation in William Faulkner," in *Mansions of the Spirit*. Edited by G. A. Panichas. New York: Hawthorn Books, 1967, pp. 17–44.

"Blessed Are the Meek: The Christian Roots of Nonviolence," *A Fellowship Reprint*. Nyack, New York: Fellowship of Reconciliation, 1967.

Breakthrough to Peace. Edited with introduction and article entitled, "Peace: A Religious Responsibility," by T. Merton. New York: New Directions, 1962, pp. 7–14, 88–116.

A Brief Comment for *The Pillar of Fire*, by K. Stern. New York: Harcourt, Brace, 1951.

"A Brief Comment on Religious Poetry," in *A New Anthology of Modern Poetry*. Edited with introduction by Selden Rodman. Revised edition. New York: The Modern Library, 1946, p. 460.

[2]In this section are included the translations, essays and excerpts of his writings, as well as the various prefaces, introductions, and forewords to books that Merton wrote.

The Christmas Sermons of Bl. Guerric of Igny. An essay by Thomas Merton; sermons translated by Sister Rose of Lima. Trappist, Kentucky: Abbey of Gethsemani, 1959, pp. 1–25.

Comments, in *War Within Man.* Edited by E. Fromm. Philadelphia: Peace Literature Service of American Friends Service Committee, 1963, pp. 44–50.

"Concerning the Collection in the Bellarmine College Library," in *The Thomas Merton Studies Center.* Santa Barbara: Unicorn Press, 1971, pp. 13–15.

"The Contemplative Life Can Be Led by All (excerpt: *Figures for an Apocalypse;* from the essay: Poetry and the Contemplative Life)," in *A Treasury of Catholic Thinking.* Edited by Ralph L. Woods. New York: Thomas Y. Crowell Co., 1953, pp. 346–47.

"The Council and Monasticism," in *The Impact of Vatican II* (Bellarmine College Studies). Edited by J. P. Dougherty. St. Louis: B. Herder Book Co., 1966, pp. 44–60.

"A Devout Meditation in Memory of Adolf Eichmann," in *New Directions in Prose and Poetry* 18. Edited by J. Laughlin. New York: New Directions, 1964, pp. 16–18.

"Distractions in Prayer," in *Springs of Devotion.* Kansas City, Missouri: Hallmark, 1969, pp. 31–32.

"The Early Legend," in *New Directions in Prose and Poetry* 18. Edited by J. Laughlin. New York: New Directions, 1964, pp. 1–9.

"Easter: The New Life," in *Harvest,* 1960. Edited by Dan Herr and Paul Cuneo. Westminster, Maryland: Newman Press, 1960, pp. 159–70.

Foreword to *Bernard of Clairvaux* by H. Daniel-Rops. New York: Hawthorn Books, 1964, pp. 5–7.

Foreword to *Burnt Out Incense* by M. Raymond, ocso. New York: J. Kennedy and Sons, 1949, pp. xi–xiii.

Foreword to *Notes on the Lord's Prayer* by R. Maritain. Edited by J. Maritain. New York: P. J. Kenedy and Sons, 1964, pp. 7–11.

Foreword to *St. Bernard of Clairvaux—Seen through His Selected Letters* by Rev. J. B. Scott. Chicago: Henry Regnery Co., 1953, pp. v–viii.

Foreword to *Vietnam: Lotus in a Sea of Fire* (translation of poems of Thich Nhat Hanh). New York: Hill and Wong, 1967, pp. vii–x.

Gandhi on Non-Violence. Edited with an introduction entitled, "Gandhi and the One-Eyed Giant," by Thomas Merton. New York: New Directions, 1964.

Introduction to *The City of God,* by Saint Augustine. New York: The Modern Library, 1950, pp. ix–xv.

Introduction to *God Is My Life: The Story of Our Lady of Gethsemani,* by S. Burden. New York: Reynal and Co., 1960, unpaged.

Introduction, entitled "A Christian Looks at Zen," to *The Golden Age of Zen,* by J. C. Wu. Published by the National War College in cooperation with the Committee on the Compilation of the Chinese Library, 1967, pp. 1–27.

Introduction to *The Monastic Theology of Aelred of Rievaulx,* by A. Hallier. Spencer, Mass.: Cistercian Publications, 1969, pp. vii–xiii.

Introduction and Commentary to *The Plague*, by Albert Camus. New York: The Seabury Press, Religious Dimensions in Literature Series, 1968.

Introduction to *The Prison Meditations of Father Alfred Delp*, by A. Delp, SJ. New York: Herder and Herder, 1963, pp. vii-xxx.

Introduction to *Religion in Wood*, by Edward D. and Faith Andrews. Bloomington, Indiana: Indiana University Press, 1966, pp. vii-xv.

Introduction and translation from the Latin to *The Solitary Life*, by Guigo the Carthusian. Worcester, England: Stanbrook Abbey Press, 1963.

Introduction and complete new translation to *The Soul of the Apostolate*, by Dom J. B. Chautard, OCSO. Trappist, Kentucky: Abbey of Our Lady of Gethsemani, 1946, pp. v-xv.

"Invisible Seeds; One's Own Virtues (excerpt: *Seeds of Contemplation*)," in *The New Treasure Chest*. Edited by J. Donald Adams. New York: E. P. Dutton and Co., 1953, pp. 409-10.

The Kingdom of Jesus by St. John Eudes. Translated by Thomas Merton. New York: P. J. Kenedy and Sons, 1946.

"Learning to Live," in *University on the Heights*. Edited by W. First. New York: Doubleday and Co., 1969, pp. 187-99.

"Letter from Thomas Merton—February, 1962," in *A Penny a Copy*. Edited by Thomas C. Cornell and James H. Forest. New York: Macmillan, 1968, pp. 207-209.

"Letters to Che: Canto Bilinque," in *Viva Che! Contributions in Tribute to Ernesto "Che" Guevara*. Edited by M. Alexandre. London: Lorrimer Publ. Ltd., 1968, p. 85.

"Marxism and Monastic Perspectives," in *A New Charter for Monasticism*. Edited by J. Moffitt. Notre Dame, Indiana: University of Notre Dame Press, 1970, pp. 69-81.

Monks Pond. Edited by Thomas Merton. Trappist, Kentucky: Abbey of Gethsemani, 1968. The magazine appeared in four issues and Merton's poetry is found in the following issues: no. 1 (Spring), pp. 26-31; no. 2 (Summer), unpaged; no. 3 (Fall), pp. 42-44, 71-78; no. 4 (Winter), pp. 73, 85-86, 87-89.

"Morte D'Urban: Two Celebrations," in *J. F. Powers*, by F. Evans. St. Louis: B. Herder Book Co., 1968, pp. 95-100.

Notes and text arrangement to *The Ox Mountain Parable*, by Meng Tzu. Lexington, Kentucky: Stamperia del Santuccio, 1960.

"Plessy vs. Ferguson: Theme and Variations," in *New Directions in Prose and Poetry* 21. Edited by J. Laughlin. New York: New Directions, 1969, pp. 201-203.

Preface to *Alone with God*, by Dom J. Leclercq. Translated by E. McCabe. New York: Farrar, Straus and Cudahy, 1961, pp. xiii-xxvii.

Préface to *L'attente dans le silence*, by Dom M. Chenevière. Paris: Desclée de Brouwer, 1961, pp. 9-13.

Préface, "Saint Bernard, moine et apotre," to *Bernard de Clairvaux*. Translated by J. de la Croix Bouton. Paris: Editions Alsatia, 1953, pp. vii-xv.

Preface to *A Catholic Prayer Book*. Edited by D. Francis. New York: Dell Publishing Co., 1958, pp. 9-12.

Preface to *In Search of a Yogi,* by Dom Denys Rutledge. New York: Farrar, Straus and Co., 1962, pp. vii–xii.

Preface to *Non Violence and the Christian Conscience,* by P. Regamy, OP. New York: Herder and Herder, 1966, pp. 7–14.

Preface and translation to *A Prayer of Cassiodorus.* Worcester, England: Stanbrook Abbey Press, 1967.

Preface to *Seul avec Dieu: La Vie érémitique,* d'après la doctrine du bienheureux Paul Giustiniani, by Dom J. Leclercq. Paris: Libraire Plon, 1955, pp. 7–18.

"The Primary Apostolate/The Apostolate of Prayer and Penance," in *The National Catholic Almanac* (50th Anniversary Edition). Washington, D.C.: Holy Name College, pp. 343–44.

"Reflections on the Character and Genius of Fénelon," in *Fénelon—Letters of Love and Counsel.* Translated and selected by J. McEwen. New York: Harcourt, Brace and World, Inc., 1964, pp. 9–30.

"The Root of War" and "Red or Dead?"—two essays, in *A Fellowship Reprint.* Nyack, New York: Fellowship of Reconciliation.

"Scattered excerpts: *Seeds of Contemplation,*" in *The American Treasury (1455–1955).* Edited by C. Fadiman, assisted by C. Van Doren. New York: Harper and Brothers, 1955, pp. 680–81.

"Seeds of Contemplation (Excerpt: *Seeds of Contemplation*)," in *The Happy Crusaders* (A Selection of readings affirming the joy of Christianity). Compiled by James Edward Tobin. New York: McMullen Books, Inc., 1952, pp. 107–10.

"Selections from *New Seeds of Contemplation,*" in *Come South Wind.* Edited by M. L. Shrady. New York: Pantheon Books, 1957, pp. 28–29, 40–41, 47–48, 57–58, 67.

Selections from the Protreptikos, by Clement of Alexandria. An essay and translation by Thomas Merton. New York: New Directions, 1963.

"The Significance of the Bhagavad Gita," in *The Bhagavad Gita As It Is.* A new translation with commentary by Swami A. C. Bhaktivedanta. New York: Macmillan, 1968, pp. 18–22.

"Solitude and Love," in *The Spirit of Man.* Edited by W. Burnett. New York: Hawthorn Books, Inc., 1958, pp. 113–19.

The Spirit of Simplicity Characteristic of the Cistercian Order—An Official Report demanded and approved by The General Chapter together with Texts from St Bernard of Clairvaux on *Interior Simplicity.* Translation and commentary by a Cistercian Monk of Our Lady of Gethsemani (Thomas Merton). Trappist, Kentucky: Abbey of Our Lady of Gethsemani, 1948.

"St John of the Cross," in *Saints for Now.* Edited by Clare Booth Luce. New York: Sheed and Ward, 1952, pp. 250–60.

Statement in *Authors Take Sides on Vietnam.* Edited by C. Woolf and J. Bagguley. New York: Simon and Schuster, 1967, p. 51.

"Student, Man-about-the-Campus, Atheist, Trappist (excerpt: *The Seven Storey Mountain*)," in *We Speak for Ourselves.* Edited by Irving Stone. New York: Doubleday and Co., 1950, pp. 415–21.

"Symbolism: Communication or Communion?" in *New Directions in Prose and Poetry 20.* Edited by J. Laughlin. New York: New Directions, 1968, pp. 1–15.

"Truly a Success as a Cistercian (excerpt: *The Seven Storey Mountain*)," in *The Catholic Bedside Book* (An Anthology about Catholics and Catholicism) Edited by B. C. L. Keelan. New York: David McKay, Co., 1953, pp. 293–94.

"The White Pebble," in *Where I Found Christ: The Intimate Personal Stories of Fourteen Converts to the Catholic Faith.* Edited by J. A. O'Brien. New York: Doubleday and Co., 1950, pp. 235–50.

"Wisdom in Emptiness: a Dialogue by Daisetz T. Suzuki and Thomas Merton," in *New Directions 17 in Prose and Poetry.* Edited by J. Laughlin. New York: New Directions, 1961, pp. 65–101.

The Wisdom of the Desert: sayings from the Desert Fathers of the fourth century. Translated by Thomas Merton. New York: New Directions, 1960.

Selected Unpublished Material[3]

"Aids to Mental Prayer."

"Camus and the Catholic Church," 1966.

"Conference on Prayer." This conference, delivered to Sisters, is on tape at the Abbey of Gethsemani.

"Conference to Sisters delivered at The Institute for Contemplative Living in the Contemporary World," (Monroe, Michigan), 1968.

"The Contemplative and the Apostolate." This conference, delivered to Novices at Gethsemani is also on tape at the Abbey of Gethsemani.

"The Inner Experience: Notes on Contemplation."

"Letter to Friends,"—Easter, 1967; Pentecost, 1967; Pre-Lent, 1968; Paschal Time, 1968; Midsummer Letter, 1968.

"Message of Contemplatives to the Modern World."

"Monastic Experience and East-West Dialogue," notes for a paper delivered at Calcutta, October, 1968.

"Prayer as Worship and Experience."

"Reflections on Houses of Prayer." Unpublished material of conferences delivered at Our Lady of Redwoods Monastery, White Thorn, California, September, 1968.

"The School of the Spirit."

[3]Because of the vast scope of this material as well as restrictions on its availability, there is included here only whatever material the author could analyze and which he felt was directly pertinent to the subject matter of the dissertation. It should be noted, however, that as regards other primary sources, all of Merton's published writings are included in the present bibliography. The writer wishes to acknowledge his indebtedness to the Trustees of the Merton Legacy Trust for permission to quote from Merton's unpublished material.

"Selections on Prayer," 1959.
"Selections on Prayer," 1961.
"Seven Words."
"Thomas Merton on Prayer at Darjeeling," 1968.
"Time-Life Bible—Introduction, 'Opening the Bible,' " 1967.

II. *Works on the Life and Thought of Thomas Merton*

Books

Baker, James Thomas. *Thomas Merton Social Critic:* A Study. Lexington, the University Press of Kentucky, 1971.
Dell'Isola, Frank. *Thomas Merton: a Bibliography.* New York: Farrar, Straus and Cudahy, 1956.
Griffin, John Howard. *A Hidden Wholeness—The Visual World of Thomas Merton.* Photographs by Thomas Merton and John Howard Griffin; text by John Howard Griffin. Boston: Houghton Mifflin Co., 1970.
Higgins, John J. *Merton's Theology of Prayer.* Cistercian Studies Series, no. 18. Spencer, Massachusetts: Cistercian Publications, 1971.
Rice, Edward. *The Man in the Sycamore Tree: The Good Times and Hard Life of Thomas Merton.* New York: Doubleday, 1970.

Articles

Allchin, A. M. "A Liberator, a Reconciler." *Continuum,* VII (1969), 363–65.
Andrews, James F. "Was Merton a Critic of Renewal?" *The National Catholic Reporter,* VI (February 11, 1970), Lenten Supplement, 1, 12–15.
Atkins, Anselm. "Reflections on Merton's Notes." *Monastic Exchange,* I (1969), 81–84.
Baciu, Stefan. "The Literary Catalyst." *Continuum,* VII (1969), 295–305.
Baird, Sr. M. Julian, R.S.M. "Blake, Hopkins and Thomas Merton." *Catholic World,* CLXXXIII (1956), 46–49.
——. "Thomas Merton and T. S. Eliot." *America,* XCII (1955), 424–26.
Baker, James T. "The Social Catalyst." *Continuum,* VII (1969), 255–64.
——. "Thomas Merton's Response to America, the Grim Reaper of Violence." *Religion in Life,* XL (1971), 52–63.
——. "The Two Cities of Thomas Merton." *Catholic World,* CCXI (1970), 151–55.
Bamberger, John Eudes, OCSO. "The Cistercian." *Continuum,* VII (1969), 227–41.
——. "A Homily." *Continuum,* VII (1969), 226.
Belford, Lee A. "Thomas Merton: Saint-Scholar." *The Witness,* LIV (January 2, 1969), 7–8.
Berrigan, Daniel, SJ. "The Trappist Cemetery—Gethsemani Revisited." *Continuum,* VII (1969), 313–18.

Bilski, Nanine. "The Difference He Made." *Continuum*, VII (1969), 320–22.

Bourne, Russell. "The Rain Barrel." *Continuum*, VII (1969), 361–63.

Bruno, Eric. OFM. "Letter to the Editor." *Spirit*, XVII (March, 1950), 23–25.

Burke, Herbert C. "The Man of Letters." *Continuum*, VII (1969), 274–85.

Burns, Flavian, OCSO. "Homélie de la messe pour le Père M. Louis (Thomas Merton)." *Collectanea Cisterciensia*, XXXI (1969), 7–8.

——. "Homily at the Mass for Father M. Louis (Thomas Merton)." *Cistercian Studies*, III (1968), 279–80.

Burton, Naomi. "I Shall Miss Thomas Merton." *Cistercian Studies*, IV (1969), 218–25.

——. "The Path to Seven Storey Mountain." *Catholic Digest*, XXIX (February, 1965), 127–32; (March, 1965), 125–31; (April, 1965), 126–31.

——. "Thomas Merton's Mountain: excerpts from *More Than Sentinels*." *Sign*, XLIV (October, 1964), 46–50.

Cameron-Brown, Aldhelm. "Seeking the Rhinoceros: a Tribute to Thomas Merton." *Monastic Studies*, VII (1969), 63–74.

Cardenal, Ernesto. "Des de la Trapa." *Abside*, XXII (1958), 314–24.

Catherine, Sr. Mary, OSU. "Letter to the Editor." *Spirit*, XVI (November, 1949), 162.

Clancy, William. "Karl Barth and Thomas Merton." *Worldview*, XII (1969), 11–12.

Conner, Tarcisius, OCSO. "Merton, Monastic Exchange and Renewal." *Monastic Exchange*, I (1969), 1–14.

Davenport, Guy. "Thomas Merton—R.I.P." *National Review*, XX (1968), 1309–1310.

Davey, William. "Thomas Merton and Dom Aelred Graham." *Integrity*, VII (April, 1953), 34–42.

Day, Dorothy. "Thomas Merton, Trappist." *Catholic Worker*, XXXIV (December, 1968), 1, 6.

——. "Thomas Merton, Trappist: 1915–1968." Reprint from *Catholic Worker*. *Catholic Mind*, LXVII (February, 1969), 30–32.

Delgado, F. "Thomas Merton: Estructura y Análisis." *Razon Y Fe*, CLXVII (1963), 39–48.

Dell'Isola, Frank. "A Bibliography of Thomas Merton." *Thought*, XXIX (1954), 574–96.

——. "The Conversion and Growth of Thomas Merton." *Cross and Crown*, XIV (1962), 53–61.

——. "A Journey to Gethsemani." *Cross and Crown*, VIII (1956), 294–310.

——. "Thomas Merton: Outlines of Growth." *Catholic Book Reporter*, I (February, 1961), 8–10.

Delteil, Chanoine Francois. "La conversion et l'ordination de Thomas Merton." *Echoes de Noble*, CXLVIII (1950), 7–10.

Dubbel, S. Earl. "In Defense of Thomas Merton." *Atlantic Monthly*, CXCI (March, 1953), 20.

Dumont, Charles, OCSO. "A Contemplative at the Heart of the World—Thomas Merton." *Lumen Vitae*, XXIV (1969), 633–46.

——. "Père Louis-Thomas Merton." *Collectanea Cisterciensia*, XXXI (1969), 3–7.

Editorial. "Benedictine v. Trappist." *Time,* LXI (February 2, 1953), 72, 74.

——. "Catholic Books." *Ave Maria,* LXXVII (1953), 642.

——. "The Death of Two Extraordinary Christians." *Time,* XCII (December 20, 1968), 65.

——. "Father Merton Denies Rumors." *Catholic World,* CLXXII (1951), iv.

——. "For I Tell You God Is Able to Raise Up Children to Abraham." *The Kentucky Alumnus,* XL (Summer, 1969), 10–12, 29, 30.

——. "Foreward." *Peace,* III (1968–69), 3.

——. "Merton Likes Monastery but He Has Reservations." *Life,* XXVI (May 23, 1949), 90.

——. "Merton's Later Life." *Peace,* III (1968–69), 13–14.

——. "Merton's Prof. to be Ordained a Priest at 60." *The National Catholic Reporter,* III (April 26, 1967), 1, 10.

——. "The Mountain." *Time,* LIII (April 11, 1949), 62–63.

——. "Mystics Among Us." *Time,* LII (October 11, 1948), 87–89.

——. "Obituary." *Publisher's Weekly,* CXCIV (December 30, 1968), 49.

——. "Thomas Merton Receives Catholic Literary Award." *Publisher's Weekly,* CLVI (October 1, 1949), 1577.

——. "Thomas Merton Today; a photo essay." *Jubilee,* XIII (1965–66), 28–33.

——. "Thomas Merton, Trappist." *Newsweek,* XXXIV (September 19, 1949), 72–73.

Evans, Illtud, OP. "Elected Speech. Thomas Merton and the American Conscience." *Tablet,* CCXX (1966), 1269–70.

——. "Thomas Merton." *Tablet,* CCXXIII (1969), 22–23.

Evans, Mary Ellen. "Poetry and Contemplation—Letter to Editor." *Commonweal,* XLVI (1947), 383–84.

Ferry, W. H. "The Difference He Made." *Continuum,* VII (1969), 319–20.

Forest, James H. "The Gift of Merton." *Commonweal,* LXXXIX (1968–69), 463–65.

Fowler, Albert. "A Visit with Thomas Merton." *Friends Journal,* VII (1961), 490–92.

Francis, Sr. Mary, PC. "Poetry and the Contemplative." *Spirit,* XXII (1955), 83–89.

Gill, Barry. "A Christmas Meditation—Letter to Editor." *Commonweal,* XLVII (1948), 349.

Gillis, James M., CSP. "Action and Contemplation." *Cross and Crown,* I (1949), 245–60.

Graham, Aelred, OSB. "The Mysticism of Thomas Merton." *Commonweal,* LXII (1955), 155–59.

——. "Thomas Merton/A Modern Man in Reverse." *Atlantic Monthly,* CXCI (1953), 70–74.

Grau, José. "Tomas Merton visto desde fuera de la Orden." *Cistercium,* CXVI (1969), 315–16.

Gregory, T. S. "Everyman's Vocation: (Father Merton's Introduction to Mystical Theology." *Tablet,* CXCVIII (1951), 489–90.

Griffin, John Howard. "In Search of Thomas Merton." *Merton Studies Center,* I (1971), 17–24.

M

——. "Les grandes amitiés." *Continuum,* VII (1969), 286–94.

——. "Merton and His Camera; excerpt from *A Hidden Wholeness: the Visual World of Thomas Merton.*" *National Catholic Reporter Supplement,* VII (November 20, 1970), 6A–7A.

Groves, Gerald. "Fourteen Years with Thomas Merton." *Critic,* XXI (April–May, 1963), 28–32.

——. "My Fourteen Years with Thomas Merton." *Catholic Digest,* XXVII (August, 1963), 48–53.

Haughton, Rosemary. "Bridge Between Two Cultures." *Catholic World,* CCIX (1969), 53–54.

Hart, Patrick, OCSO. "Last Mass in the Hermitage." *Continuum,* VII (1969), 213–15.

——. "Last Mass in the Hermitage." *Monastic Exchange,* I (1969), 85–86.

——. "Last Mass in the Hermitage—A Memory of Thomas Merton." *New Book Review,* (October, 1969), 3–4.

——. "Thomas Merton." *The Lamp,* LXIX (1970), 2.

——. "Thomas Merton's East-West Dialogue." *Monastic Exchange,* II (1970), 18–20.

Horrigan, Alfred F. "Thomas Merton Studies Center." *Merton Studies Center,* I (1971), 7–11.

Jocelyn, Sr Mary, OSB. "Thomas Merton: Poet of Contemplation." *America,* LXXXIII (1950), 420–22.

Julie, Sr., OP. "New Directions Present a Catholic Poet." *America,* LXXIII (1945), 316–18.

Julie, Sr Rosemarie. "Influences Shaping the Poetic Imagery of Merton." *Renascence,* IX (1957), 187–97, 222.

Kelly, Richard. "Thomas Merton and Poetic Vitality." *Renascence,* XII (1960), 139–42, 148.

Kelty, Matthew. "Letter from Gethsemani." *Monastic Exchange,* I (1969), 86–89.

——. "Some Reminiscences of Thomas Merton." *Cistercian Studies,* IV (1969), 163–75.

——. "Thomas Merton, mon confrère, mon ami." *Collectanea Cisterciensia,* XXXI (1969), 233–42.

Landy, Joseph. "The Meaning of Thomas Merton." *America,* LXXXVIII (1953), 569–70.

Lansdell, Sarah. "In Search of Thomas Merton." *The Courrier Journal and Times Magazine,* (December 7, 1969), 47–48, 50, 52, 54.

Lauras, Antoine. "Le Cardinal et le Trappiste; Aspects du Catholicisme aux États-Unis." *Etudes,* CCLXXI (1951), 368–78.

Leclercq, Jean. "Derniers souvenirs." *Collectanea Cisterciensia,* XXXI (1969), 9–14.

LeFrois, Bernard J., SVD. "The Function of Mariology." *American Ecclesiastical Review,* CXXXVI (1957), 242–45.

Lentfoehr, Sr M. Thérèse, SDS. "Letter to the Editor." *Spirit,* XVII (March, 1950), 20–23.

——. "The Spiritual Writer." *Continuum,* VII (1969), 242–54.

Lissner, Will. "Toast of the Avant-Garde: a Trappist Poet." *Catholic World*, CLXVI (1948), 424–32.

Lowell, Robert, "The Verses of Thomas Merton." *Commonweal*, XLII (1945), 240–42.

MacEoin, Gary. "Thomas Merton: the Usefulness of the Useless." *Ave Maria*, CIX (1969), 6–7.

Mansfield, Margery. "Letter to the Editor." *Spirit*, XVII (May, 1950), 62.

Marie, Sr Consuela, SBS. "Merton or Toynbee?" *Xavier University Studies*, I (1961–62), 34–38.

Marty, Martin E. "To: Thomas Merton. *Re:* Your Prophecy." *The National Catholic Reporter*, III (August 30, 1967), 6.

Materer, Timothy. "Merton and Auden." *Commonweal*, XCI (1969–70), 577–80.

Mayhew, Alice. "Merton against Himself." *Commonweal*, XCI (1969–70), 70–74.

McCarthy, Coleman. "Old Order Changeth—Trappists Open up to World." *Louisville Times* (January 9, 1969), A13.

——. "Renewal Crisis Hits Trappists." *The National Catholic Reporter*, IV (December 13, 1967), 1, 5.

McCauliff, George A. "Letter to the Editor." *Spirit*, XVII (May, 1950), 62–63.

McDonnell, Thomas. "An Interview with Thomas Merton." *Motive*, XXVII (October, 1967), 32–41.

——. "An Interview with Thomas Merton." Reprint from *Motive*. *U.S. Catholic*, XXXIII (March, 1968), 28–34.

——. "The Poetry of Thomas Merton." *Spirit*, XXV (March, 1958), 23–30.

——. "Thomas Merton and the Franciscans." *Cord*, VI (1956), 9–13.

Moffit, John. "New Charter for Monasticism." *America*, CXX (1969), 60–64.

——. "Thomas Merton: The Last Three Days." *Catholic World*, CCIX (1969), 160–63.

Morrissey, Jim. "Talks with and about Thomas Merton: Monk, Man and Myth." *Courier-Journal Magazine* (Louisville, Kentucky), (January 23, 1966), 15–16, 20, 25.

Morrison, Richard. "Thomas Merton: The Man and His Meaning." *Laurel* (Spring, 1965), 14–19.

Moulton, Herbert E. "Thoughts on Thomas Merton's *No Man Is an Island*." *Torch*, XL (June–July, 1956), 5–7.

Pallis, Marco. "Thomas Merton—1915–1968." *Studies in Comparative Religion*, III (1969), 138–46.

Peloquin, C. Alexander. "To Remember." *Liturgical Arts*, XXXVII (1969), 52–53.

Rice, Ed. "Thomas Merton." *Sign*, XLVIII (February, 1969), 29–37.

Ross, Ilona. "Our Lady's Liveryman." *The Flame*, III (Autumn, 1964), 15–21.

Rutledge, D., OSB. "Thomas Merton and His Critics." *Clergy Review*, XXXVIII (1953), 671–78.

Saward, Sr Anne, OCSO. "Tribute to Thomas Merton." *Cistercian Studies*, III (1968), 265–78.

Shaddy, Virginia M. "Thomas Merton and *No Man Is an Island*." *Catholic World*, CLXXXIV (1956–57), 51–56.

Shenker, Israel. "Thomas Merton Is Dead at 53; Monk Wrote of Search for God." *The New York Times* (Wednesday, December 11, 1968), 1, 42.

Stark, Philip M., sj. "A Summer at Gethsemani." *Continuum*, VII (1969), 306–12.

———. "Two Poems to a Dead Brother: Catullus and Thomas Merton." *The Classical Bulletin*, XXXVIII (April, 1962), 81–83.

Steindl-Rast, David. "Recollections of Thomas Merton's Last Days in the West." *Monastic Studies*, VII (1969), 1–10.

Stevens, Clifford. "Thomas Merton: an Appraisal." *American Benedictine Review*, XVIII (1967), 223–26.

———. "Thomas Merton, 1968: a Profile in Memoriam." *American Benedictine Review*, XX (1969), 7–20.

Strahan, Speer. "Thomas Merton: Poet." *Ave Maria*, LXV (1947), 231–34.

Thielen, James A. "Thomas Merton: Poet of the Contemplative Life." *Catholic World*, CLXIX (1949), 86–90.

Tobin, T., cssr. "Catholic Author of the Month/Thomas Merton." *Liguorian*, XXXVII (1949), 443–44.

Toelle, Gervase, o.carm. "Merton and the Critics." *Renascence*, II (1950), 139–46.

———. "Merton: His Problem and a Solution." *Spirit*, XVI (July, 1949), 84–89.

VanDoren, Mark. "Thomas Merton." *America*, CXX (1969), 21–22.

———. "Thomas Merton—Monk." *Columbia Forum* (Spring, 1969), 44.

Walsh, Daniel. "Thomas Merton: The Sense of Mystery." *Saint John's*, IX (Summer, 1969), 13–19.

Weiss, Frank J. "Of Thomas Merton: His Word and His Spirit." *Carroll Quarterly*, I (1948), 4–13.

Worland, Carr. "Death of a Peacemaker." *Catholic Library World*, XL (1969), 421–43.

Young, E. B. "Fr. Thomas Merton on the Monastic Life—Letter to Editor." *Tablet*, CCI (1953), 500.

Zaehner, R. C. "Can Mysticism Be Christian?" *New Blackfriars*, XLVI (1964–65), 21–31.

Zahn, Gordon. "The Peacemaker." *Continuum*, VII (1969), 265–73.

Book Reviews[4]

Callahan, Daniel J. "Unworldly Wisdom." *Commentary*, XXXIX (April, 1965), 90, 92–94.

Conner, Tarcisius, ocso. "The Man in the Sycamore Tree." *Monastic Exchange*, II (1970), 7–10.

[4]Here again, because of the large number of such reviews, this writer has judged it necessary to include only those directly pertinent to the present dissertation.

Connolly, Francis X. "The Complete Twentieth-Century Man; review of Seven Storey Mountain." *Thought*, XXIV (1949), 10–14.

de Lenval, Hélenè Lubienska. "Moisson de Silence." *La Vie Spirituelle*, LXXXIV (1951), 616–627.

———. "Le Pain des Psaumes." *La Vie Spirituelle*, XCI (1954), 410–12.

Editorial. "Action and Contemplation in St. Bernard." *Theology Digest*, III (1955), 100.

———. "Merton's Newest." *Newsweek*, XLI (February 9, 1953), 80.

———. "Prayer for a Miracle." *Newsweek*, LIII (February 16, 1959), 106.

———. "Thomas Merton's Early Novel." *Publisher's Weekly*, CXCV (April 28, 1969), 67–68.

———. "White Man's Culture." *Time*, LII (November 29, 1948), 81–82.

Forest, James. "A Circus of Mertons." *Commonweal*, XCII (1971), 400–403.

———. "The Frozen Rainbow." *Critic*, XXVIII (1970), 86–88.

Gilbert, Sr. M., snjm. "Fusion and Fission: Two by Merton." *Sewanee Review*, LXXII (1964), 715–18.

Gregory, Horace. "Life and Poems of a Trappist Monk." *New York Times Book Review* (October 3, 1948), 4, 33.

Kinish, David. "Review Article: The Climate of Monastic Prayer." *Benedictines*, XXV (1970), 128–134.

Krikorian, Y. H. "The Fruits of Mysticism." *New Republic*, CXXI (September 12, 1949), 17–18.

Lentfoehr, Sr. M. Thérèse, sds. "Flash of Dark Lightning." *Renascence*, VII (1954), 103–108.

———. "From Harlem to Gethsemani." *Renascence*, XII (1960), 149–53.

———. "If You Are Looking . . . Look Inside Yourself." *Books on Trial*, X (1951–52), 66–67.

———. "Merton Indexed: Thomas Merton: A Bibliography." *Renascence*, X (1957), 38–41.

———. "Merton's Jonas." *Renascence*, VI (1953), 44–52.

———. "Notes and Meditations." *Books on Trial*, XIII (1955), 311–12.

———. "Out of Gethsemani." *Renascence*, XV (1962), 46–50.

———. "Patristic and Titanic." *Renascence*, XIV (1962), 218–22.

Margaret, Helene. "Exciting Autobiography Condemns Modernism." *Books on Trial*, VII (1948), 133, 144.

McSorley, Joseph. "The Cistercians." *Catholic World*, CLXX (1949), 198–203.

Michelfelder, William. "A Search beyond the Self." *The Saturday Review of Literature*, XLIII (September 24, 1960), 24.

Murray, Michele. "Recalling the Artist and Monk Who Lives On." *National Catholic Reporter*, VII (February 19, 1971), 11.

Pennington, M. Basil, ocso. "The Climate of Monastic Prayer." *Theological Studies*, XXXI (1970), 207–8.

Rago, Henry. "From the Belly of the Whale." *Commonweal*, LVII (1952–53), 526–29.

Redman, Ben Ray. "In the Belly of a Paradox." *The Saturday Review of Literature*, XXXVI (February 21, 1953), 45–46.

Theall, Bernard, osb. "The Sign of Jonas." *Books on Trial*, XI (1953), 189, 208.

Articles Appearing in Books

Berrigan, Daniel. Foreward to *The Politics of the Gospel,* by Jean Marie Paupert. Translated by Gregor Roy. New York: Holt, Rinehart and Winston, 1969, pp. vii–xviii.

Bridges, Hal. *American Mysticism* (From William James to Zen). New York: Harper and Row, 1970, pp. 65–72.

Burr, Nelson R. *A Critical Bibliography of Religion in America.* 4 vols. Princeton, New Jersey: Princeton University Press, 1961, vo.l 4, pp. 927–28.

Burton, Naomi. Foreward to *My Argument with the Gestapo: a macaronic journal,* by Thomas Merton. New York: Doubleday, 1969, pp. 7–11.

———. *More Than Sentinels.* New York: Doubleday, 1964, pp. 238–53, 313–16.

De Pinto, Basil, OSB. "In Memoriam: Thomas Merton 1915–1968," in *The Cistercian Spirit—A Symposium.* Edited by M. Basil Pennington, OCSO. Spencer, Mass.: Cistercian Publications, 1969, pp. vii–x.

Leary, Paris and Kelly, Robert. *A Controversy of Poets: an anthology of contemporary American Poetry.* New York: Doubleday-Anchor Books, 1965, pp. 542–43.

Leclercq, Jean, OSB. Introduction to *Contemplation in a World of Action,* by Thomas Merton. New York: Doubleday, 1971, pp. ix–xx.

Moffitt, John, "Thomas Merton: The Last Three Days," in *New Theology No.* 7. Edited by Martin E. Marty and Dean G. Peerman. New York: Macmillan, 1970, pp. 125–34.

Steere, Douglas V. Foreward to *The Climate of Monastic Prayer,* by Thomas Merton. Spencer, Mass.: Cistercian Publications, 1969, pp. 13–27.

———. Foreword to *Contemplative Prayer,* by Thomas Merton. New York: Herder and Herder, 1969, pp. 7–14.

Thornton, Francis B. *Return to Tradition—A Directive Anthology.* Milwaukee: Bruce Publishing Co., 1948, pp. 850–52.

Vitale, Philip H. *Catholic Critics.* 2 vols. Chicago: Auxiliary University Press, 1961, vol. 2, pp. 13–26.

Waugh, Evelyn. Foreword to *Elected Silence,* by Thomas Merton. London: Hollis and Carter, 1949, pp. v–vi.

Zahn, Gordon C. Introduction to *Thomas Merton on Peace.* Edited by Gordon C. Zahn. New York: McCall Publishing Co., 1971, pp. ix–xli.

Doctoral Dissertations

Baker, James Thomas. "Thomas Merton: The Spiritual and Social Philosophy of Union." Unpublished Ph.D. dissertation, Florida State University, 1968.

Campbell, Susan Margaret. "The Poetry of Thomas Merton: a Study in Theory, Influences and Form." Unpublished Ph.D. dissertation, Stanford University, 1954.

McInerny, Dennis Quentin. "Thomas Merton and Society: A Study of the Man and his Thought against the background of Contemporary American Culture." Unpublished Ph.D. dissertation, University of Minnesota, 1969

Unpublished Masters' Theses

Flaherty, Luke. "Mystery and Unity as Anagogical Vision in Thomas Merton's *Cables to the Ace:* A Critical Explication." Unpublished Master's dissertation, University of Louisville, 1966.

Gavin, Sr. Rosemarie Julie, SNDN. "An Analysis of Imagery in Selected Poems of Thomas Merton." Unpublished Master's dissertation. The Catholic University of America, 1951.

Hergott, Alvin W. "Thomas Merton and the Image of Man." Unpublished Master's dissertation, University of Saskatchewan, Regina, 1971.

Unpublished Material

Chester, Sr. Mary Aquin. "Letter to Friends *re* Monroe Conference on Contemplative Living in the Contemporary World." January 25, 1969.

Hart, Patrick, OCSO. A Foreword and Postscript to *Thomas Merton's Asian Journal,* January, 1970. This book is to be published shortly by New Directions.

Walsh, Daniel C. "Homily for the Funeral Mass of Father Louis Merton, OCSO." December 17, 1968.

CISTERCIAN FATHERS SERIES

Under the direction of the same Board of Editors as the CISTERCIAN STUDIES SERIES, the CISTERCIAN FATHERS SERIES seeks to make available the works of the Cistercian Fathers in good English translations based on the recently established critical editions. The texts are accompanied by introductions, notes and indexes prepared by qualified scholars.

Bernard of Clairvaux
> Treatises I
>> Introductions: Jean Leclercq, Chrysogonus Waddell, M. Basil Pennington
> On the Song of Songs I
>> Introduction: Corneill Halflants
> On the Song of Songs II
>> Introduction: Jean Leclercq

Aelred of Rievaulx
> Treatises, Pastoral Prayer
>> Introduction: David Knowles
> On Spiritual Friendship
>> Introduction: Anselm Hoste

William of St Thierry
> On Contemplating God, Prayer, Meditations
>> Introductions: Jacques Hourlier, J. M. Déchanet
> Exposition on the Song of Songs
>> Introduction: J. M. Déchanet
> Golden Epistle
>> Introduction: J. M. Déchanet

Guerric of Igny
> Liturgical Sermons: 2 vols.
> Introduction: John Morson and Hilary Costello

CISTERCIAN PUBLICATIONS
Spencer, Massachusetts 01562